Anna A. Novokhatko
A Guide to Classics and Cognitive Studies

Anna A. Novokhatko

A Guide to Classics and Cognitive Studies

Reviewing findings and results

In cooperation with Douglas Cairns, Angelos Chaniotis and David Konstan

DE GRUYTER

ISBN 978-3-11-157696-1
e-ISBN (PDF) 978-3-11-157737-1
e-ISBN (EPUB) 978-3-11-157822-4

Library of Congress Control Number: 2024942392

Bibliographic information published by the Deutsche Nationalbibliothek
The Deutsche Nationalbibliothek lists this publication in the Deutsche Nationalbibliografie; detailed bibliographic data are available on the internet at http://dnb.dnb.de.

© 2025 Walter de Gruyter GmbH, Berlin/Boston
Cover image: Painting and photo © Gela Samsonidse, untitled, 2004, http://gela-samsonidse.de

www.degruyter.com

In gratitude for my students – past, present and future

Acknowledgments

This book was originally written at the request of various students with whom I discussed cognitive approaches to ancient sources and the role of cognitive science in the humanities today. From these discussions, the structure of the current volume was born.

I would like to express my gratitude to all those who provided support, help, and encouragement throughout this process. I begin by acknowledging the contributions of David Konstan, who sadly passed away several months ago. He was a constant source of inspiration, wonderfully open-minded, always encouraging and enthusiastic. David not only read his own interview script in this book and provided valuable feedback, but also read the entire manuscript and made numerous helpful comments and suggestions.

Douglas Cairns was for many years a constant support, offering constructive suggestions, corrections and ideas that were of great benefit for me. Finally, I want to extend my gratitude to Angelos Chaniotis for agreeing to be part of the team despite his ongoing commitments on excavations. His encouragement was extremely useful.

Apart from these three participants and contributors to the volume, other colleagues and friends have commented on the text at various stages, adding valuable information, commenting on and correcting arguments. Peter Meineck was extraordinary and the book would look completely different without his reading. Anne-Sophie Noel kindly offered her sharp critical eye, reading and commenting on a considerable part of the manuscript.

My colleagues and friends in numerous 'cognitive classics' discussions over long time have been Suzanne Adema and Chiara Fedriani. I always have so much to learn from them.

The expertise of the anonymous readers was especially useful and proved invaluable as I made final revisions.

I will not of course be able to mention everyone who has inspired me, influenced my train of thought, helped through discussion or consultation on the bibliography during the preparation of this book. Among so many others, I am very grateful to Eric Cline, Margaret Miller, Naomi Weiss, Evert van Emde Boas, Jennifer Devereaux, Bernhard Zimmermann, Antonios Rengakos, Hildegund Schaab, Florence Low, Al Duncan, Emmanuela Bakola, Panayotis Pachis, Karoline Reinhardt, Pia Campeggiani, and Virginia Mastellari. I would also like to thank Chiara Zanchi and Eleonora Athanasiadou.

I am deeply indebted to the publisher, De Gruyter, and especially to Serena Pirrotta, who handled the whole process with the utmost professionalism. The project manager, Anne Hiller, as well as Alexandra Koronkai-Kiss, Andrea Jost and Ulla Schmidt, worked with efficiency and competence.

After countless lovely chats with my sister, Ekaterina Novokhatko, on the topics of the mind and emotions, I have come up with various important thoughts. Gela Samsonidse and Georges Salameh sent me beautiful images of their work. The professional and prompt help of colleagues from the British Museum in London, the Ephorate of Antiquities of Achaia in Greece and the National Archaeological Museum of Naples was amazing.

I cannot thank all these people and many others sufficiently. Any errors remain, of course, my own responsibility.

Thessaloniki, September 2024

Contents

Acknowledgments —— **VII**

List of figures —— **XI**

Introduction: Why the Search for Cognition in Classical Studies? —— **1**
        Cognitive linguistics —— **11**
        Memory and cognition —— **16**
        Theory of mind —— **19**
        Cognitive poetics —— **21**
        Artificial intelligence and Classics —— **23**
        Towards a constructive dialogue? —— **28**

Chapter 1 Objects acting: Ancient sources and 'material turn(s)' —— **32**
1.1   General premises —— **33**
1.2   Cognitive archaeology and ancient material —— **37**
1.3   Material engagement and "how things shape the mind" —— **39**
1.4   "Material turn" and the interpretation of texts —— **44**
1.5   Embodied perception —— **52**

Chapter 2 Spatial perception and ancient sources —— **58**
2.1   Space and social cognition —— **60**
2.2   Theoretical preconditions —— **63**
2.3   Ancient theatre as place and space: a case study —— **65**
2.4   Literary sources and the perception of space and place —— **70**

Chapter 3 Imaginations, visions, and perception —— **77**
3.1   Cognitive approaches to viewing in ancient dramaturgy and theatre —— **77**
3.2   Cognitive vision in ancient sources —— **86**
3.3   Conceptual theory of metaphor and ancient texts —— **97**

Chapter 4 Experience and the senses —— **106**
4.1   Experientiality and evidentiality in language —— **106**
4.2   Experience and 'sensory turn' in the Classics —— **110**
4.3   'Religious experience' and cognitive science —— **114**
4.4   Choruses as vehicles of social, political, and religious life —— **121**

Chapter 5 Emotions and ancient sources: conversations with David Konstan, Angelos Chaniotis, and Douglas Cairns —— 125
5.1   David Konstan —— **131**
5.2   Angelos Chaniotis —— **138**
5.3   Douglas Cairns —— **145**

Conclusion: Off to new shores? —— 157

Bibliography —— 163

General Index —— 206

Index of Greek and Latin passages —— 210

List of figures

Figure 1. *Warriors rowing and wild birds flying overhead. Sherd of a Mycenaean krater with remains of a scene. Voudeni, first half of 11th century BCE. The Archaeological Museum of Patras. © Ministry of Culture, Ephorate of Antiquities of Achaia* —— **7**

Figure 2. *The making of Pandora. Red-figured calyx-krater, circa 460–450 BCE. London, British Museum 1856,1213.1. © The Trustees of the British Museum* —— **27**

Figure 3. *Philoktetes on Lemnos. Terracotta squat lekythos (oil flask), circa 420 BCE. New York, Metropolitan Museum of Art 56.171.58. © OA Public domain https://www.metmuseum.org/art/collection/search/254917, last access June 11th 2024* —— **45**

Figure 4. *Gela Samsonidse, untitled, 2003, oil on canvas, 240x200 cm. © Gela Samsonidse* —— **47**

Figure 5. *Masks. Courtesy of Peter Meineck, Aquila Theatre, photography by Richard Termine* —— **49**

Figure 6. *The Temple of Zeus at Stratos, Agrinio, circa 321 BCE. Photography by © Georges Salameh* —— **62**

Figure 7. *The Theatre of Thorikos, north of Lavrio, circa 525–480 BCE. Photography by © Georges Salameh* —— **67**

Figure 8. *Naples birds krater. © Museo Archeologico Nazionale di Napoli 205239, formerly Malibu 82.AE.83, courtesy of the Italian Ministry of Culture, photography by Giorgio Albano* —— **84**

Introduction: Why the Search for Cognition in Classical Studies?

> *I think we're only at the beginning.*
> Douglas Cairns

This book is intended primarily as an explanatory introduction for students, but more generally for anyone interested in a new and rapidly growing field. The field is very attractive because it is multidisciplinary and open to diverse discussions and questions, whilst also being challenging and very complex. In a time of "growing excitement about the brain", interest in a dialogue between modern natural science research on human cognition and research in the humanities has been expressed for some years now.[1]

Cognitive studies examine the production and perception of information in interdisciplinary contexts that encompass thinking and feeling, in humans and in animals and even in machines. In this sense, there is a growing awareness that cognitive science offers insights for a new understanding of the classical world and its sources, and of classical literature and conventions.[2]

First of all, what do we mean by 'cognitive'? 'Cognitive' is, after all, a broad term that refers to the interest in and engagement with active mental processing by which we explain and interpret human behaviour.[3] Given the enormous diversity of research programmes on mental processing, 'cognitive studies' is used as an umbrella term throughout this book. It is an interdisciplinary endeavour akin to 'cultural studies', bound together by a set of shared concerns, affiliations and references, rather than a cohesive body of knowledge unified by agreed parameters and methodologies.

As Felix Budelmann recently pointed out in his writing on cognitive approaches to literature, "Like feminist criticism, poststructuralist criticism, or New Materialism, cognitive literary studies, and indeed the cognitive humanities as a whole, are a set of loosely connected enterprises rather than a focused programme of research. What holds these enterprises together, and justifies the umbrella term, is a shared interest in cognition, and in dialogue with research into

---

[1] See Noë 2009, xi.
[2] Thagard 2021. See three collected volumes dealing with the exchange between classicists and cognitive studies: Lauwers, Schwall and Opsomer 2018, Anderson, Cairns and Sprevak 2019, and Meineck, Short and Devereaux 2019a. See also the growing bibliography on the blog https://cognitiveclassics.blogs.sas.ac.uk, last access June 3rd 2024.
[3] Richardson 2004, 1–2. See also Louwerse and Van Peer 2009; Schneider 2000 and Schneider 2012, 117–120; Zunshine 2015b.

cognition in other subjects".[4] The traditional understanding of the human mind and behaviour in terms of Cartesian dualism has been actively criticised in recent years, and new models for conceptualising cognition, emotion and behaviour have emerged.[5] Cognition is no longer contrasted with feelings: it includes perception, intuition, and emotion insofar as they are related to how someone gathers knowledge about the environment and finds their way through it. New questions about literature, language, material culture, performance and religion come about by incorporating information from physiology and cognitive processes. In turn, the humanities, and ancient studies in particular, can also help neuroscientists and experimentalists – people who work in the fascinating field of scientific research into the structure and function of the nervous system and brain – gain important insights into the structure of the brain. To give an example, it might be of interest to consider the lifestyles and patterns of behavior, conversation and dealing with emotional crises in Classical Athens during Pericles' time, or in Nero's Rome. It may also be beneficial to consider instances where individual emotions appear to align with collective sentiments. In a modern context, scientific insights from a variety of societies, particularly those facing political challenges and personal struggles, can be valuable. By comparing these patterns with our own society, we might be able to gain some inspiring insights for both classicists and experimentalists.

Finally, some distinctions should be made in the fuzzy use of 'cognitive' terminology. Basically, cognitive science, cognitive approaches, cognitive research, cognitive theories and cognitive studies are all used interchangeably when applied to Classics. A strict distinction should actually be made between the empirical/scientific and theoretical nature of the material on which scholars base their use of the term.[6] In particular, the term 'cognitive science' will be used in this book to refer to empirical research (encompassing neuroscience and psychology, which involve empirical, data-driven research methods similar to those used in biology or chemistry, as well as theoretical, computational, and philosophical approaches) which is often the case in religious studies.[7]

I will discuss the cognitive approaches to the Classics that have been applied in recent decades, and the interaction of cognitive theories with classical studies in general and at different levels. In the rare cases where I refer to 'cognitive science' as it is commonly understood (such as clinical neuroscience), these studies have

---

[4] Budelmann 2023, 1.
[5] See Damásio 1994 and e.g. cross-disciplinary contributions in Scarinzi 2015. See also below p. 4–5, 8–9, 41, 52.
[6] See a good methodological overview in Budelmann 2023, 7–18.
[7] See p. 114–121 below.

also been carried out in recent years, but it is still far from being an established practice.[8]

The scepticism of many classicists towards so-called cognitive approaches is clear. Is there a chance to convince those with other opinions that cognitive concerns are important in the Classics, or will cognitive approaches ultimately prove fruitless and unnecessary? Or is this a case of pouring "old wine into new wineskins"? Is there anything new to say when applying these findings, or are the results pretty much the same as the way a good old-fashioned philologist would read in the sources? And more generally, what are the limits and possibilities of a dialogue between classicists and cognitive scientists? What can empirical studies contribute to the analysis of texts, performance, religion, ancient cultures, and cultural artefacts?

'Cognitive' approaches are by no means something that is only now being developed. The Roman grammarian, rhetorician and jurist Marcus Cornelius Fronto is known to have taught the young Roman emperor Marcus Aurelius rhetoric according to a special method. It seems that his approach was somewhat unique, as it is not mentioned in the Progymnasmata manuals, preliminary rhetorical exercises designed to prepare students for writing declamations. Marcus is instructed to develop an idea or conceptual domain using contemporary terminology from the field of metaphor studies and relate it to another given domain, to a given *imago*. In other words, Fronto gives his pupil a set of what we now call cognitive metaphors to use in his language. Marcus now has to find and describe a situation that matches a suggested *imago* (*Epist. ad M. Caes. et Inv.* 3.7 and 3.8, 139–140 CE).[9] Letter 3.8 is particularly interesting because here Fronto explains the technique of working out thought patterns. Marcus does not know how to use a particular *imago* and Fronto helps him.

> Front. *Ad Marc.* 3.8.1
>
> *Imaginem, quam te quaerere ais, meque tibi socium ad quaerendum et optionem sumis, num moleste feres, si in tuo atque in tui patris sinu id futurum quaeram?*
>
> As for the image you say you are looking for and want me to help you find, would you mind if I looked for it in your chest and in your father's chest?

Fronto is certain that searching for mental images in one's imagination, with the area of the breast or heart as a possible starting point, is the way forward. The imagination can be expanded to denote the mind more generally. As we soon

---

[8] See p. 114–121 and 6–9 below.
[9] Van den Hout 1999, 108–112 and Novokhatko 2024.

learn, the given image is of an island (*insula*), for which Fronto creates a further image: "As the island lies in the sea and holds back the waves, so your father carries the work of the kingdom on his shoulders" (Front. *Ad Marc.* 3.8.1). He adds, however, that Marcus is free to use this *imago* in different ways (*hac imagine multimodis uti potes*, Front. *Ad Marc.* 3.8.1). So, what exactly does *imago* mean here (Fronto also frequently uses the Greek εἰκών as an equivalent)?[10] The *imago* is sought and found in the chest or mind of Marcus and in that of his father.

It is clear that the *imago* is created by the imaginative power of the narrator and then of the narratee. Then there is the transfer of the *imago* to an appropriate domain. In terms of the theory of conceptual metaphor established by George Lakoff and Mark Johnson, Fronto provides Marcus with 'source domains', i.e. the conceptual domains from which the metaphorical expressions originate, in this case the *insula*, and asks him to find various appropriate 'target domains', such as in this case the emperor and his duties.[11] The 'target domain' is the quality or experience described or analogised by the 'source domain'. Marcus is asked to continue the exercise by trying to find the 'source domains' and apply them to the 'target domains' ("Send me the images you searched for and found with the same method by which the matter was demonstrated", *tu quas εἰκόνας in eandem rem demonstrata ratione quaesiveris et inveneris, mittito mihi*, Front. *Ad Marc.* 3.8.1).

We will return to this passage later when discussing the cognitive treatment of metaphor. Fronto is just one example of many that demonstrate the insights and overlaps between ancient theoretical discourse and contemporary cognitive approaches, including discussions of memory, imagination, emotions and perception.

Before discussing the structure of this book and the fields where cognitive theories and classical studies have enjoyed fruitful interaction, I will lay out a brief history of the field to cement some significant terms.

It is often thought that during the ancient and medieval periods, the prevailing mode of thought was dualism, where the mind is seen as distinct from the body.[12] However, as cognitive approaches to classical and medieval texts reveal, the reality

---

[10] On the use of *imago* and εἰκών in Fronto, see Schmitt 1934, 18–36.
[11] The theory of conceptual metaphors states that our mind works primarily in two domains: a 'source domain' from which we draw a mental image, and a 'target domain' that we want to understand (e.g. LIFE IS A JOURNEY, where LIFE is a 'target domain' and the JOURNEY is a 'source domain'). See Lakoff and Johnson 1980, Lakoff and Turner 1989, and Kövecses 2010. On the island metaphor here in Fronto see particularly Poignault 2002 and Ronnick 1997, 240–241. See below p. 88–91.
[12] While the bibliography is extensive, for the sake of clarity and coherence, a helpful resource for this book could be *Descartes' Error* by António Damásio (1994), in which he sees René Descartes' separation of mind and body (the famous mind-body dualism) as an error because thought requires guidance from emotions that are mediated by the body (Damásio 1994). See below p. 41, 52. See also Scarinzi 2015.

was in fact much more complex and nuanced, and classical thought was never purely and merely 'dualistic'. Nevertheless, it could be argued that the intellect was thought to be most obviously resistant to a materialistic account, and that, particularly from Descartes onwards, the main challenge to materialist monism was the concept of 'consciousness'.

The growing popularity of mechanisation in science in the 19th century led to some thought-provoking questions being raised about the body-mind relationship. As machines became more involved in decision-making and problem-solving, it seemed that these challenges were becoming more prevalent.

It has been for a long time an intriguing question whether a machine could be able to think. Could it be that the mind itself is a thinking machine? It could be argued that the idea that the mind is a machine is, in itself, a cognitive metaphor. It seemed increasingly plausible that the mind might be understood as a computational system, a possibility that led to the development of the computational theory of mind. In 1943, Warren McCulloch and Walter Pitts proposed a model of real processes in neuronal structures to clarify whether the brain could really compute the Turing-computable functions.

In the 1960s, Turing computation took centre stage in the emerging interdisciplinary field of cognitive science, which includes computational theory of mind, drawing upon a range of disciplines, including psychology, computer science, linguistics, philosophy, game theory and behavioural economics, anthropology, and neuroscience. Core mental processes such as reasoning, decision-making and problem solving are analogous in significant ways to computations executed by a Turing machine.

This approach was subsequently designated the 'first wave' or 'first generation' of cognitive theories, which posits that the mind is focused on machine-like processes that generate knowledge about the world. The subsequent 'wave' or 'second generation' of cognitive theories postulates that mental processes are linked to biological and physiological phenomena as well as cultural practices. The term 'distributed cognition' is typically employed to describe this approach, which provides a framework and method for studying human-object interactions.[13] Cognition is thus not limited to the brain and biological brain structure. It also consists of external devices and arenas, multi-person work teams, and ritual, mythical or scien-

---

[13] Scholz 2013. On distributed cognition and the humanities, cf. Anderson, Wheeler and Sprevak 2019.

tific systems that elicit interpretations of the real world as a feedback loop. These set the mind in a continuous flow, both in and out and back again.[14]

Distributed cognition theory is a vast interdisciplinary field of cognitive science. According to this theory, mental representations, which are supposed to be located in the individual brain, are in fact distributed throughout the socio-cultural system, which is essentially the means by which we think through and perceive the surrounding world.[15] In this way, distributed cognition can reveal the complex interdependencies between people and objects. As with enactivism, the embodied cognition approach emphasises the interconnectedness of body and environment in cognition processes. This includes not only somatic, but also neural, emotional and affective processes, motor control, proprioception and kinaesthesia.[16] It is also important to understand the way in which the body is connected to its social and physical environment.[17]

It might also be helpful to mention the seminal article, 'The extended mind', published by Andy Clark and David Chalmers in 1998. This text opens with a thought-provoking question: "Where does the mind stop and the rest of the world begin?"[18] Clark and Chalmers put forth the idea that cognitive states and processes could be more expansively conceived in terms of their spatial dimensions. Their theory of extension considers the boundaries within which cognition takes place, specifically in terms of space. It is also possible that cognition may happen outside the skull, in the 'centre' or the 'covering'. It seems that there is a growing body of evidence suggesting that mental processes may not be limited to the brain, but may extend into the body and into its environment.

At the Archaeological Museum of Patras this year I found a remarkable sherd of an 11th century BCE Mycenaean krater unearthed in Voudeni (Fig. 1). The scene is unmistakably vivid and interactive, with birds and humans shown as equal agents, merging into one another. This is an example of distributed cognition. Two rowing warriors are depicted, as are two helmets resembling hedgehogs, featuring low crests and decorative bosses. The warriors are holding a long stem in a rowing motion. Each warrior has a bird above his head that also resembles a hedgehog, looking in the opposite direction. The bird is shown with long legs

---

14 Lyre 2013. The theory of distributed cognition inspired the philosopher Andy Clark, who soon proposed his own version of the theory, which he called 'extended cognition'. See Clark 2008, Clark 2015. Cf. also Walter 2013 and Kiverstein 2018.
15 Zhang and Patel 2006.
16 Van Duijn 2012, Canino e.a. 2022.
17 See e.g. Clark and Chalmers 1998, Zhang and Patel 2006, and Ross, Spurrett, Stephens, Kincaid 2007.
18 Clark and Chalmers 1998, 7.

and a high neck, a fringed jewel on the back (attributed to the thorax), and one eye.[19]

Fig. 1: *Warriors rowing and wild birds flying overhead.* Sherd of a Mycenaean krater with remains of a scene. Voudeni, first half of 11th century BCE. The Archaeological Museum of Patras. © Greek Ministry of Culture, Ephorate of Antiquities of Achaia.

The distributed cognition approach thus focuses on how cognition extends into the environment through a mix of social means and technology.[20] It is a platform for cognitive research that embraces mediation between people, artefacts, and their surroundings. In addition, distributed cognition theory is an approach that helps shape the social aspects of cognition, focusing on the individual, the environment, and the media that people use to communicate with each other or to achieve complex goals.

A recent edited volume explores how cognition is conceived, explicitly or implicitly, as distributed across the body, the brain and the wider world, for example

---

19 See Kolonas 2020, 174–175, 178. On the context of such scenes, see also Cline 2024, 134–135 with further bibliography.
20 Yakhlef 2008, Michaelian and Sutton 2013.

in Greek and Roman technology and science (Courtney Roby, Andrew Riggsby and William Michael Short), medicine (George Kazantzidis), theatre (Peter Meineck and Diana Ng), philosophy (Christopher Gill) and literary criticism (Luuk Huitink).[21] A number of models are presented, which differ in whether cognition is embodied or relates to objects or devices in the world. Because most of the concepts and methods discussed in the volume have had an impact on modern thought, the study of the distributed nature of human cognition in antiquity and the contemporary study of cognition and neuroscience and their interaction with the classical texts are both of particular importance. In a nutshell, the papers explore the historical foundations of the theoretical understanding of how we are made to think.

With regard to the philosophy of mind, there are a number of different, partly overlapping, partly diverging, theories on the embodiment of the mind, to which distributed cognition is closely related. These can be described as the four 'E's', or the '4E cognition' paradigm (*E*-mbodied, *E*-mbedded, *E*-nacted, *E*-xtended).[22] This model emphasises the role of the sensorimotor system and the physical and social environment. It includes a broad perspective on the interactions between body, mind, and environment, from the 'extended mind' to tools and social interaction through to action-orientated processes.[23]

As described by Mark Rowlands, mental processes are: 1) 'embodied' in the sense that they are supported by all bodily states, including not only the brain but also more general bodily processes; 2) 'embedded' in their environment and only work in the relevant external environment; 3) 'enacted', in the sense that they include not only thinking but also acting and interacting, and not only neural but also corporeal processes; (4) 'extended' in the physical environment and include tangible and intangible resources (e.g. storing and writing data on computers).[24]

The current debate on the '4E cognition' and on embodiment is once again primarily transdisciplinary, shaped by recent findings from research into robotics and artificial intelligence as well as evolutionary biology and cognitive studies. However, the discussion also involves philosophical theories, and in particular phenomenological theories of the 20th century.

Although the Cartesian dichotomy between a material, world-bound body and an immaterial, thinking mind has already disputed considerably earlier, it seems

---

[21] Anderson, Cairns and Sprevak 2019. See also Roby 2019, Riggsby 2019, Short 2019, Kazantzidis 2019, Meineck 2019, Ng 2019, Gill 2019, Huitink 2019.
[22] Newen, De Bruin, Gallagher 2018 with further bibliography.
[23] See below p. 33–44. See also Gallagher 2005, Wheeler 2005, Zahavi 2014, Hutto and Myin 2012, Colombetti 2014, Colombetti and Roberts 2015. On enactivism, see above p. 6.
[24] Rowlands 1999, Rowlands 2010.

fair to say that Descartes remains the main addressee of '4E theorists'. It could be suggested that the fundamental premise of embodiment theories is to challenge the Cartesian dualism that has been fundamental to our understanding of science and the world. '4E theorists' argue that cognitive abilities are also influenced by physical abilities and interaction with the environment.

Embodiment theories, which will frequently appear in this book, claim that we are corporeal beings embedded in our environment. It is a fact that our cognitive capacity and intelligent abilities depend on this embedding and embodiment. The other important concept developed out of the '4E cognition' paradigm, enactivism, suggests that cognitive actions may arise from an interaction between the body, the mind, and the environment.[25] The environment is shaped and conceptualised by the dynamic sensorimotor processes of the human being. The key point is that the living being produces and determines its own problematic space, and this space does not exist independently, nor is it populated by organisms that have fallen from the sky, so to speak.[26] Rather, the organisms and their environment are inextricably linked and interconnected through mutual influence.

The introduction of the term 'enactivism' is connected to the coinage 'enaction' by Francisco Varela, Evan Thompson and Eleanor Rosch in their seminal book *The Embodied Mind: cognitive science and human experience* (1991). The authors suggest that our understanding of cognition can only be complete if we find a common ground for our understanding of the mind between science and experience. Cognition is thus "not the representation of a pre-given world by a pre-given mind but is rather the enactment of a world and a mind on the basis of a history of the variety of actions that a being in the world performs".[27] Enactivism is closely related to the human capacity to experience the world and to interact with other bodies in the surrounding world. The bodies are associated with the potential for interaction with the environment, which can be measured by the neural activity linked to anticipatory movement during perception.

Enactivism is often seen as the 'second generation' branch of the study of embodied cognition. It is presented as a counter-model to cognitivism (cognition as the analogue of information processing), computationalism (the 'first-generation' model of the mind as a computational information processing system) and the Cartesian mind/body dualism.[28]

---

25 Kyselo 2013 with further bibliography.
26 Varela, Thompson, and Rosch 1991, 198.
27 Varela, Thompson, and Rosch 1991, 9. See also the revised 2017 edition.
28 Stewart, Gapenne, Di Paolo 2010, Di Paolo, Rohde, and De Jaegher 2010, Gallagher 2017, Di Paolo 2018, Di Paolo, Cuffari, De Jaegher 2018. On the 'first' and 'second-generation' models, see below p. 16.

To sum up, enactivism is concerned with the interaction between mind, emotions, body and environment, and considers them to be inextricably intertwined. The 'second-wave' cognitive tendencies, including distributed cognition, '4E cognition', embodiment and enactivism, are the way forward when it comes to analysing classical texts and objects according to a cognitive framework. They offer the possibility of a variety of innovative readings of well-known passages.

The aim of this book is to give the reader an overview of the main perspectives and research of the last few decades from the fruitful collaboration between Classics and cognitive studies. It grew out of my students' questions: What exactly is the cognitive turn? Why is it of interest? I have taught several courses providing a general introduction to the topic, which try to explain what has been going on in Classics and related disciplines in recent years. The present book is intended as a stocktaking of cognitive studies in various branches of ancient studies, such as literary criticism and poetics, linguistics, ancient history, and archaeology.

Four major research areas or clusters are chosen for the presentation of each of the chapters of this work. Thus, chapter one discusses recent studies of materiality and material agency connected to the human mind, chapter two the so-called 'spatial turn' and cognition and the perception of space and place in relation to antiquity, chapter three imagination and vision and cognitive approaches to seeing, while chapter four considers experience and experientiality and the 'sensory turn' as applied to ancient sources. Finally, the fifth chapter is a special case and thus is in a different medium. Emotions are an indispensable part of historical and literary studies and form the background for all the above-mentioned thematic complexes. The work of three well-known pioneers of the study of emotions in the ancient world, David Konstan, Angelos Chaniotis, and Douglas Cairns, has considerably influenced the interplay and the dialogue between classical studies and cognitive approaches in recent decades in various direct and indirect ways. Therefore, I decided not to merely repeat their studies, but to change the format and create a kind of platonic dialogue in which the voices of the narrators merge with the thread of this book, and even dictate and determine it. In chapter five, I put forward some important methodological points for discussion with them and publish our conversations with their kind permission. The interviews took place in the spring of 2023 and will be published as a podcast alongside the printed version of this book. I asked these three scholars the same or very similar questions, often the same questions that my students have been asking me. The reader will see, however, that their answers are quite different to each other, and I believe that publishing our conversations in this form constitutes a particularly valuable part of this book.

The book is by no means intended to be the only, and much less so the definitive, assessment of the scholarship on the subject. Rather, it is an attempt to take stock of a rapidly evolving and highly controversial field that is currently in full bloom. It mainly discusses what has already been done in this field, and these questions are addressed from methodological and epistemological points of view. It is thus meant as a contribution to the evaluation of the phenomenon and of the processes that have taken place in Classics over the last twenty years. I discuss here only those concepts that have been elaborated particularly fruitfully with reference to classical sources. Ancient disciplines, as we know, are in the process of being questioned and reconsidered, and many modern theories are in the process of being applied to ancient material. In the case of cognitive studies, this is partly the point, but it is also an ongoing dialogue, and one might suggest that cognitive studies, can and will benefit from the study of ancient sources.

Some areas related to cognitive research are mentioned several times below, but are not covered in separate chapters. Here I will briefly outline some trends, including memory research, theory of mind, artificial intelligence and digital humanities, as well as the links between these areas and classical studies.

Cognitive linguistics

In recent decades, an increasing number of linguists have begun to apply concepts from cognitive linguistics to the analysis of ancient Greek and Latin, emphasising the opportunities that this can offer for our understanding of the classical languages. However, the juncture 'cognitive linguistics' is scientifically and terminologically controversial; there is no agreement on what it means exactly.[29] When analysing natural language, it assumes that language is a tool for organising contexts, processing information, and communicating.[30]

In cognitive linguistics, language is seen as a necessary part of the human cognitive faculty. As paradigmatically presented in the more recent handbooks, the following areas are therefore of particular importance for cognitive linguistics: "the structural features of natural language categorisation" (such as systematic polysemy, cognitive models, prototypicality, mental imagery and metaphors); "the

---

[29] Schwarz-Friesel 2012. See also Geeraerts and Cuyckens 2007b and Barcelona and Valenzuela 2011.
[30] Geeraerts 2006. The field is vast and thriving. Fundamental primers include: Taylor 1989, Ungerer and Schmid 1996, Dirven and Verspoor 1998, Lee 2001, Croft and Cruse 2004, Evans and Green 2006, Geeraerts and Cuyckens 2007a, Evans, Bergen, and Zinken 2007, Rickheit, Weiss, and Eikmeyer 2010, Brdar, Žic Fuchs, and Gries 2011, Littlemore and Taylor 2014, Dabrowska and Divjak 2015, Dancygier 2017, Thiering 2018, Dabrowska and Divjak 2019. Cf. also the journal *Cognitive Linguistics* (https://www.degruyter.com/journal/key/cogl/html?lang=de, last access June 3rd 2024).

functional principles of linguistic organisation" (such as iconicity and naturalness); "the conceptual interface between syntax and semantics" (studied by cognitive grammar); "the experiential and pragmatic background of language use"; "the relationship between language and thought", including also issues of relativism (e. g. the well-known variety of snow designations in the Inuit Eskimos language) and "conceptual universals" (such as nouns and verbs in all natural languages or consonants and vowels in all spoken languages).[31]

Cognitive linguistics originated with Noam Chomsky's critical review of B. F. Skinner's *Verbal Behavior* in 1959.[32] Chomsky's departure from behavioural psychology and his consequent antagonism to behaviourism contributed to a shift in the focus of psychology from empiricism to mentalism. The new fields of cognitive psychology and cognitive science then emerged.[33] In the 1980s, George Lakoff and Ronald Langacker launched the so-called 'Lakoff-Langacker Agreement', proposing to jointly oppose Chomsky's "generative grammar" as a cognitive science under the name of "cognitive linguistics".[34] According to the Agreement, cognitive linguistics does not regard syntax as an independent cognitive model subject to its own internal regulations and involving its own kind of mind representations, as is the case with Chomsky's approach, but rather examines syntactic and semantic structures of language in the context of ubiquitous and general human cognitive, biological and sensorimotor abilities.[35] In cognitive linguistics, language is therefore analysed on the grounds of neuroscientific findings, biology, experimental psychology, psycholinguistics, philosophy of mind, and other related academic fields that deal with the interaction of humans with their environment.

Consequently, there are three competing approaches within cognitive linguistics today: first, the Lakoff-Langacker approach (cognitive linguistics in terms of embodied cognition), which was one of the strongest drivers of the "second wave" of linguistic science.[36] Chomsky's "generative grammar" is the second. The third approach is that proposed by those linguists whose research falls outside the scope of the other two (Monika Schwarz-Friesel being the main proponent). They claim that cognitive linguistics should be assessed for its evidential value

---

[31] Geeraerts 2022, 178.
[32] Chomsky 1959.
[33] MacCorquodale 1970.
[34] Lakoff 1987a, Lakoff 1987b, Langacker 1987. See Harris 2021.
[35] Meineck, Short, and Devereaux 2019b, 5–7.
[36] On the contrast between the "second generation/wave" and the "first generation/wave" under the influence of the computational theory of mind, see below f. 52, and in particular Kukkonen and Caracciolo 2014.

rather than its theoretical value and should be considered as a whole field of scientific enquiry.[37]

As part of the entire human cognitive apparatus, language has an important impact on the formation and structuring of our knowledge of the world and helps us to conceptualise and organise the world we experience and create into cognitive units. Furthermore, language transports and 'translates' this information into a formal process that allows it to be communicated to others.[38] Therefore, everything that is expressed linguistically is somehow related to the experienced world, albeit at different levels of abstraction. It should be stressed that, according to the embodied hypothesis, meanings are not conceived as mere visual representations of the world.[39] Instead, since meaning in generative semantics is understood as 'mental representations', it always entails the expression, explanation and interpretation of the experienced world.[40] In this respect, language is not only a store of meaning, but also a form and a way of categorising and organising knowledge. Language not only reflects objective reality, but also organises and structures the world through its categorical functions. Above all, language is a form of knowledge management. It reflects the demands, requirements, concerns and expectations of individuals and cultures.[41]

In this sense, some conceptual phenomena are widely recognised as core components of cognitive linguistics. Some of the concepts mentioned above will be familiar to non-linguists, as they are common in literary criticism. In any case, this shows that cognitive approaches tend to unite rather than divide the disciplines, and that they create new intersections and crossroads where research can become complex and interdisciplinary. Perhaps the most current concepts in cognitive linguistics are prototypicality (categorisation of proto-images or obvious and stable concepts), metaphor (mapping from one conceptual domain to another), metonymy (mapping within a cognitive domain), embodiment (linguistic knowledge shaped by the individual's experience of the world), perspectivisation (the process of describing an object from the speaker's point of view), and mental spaces (partial formations created in thought and speech for the purpose of localised understanding and action).[42]

---

[37] See in detail Schwarz-Friesel 2012.
[38] Talmy 2000.
[39] On embodied language, see Dove 2014 and Johnson 2018.
[40] Mocciaro and Short 2019b, 1–2.
[41] Geeraerts and Cuyckens 2007b, 5.
[42] Basic concepts and models are excellently presented and discussed in Geeraerts and Cuyckens 2007b.

In the last few years, the theories and practices of cognitive linguistics have often been applied to the study of Greek and Latin language and culture. The way people use their language says a lot about how they think. In particular, a cognitive grammar requires that its conceptual constructions are based on language in its psychological and societal circumstances of use.

This has led to the development of frameworks and pragmatic/contextual phaenomena that are crucial to the study of pragmatics, sociolinguistics (on social registers, gender or politeness), and discourse analysis in ancient languages, such as word order, discourse markers, speech acts, and particles.[43] The analysis of linguistic data in Greek demonstrates the usefulness of a pragmatic approach: for example, linguistic and non-linguistic devices are used to analyse illocutionary power and modality in ancient languages. The different stages of the diachronic development are formally reflected in the linguistic context (use of negation, word order, modality in subordinate clauses, etc.).[44]

Deverbal pragmatic markers are also studied, for example, procedural elements derived from verbs whose form has been fixed and which have acquired new intersubjective meanings (e.g. Greek ἄγε "come on", Latin *quaeso* "please"). They can be explored in terms of politeness markers as their main function, which mitigates the illocutionary power of commands and requests, and they also can be explored in terms of their sociolinguistic distribution.[45] As the data suggest, these markers convey a range of meanings far beyond politeness and the illocutionary effects of attenuation. They communicate a range of personal attitudes, a reinforcement of pragmatic power and even a mocking rudeness, a kind of pragmatic inversion.

Cognitive linguistics offer a comprehensive framework for elucidating certain grammatical patterns that characterise Greek and Latin. Similarly, other embodied aspects of their linguistic structure concern the interface between morphosyntactic and lexical structure. Students of Classics are familiar with the syntactic and grammatical arrangements around which the teaching of grammar is traditionally

---

[43] Discourse analysis in ancient languages has been studied extensively in recent decades. Here are some of the most important works, with numerous (also very valuable) essays omitted: Porter and Carson 1995, Kroon 1995, E. Bakker 1997, E. Bakker and Kahane 1997, Raccanelli 1998, Boegehold 1999, Porter and Reed 1999, E. Bakker 2005, S. Bakker and Wakker 2009, Lee 2010, Raccanelli 2010, Raccanelli 2012, Ghezzi and Molinelli 2014, Nordgren 2015, Barrios-Lech 2016, Denizot and Spevak 2017. For an overview, see also Perdicoyianni-Paléologou 2014.
[44] Cf. Revuelta Puigdollers 2017. On neuroscientific studies applied to communication settings in Homer, see Giordano 2022.
[45] Cf. Fedriani 2017, Zakowski 2018. For politeness markers in Greek and Latin, see various contributions in Unceta Gómez and Berger 2022.

structured: circumstantial, temporal, and causal clauses; final and conditional clauses; gerunds, gerundives and supinals, and so on. In this field, Silvia Luraghi has done pioneering work on case systems, prepositions and semantic roles in ancient languages. These are related to specific schemes of movement and force and their metaphorical meanings.[46] In similar vein, Greek particles and the verbal tense system were analysed by Anna Bonifazi using methods of cognitive construction grammar.[47]

Klaas Bentein has published many case studies on cognitive approaches to linguistic constructions. For example, he discusses constructions in ancient Greek that are made up of a verb form and a present participle, an aorist or perfect tense.[48] Thus, by adopting a cognitive framework, he provides a semantic description of those uses in which the participle has an 'adjectival' function. A special kind of conceptual integration, in which only one component state of the verb is elaborated by the participle, is the so-called 'property reading', and property predication, which can be characterised by a low degree of transitivity, is typically involved in the adjectival periphrase.[49]

In another project, Bentein examines interpersonal relations and social interactions in Greco-Roman and Late Ancient Egypt (third century BCE – seventh century CE) through Greek documentary papyri, innovatively using the linguistic framework of historical politeness by incorporating a multimodal dimension.[50] In contrast to the literary sources, the documentary papyri offer an insight into daily life of all social classes. Moreover, since they are original, they can be interpreted on the basis of their external characteristics. The study focuses on a selection of document types (such as private and official letters, orders and petitions) from the city of Oxyrhynchos, one of the most important papyrological sites. These are examined to understand how politeness, apart from linguistic formulas and customs, can also be conveyed through the external features of written communication, such as the material and visual aspects of a text, and even through non-verbal and intangible communication (e.g. gestures and facial expressions).

Methodologically, cognitive linguistics treats language primarily as a system of categories and focuses on analysing the logical and empirical foundations of these categories. At the level of form, structures are examined not as independent units

---

46 Cf. Luraghi 2003, Luraghi 2010; Luraghi 2014; Luraghi 2022.
47 Cf. Bonifazi 2001, Bonifazi 2008, Bonifazi 2009, Bonifazi 2012, Bonifazi 2018, Bonifazi 2019, Bonifazi 2021.
48 Cf. Bentein 2016, Bentein, Janse, and Soltic 2017, Bentein 2020.
49 See also Hopper and Thompson 1980.
50 Bentein 2015a, Bentein 2015b.

but as reflecting levels of conceptual ordering, categorising principles, operating mechanisms, and the influences of experience and environment.

Memory and cognition

This is another crucial area that cannot be overlooked. Memory research is an important part of distributed cognition theory, which examines the ways in which we embed experiences of memory, facts or knowledge in the objects, people and tools around us. Memory enables us to store information and recall it later, and it is assumed to consist of short-term and long-term memory. As is well known, memory has gained in importance in recent decades in history, cultural studies, anthropology and, of course, in science. Like psychologists, cognitive scientists study memory, but are more likely to focus on how it might affect cognitive processes and the relationships that link cognition and memory.[51] Memory studies were particularly popular in the so-called 'first wave' of cognitive studies, mentioned above, when scholars applying them to classical sources focused on the creation, transmission and reception of literary heritage.[52]

Astrid Erll outlines approaches to memory research in the 20th century and distinguished between three phases of memory research: in the 1920s and 1930s, Maurice Halbwachs, Aby Warburg, and Frederic Bartlett wrote fundamental works on "collective memory" (*mémoire collective*); the second wave, in the 1980s and 1990s, was associated with Pierre Nora's work on *lieux de mémoire* and national memory in a broader sense, and with Jan Assmann's coinage of 'cultural memory'; finally, in recent decades the third has focused on post-colonial, transnational, transcultural, and multi-directional approaches.[53] In more recent studies, we have witnessed the emergence of a fourth phase that posits the post-human ecologically and leaves anthropocentric concepts aside.[54]

---

51 Markowitsch, Enlegen, Tscherepanow, Welzer 2013. Bjork and Bjork 1996, Slotnick 2017.
52 The 'first wave' or 'first generation' focused on machine-like processes that generate knowledge about the world: attention, categorisation, reasoning, learning, thinking, decision making, problem solving, perception, language comprehension and memory. The 'second wave' or 'second generation', on the other hand, linked mental processes to biological and physiological phenomena as well as cultural practices; it regarded the mind as an enactive evolutionary system and generally worked within the framework of enactivism (see p. 8–10 above). See Kukkonen and Caracciolo 2014.
53 Erll 2011b.
54 Bond, Craps, Vermeulen 2016.

According to Aleida and Jan Assmann, 'communicative/social memory' and 'cultural memory' are the two components of 'collective memory'.[55] The term 'cultural memory' refers to the traditions that are part of us, "the texts, images and rites that have been hardened over generations, in centuries, sometimes even millennia of repetition, and that shape our awareness of time and history, our view of ourselves and the world".[56]

Meanwhile, 'communicative memory' is limited to the oral tradition and the lived experiences of contemporary witnesses of the last three generations and, according to Assmann, covers at most the previous eighty years.[57] It is close to everyday life and bound to groups. 'Cultural memory' encompasses the archaeological and written legacy of humankind. It refers to a mythical prehistory. It is passed on orally, in writing, normatively and narratively. In contrast to communicative memory, it is highly formal and structured. Central concepts of 'cultural memory' are tradition and repetition. In oral societies, 'cultural memory' is passed on by memory experts and manifests itself in commemorative days and religious festivals.[58]

Memory studies have stimulated lively research in the Classics. However, although this conversation is longstanding and complex, far from all studies of memory are directly related to cognitive research. For example, literacy in the ancient world is in itself a subject closely linked to memory. The technique of writing alone, the encoding and decoding of symbols, the interpretation of meanings, the systems of retrieval and representation that organise the storage of meanings, and memory are seen as a complex and necessary fusion of different skills for reading and writing.[59] The relationship between writing, song and memory in the ancient world has taken centre stage for decades, culminating in the Parry-Lord studies of oral poetry. This has recently been explored from the perspective of psychology and cognition.[60] The writing tools we use have an effect on what we write, they shape and influence the writing process, and last but not least, our mind and our body, our hands, interact closely with writing tools. What exactly

---

55 The distinction between 'communicative' and 'social' memory is complicated and handled differently in the various schools of thought. Cf. Assmann and Assmann 1994, Erll 2011a, 27–35, Denschlag 2017, 17–42.
56 Assmann 2006a, 70.
57 Assmann 1992, Erll 2008.
58 Erll and Nünning 2008. On recent developments in cultural memory studies, see Crownshaw 2016.
59 E.g. see Ong 1982, Goody 1988, Finnegan 1988, Le Goff 1992, Assmann 2006b. As Douglas Cairns notes, the bibliography on this subject is extensive, but very little of it relates explicitly to cognitive science: Cairns 2019, 21f. 16 with further bibliography. Cf. also Short 2019b, 95–98.
60 Small 1997, Livingstone 2011, Hernández Garcés 2021.

is going on here? Writing and reading are deeply cognitive, and the tasks required of memory evolve and transform with the growth of literacy skills and technologies.

Elizabeth Minchin's pioneering monograph on memory studies and some applications of cognitive science to the *Iliad* and the *Odyssey*, for example, initiated cognitive approaches to memory and ancient texts.[61] A poet working in an oral tradition could maintain the momentum and rhythm of his song and create a story that would fill a long span of time. Such singers are still alive today and their memory is phenomenal.

Recently, some scientific insights from cognitive psychology and linguistics have become available to us through studies on the functioning of the brain, and we can learn how memory contributes to the composition and performance of orally transmitted poetry. Minchin has repeatedly and convincingly demonstrated how the poet in an oral tradition uses different memory resources, such as episodic, auditory, visual and spatial memory, to assist both in the process of creating and composing a song and at the moment of performance.[62] The cognitive implications of orality and writing are rooted in a number of earlier studies of the contribution of oral tradition and written records to the preservation of memory (see e.g. Short's analysis of function of *mnēmōn* as a databank in archaic Greece).[63]

A number of projects are currently underway that examine historiography and memory, trauma and remembrance, as they are constructed and circulated. Traumatic histories can lead to compassion and grief, but also to positive emotions such as hope and encouragement.[64]

Tragedy is an essential aspect of memory and cognitive thinking. Tragic heroes on stage are figures defined by their past who represent types of memory in theatre. In light of recent discussions, it has been aptly suggested that "if we examine the memories communicated onstage in terms of contemporary ideas about the construction and presentation of memory, we can see more clearly both what is

---

[61] Minchin 2001, Minchin 2005, Minchin 2007, Minchin 2008, Minchin 2016. On the "theatre of memory" in the *Iliad*, see also Clay 2011.
[62] E.g. Minchin 2019.
[63] Short 2019b, 96–99. See more generally Havelock 1963, Havelock 1986. Cf. also the series *ScriptOralia* published by Narr Verlag (Tübingen), which originated as the publication organ of the Freiburg Collaborative Research Centre "Transitions and Fields of Tension between Orality and Writing" (*Übergänge und Spannungsfelder zwischen Mündlichkeit und Schriftlichkeit*), as well as the series *Orality and Literacy in the Ancient World* published by Brill. Both series contain various volumes on memory research on ancient sources.
[64] See for example Meineck and Konstan 2014, Caston and Weineck 2016, Proietti 2019, Cecchet, Degelmann, and Patzelt 2019, Proietti 2021, Proietti 2022.

at stake when a character engages in an act of memory and how differences in memory can be indicative of broader differences in perspective".[65]

Theory of mind

Another area related to both memory studies and cognitive theories is the theory of mind. It is a model in psychology for the ability to understand other people's mental and emotional states as a possible cause of behaviour, which helps explain and predict one's own or others' actions. In literature one can find various paraphrases of this term, such as understanding of other people's consciousness, theory of intentions, theory of consciousness, and so on, with consciousness being understood as "the locus of remembering, imagining, and feeling".[66] It is a system of representations of mental phenomena (*metarepresentations*) that develops intensively in childhood. To possess a mental state model means to be able to perceive both one's own experiences (belief, desires, intentions, emotions, thoughts, knowledge, etc.) and those of other people. Theory of mind thus interacts with the capacity for empathy or sympathy: a crucial awareness develops that others' experiences could and should be different from one's own.[67]

In recent decades, the theory of mind has borne particularly rich fruit in its engagement with narratology, which has been declared indispensable to our reading and interpretive process, while narrative has been described as a "description of fictional mental functioning".[68] Alan Palmer focuses on the social nature of thinking and uses theory of mind as a tool to respond to narratives in order to navigate the social world. From another perspective, Lisa Zunshine sees 'mindreading', the development of new cultural and social relations to make the audience imagine the intricate state of mind of characters and narrators, as an inference about mental state made from behaviour, and therefore necessary for normal human communication.[69] Her recent monograph brings together cognitive science, ethnography and literary history to examine patterns of 'mindreading' in a range

---

65 Van Essen-Fishman 2023, 99.
66 Chafe 1994, 38. See also Blackmore and Troscianko 2018.
67 The discovery and development of theory of mind largely took place through research on animals and young children. See Premack and Woodruff 1978.
68 Palmer 2004, 12, and Palmer 2010, 9. On the theory of mind applied to narratology, see Mar, Djikic and Oatley 2008, Oatley 2009, Herman 2011, Leverage e.a. 2011, Pagan 2014.
69 Zunshine 2006. On 'mindreading', see Apperly 2011, Chesters 2014, Lavelle 2022. For the application of the theory to classical studies, see Ruffell 2008, and Budelmann and Easterling 2010 and below p. 21.

of literary works, from *The Epic of Gilgamesh* to Ralph Ellison's *Invisible Man*.[70] Zunshine suggests that states of mind are 'embedded' in each other, and compares this with the real paradigms studied in cognitive psychology. It is particularly worth noting that the mind-reading of others can be both transparent and false, with the possibility of misunderstanding deserving special evaluation.[71]

One of the most prominent examples of applying of the theory of mind to classical texts is Ruth Scodel's work on Homer.[72] She looks at how Homeric characters interact with each other throughout the story, focusing in particular on their social behaviour, what opponents think of the hero, but more importantly, what 'others' think of him. Characters tend to control how others judge them, which is why Homeric heroes carefully manipulate their words. They are constantly engaged in a process of mindreading, and their psychology is much more complicated than previously thought. This study is therefore an important contribution to the serious contemporary debate about whether and how deeply we can know other people's minds.

Scodel's model of thought is part of a long tradition of cognitive psychological readings of the *Iliad* and the *Odyssey* that began, perhaps, with Bruno Snell's seminal postwar work *The Discovery of the Mind* ("Entdeckung des Geistes", 1946), but was further developed and scientifically grounded by Elizabeth Minchin (discussed above), and culturally popularised by the clinical psychiatrist Jonathan Shay.[73] It is clear that psychiatry and psychoanalysis are inextricably linked with the theory of mind, which is focused on the ability to understand mental states and behaviour.

More recently, several volumes have explored the rich interaction between theory of mind and classical texts, or perhaps psychoanalysis and classical texts is more apt given the increasing use of terms such as depression, trauma, therapy with reference to ancient sources. These scholars argue that the study of Classics can enable psychologists to ground their science in historical, literary and philosophical frameworks, including Peter Meineck and David Konstan (*Combat Trauma and the Ancient Greeks*, 2014), Jeroen Lauwers, Jan Opsomer and Hedwig Schwall (*Psychology and the Classics: A Dialogue of Disciplines*, 2018), and more

---

70 Zunshine 2022.

71 For a sketchy analysis of Palmer and Zunshine's work on the application of the theory of mind to narratology, see Grethlein 2023b, 83–87. Grethlein also argues at length for certain limitations of the theory of mind when applied to the narratological analysis of ancient texts.

72 Scodel 2008, Scodel 2012, Scodel 2014. In a recent publication, Scodel applied attribution theory, which is closely related to the theory of mind and examines how people assign causes to actions and outcomes, to the exchange between Antigone and Ismene in Sophocles' *Antigone*, see Scodel 2023.

73 Snell 1946, Minchin 2001, Minchin 2007, Shay 1995, Shay 2002.

narrowly by Konstantinos I. Arvanitakis (*Psychoanalytic Scholia on the Homeric Epics*, 2015), Charles Underwood (*Mythos and Voice: Displacement, Learning, and Agency in the Odyssey*, 2018), and Joel Christensen (*The many-minded man: the Odyssey, psychology, and the therapy of epic*, 2022).

In the field of Greek tragedy, a seminal 2010 article by Felix Budelmann and Pat Easterling made a valuable contribution to the application of theory of mind to reading classical texts.[74] They consider the ways in which spectators engage with the thoughts, feelings and intentions of the 'characters', with the aim of understanding how these elements are perceived and received by the audience. In Old Attic comedy, Isabel Ruffell applied the theory of the mind to the audience's perception of emotion. When comic audiences engage with a performance, they are not analysing the jokes of realistic characters, but the comic causation, which includes the characterisation itself. An important criterion for assessing audience response is to track the audience's emotional involvement.[75]

While researchers in cognitive literary studies actively seek professional exchanges and forums, they do not strive to develop the same methods and tools, as they mostly work in spheres that are very distant from each other in terms of content. The human mind is undoubtedly complex, and there is still much to be discovered about it. Nevertheless, the search for a grand unified theory of cognition and literature is a worthy endeavour. However, without a solid theoretical foundation in cognitive studies, it is impossible to fully understand the world we live in.[76] These multifaceted views have undoubtedly shaped the development of cognitive approaches in literary studies over the last decade, despite the lack of overall consensus.

Cognitive poetics

One of the specific terms coined to describe this fusion of some principles of cognitive science, especially cognitive psychology, with the interpretation of literary

---

74 Budelmann and Easterling 2010.
75 See especially Ruffell 2008, 45–50.
76 The cognitive methods that emerged in the 1980s and are used in literature interpretation are numerous. See, for example, Fludernik 1996, Stockwell 2002, Zunshine 2006, Tsur 2008, Brône and Vandaele 2009a, Sanford and Emmott 2012, Armstrong 2013, Bernini and Caracciolo 2013, Calabrese and Ballerio 2014, Ryan 2015, Zunshine 2015a, Zunshine 2015b, Cave 2016a, Cave 2016b, Lavocat 2016, Garratt 2016, Burke and Troscianko 2017, Tsur 2017, Kukkonen 2017, Armstrong 2020, Zunshine 2022.

texts is 'cognitive poetics'.[77] Cognitive poetics draws on the modern principles of cognitive linguistics and ties in with reader-oriented criticism.[78] Above all, the narratological insights of literary criticism invite engagement with linguistic studies on discourse analysis and the experiential character of language.[79] As will be shown below, there are many commonalities between cognitive poetics and cognitive linguistics, such as deixis, schema, writing and its role in reading, attention and the like.[80] It is therefore not surprising that the most important names in the work on cognitive poetics partly overlap with those who wrote the key works on cognitive linguistics.

Of course, literary scholars can only work together with cognitive scientists to a limited extent. As Nancy Easterlin has rightly pointed out, the nature and diversity of literary works contradict a programmatically scientific approach to them, because the complex cognitive process of generating and consuming is always subjective and interpretative.[81] Furthermore, cognitive science requires long preparation and demanding training. The – in many ways formidable – separation between the natural sciences and the humanities leads to significant differences in thinking about the world. A significant branch of cognitive science emerges from philosophy and psychology. This provides a solid theoretical foundation that could potentially lead to the unification of these fields, as evidenced by the distributed cognition projects mentioned above.[82]

The work of Evert van Emde Boas should also be seen within a general framework of cognitive poetics (or cognitive stylistics). In several publications he carried out cognitive and experimental studies on the Greek language, in particular on the language of Greek tragedy. Van Emde Boas works with the notion 'mind style', borrowed from the theory of cognitive stylistics, and claims that the way people speak on stage or in speeches reveals a lot about their way of thinking and their character. Van Emde Boas claims that an author shapes his characters through their use of language, showing how the characterisation of narrators is determined by their speaking style and 'linguistic behaviour'.[83]

---

[77] It seems that the term was coined by the Israeli literary critic Reuven Tsur, see Tsur 1983.
[78] Vgl. Jauß 1982, Jauß 1967, Jauß 1994, Jauß 1998, Iser 1971, Iser 1972, Körtner 1994, Semsch 2005, Winko und Köppe 2008. Also see below p. 28, 109.
[79] E.g. Allan and Bijs 2007, van Gils, de Jong, and Kroon 2019, De Bakker and De Jong 2022.
[80] Major introductory works on cognitive poetics and stylistics include: Semino and Culpeper 2002, Stockwell 2002, Zunshine 2006, Gavins and Steen 2003, Stockwell 2007, Freeman 2007, Tsur 2008, Boyd 2009, Brône and Vandaele 2009a, Vermeule 2010, Gottschall 2012.
[81] Easterlin 2012, 6.
[82] See above p. 6–10.
[83] E.g. see on Euripides Van Emde Boas 2017, on Sophocles Van Emde Boas 2021, and on Lysias Van Emde Boas 2022.

'Mind style' was introduced by Roger Fowler in 1977 to describe "any distinctive linguistic representation of an individual mental self".[84] In literary studies, it is also used to analyse the thoughts, ideas and values of characters based on what they say and how exactly they use language.[85] Of course, the term 'mind style' is closely associated with research on theory of mind discussed above, and its placement here in the discussion of cognitive poetics is rather conventional, perhaps because it is more linguistic and less philosophical, if such a distinction makes any sense in studies of mind and language.

Cognitive literary scholars build on the insights of cognitive science, but approach them critically and pragmatically, examining them in the context of their own discipline. In addition, cognitive literary criticism encompasses a wide range of studies such as gender studies, postcolonial studies, narratology and ecocriticism. The application of two fields that are already highly interdisciplinary, such as literary criticism and cognitive science, inevitably leads to a great diversity of paradigms and approaches. The diversity is so great that both sceptics and advocates of cognitive approaches say: "Anything can be cognitive!" Indeed, material engagement theory and cognitive narratology, for example, have at a first glance little in common, either in terms of the cognitive science research areas they draw upon or the theoretical paradigms they develop.[86] And yet, as will be argued below, there are key features of cognitive approaches to literature that unite all these views.

Artificial intelligence and Classics

Just as artificial intelligence is one of those fashionable terms that people talk about everywhere, it is also very popular in connection with classical antiquity; however, it is actually a very difficult term to understand.[87] AI research is generally considered a sub-discipline of cognitive science.[88] AI does fantastic things when the rules are clear and there is lots of training data, but it will only ever do exactly

---

[84] Fowler 1977, 103.
[85] Semino 2002, Semino 2005, Semino 2007. See also Leech and Short 1981, chapter 6 "Mind style", and Pillière 2013 on the use of the notion in scholarly research.
[86] See below p. 39–44.
[87] For a stimulating discussion of what AI is and is not, see the general overview by philosopher Karoline Reinhardt and data scientist Bernhard Knapp (13 May 2022): https://www.forbes.at/index.php/artikel/WAS-IST-KI-NICHT.html?fbclid=IwAR1TJFM_3Mkmv1WSXyAJygkgsFD_mEhw8kfIP2-3NvW1HwZDh0pN9Md0u-k, last access June 3rd 2024.
[88] Schmid 2013. See also Rohde 2013 and Frankish and Ramsey 2014.

what it has been trained to do. Ultimately, it remains a construct of metals and electrical impulses, and behind every step and click is the influence of human intelligence. The artificial system that we have created to perform a specific task can even learn (an obvious and prominent example is a type of large language model *Generative Pre-trained Transformers*) although it seems to have no mind or motivation of its own. These are all open questions that may be thought-provoking. Indeed, the debates on computational mind that have emerged in the 1960s have already brought these questions to the fore.[89]

Computational modelling explores how human intelligence might be built. There is a debate in the field as to whether it is better to think of the mind as a vast set of tiny but singularly weak items (such as neurons) or as a set of overarching constructs such as schemas, symbols, rules, plans, and patterns.[90] The former relies on connectionism to explore the mind (learning associations from data as a crucial process for understanding behaviour), while the latter focuses on symbolic artificial intelligence (using knowledge in learning to produce intelligent behaviour). One way of looking at this is whether a machine can accurately simulate a human brain without the neurons that make it up.

There are at least two ways of looking at the interaction between AI and Classics. One is to see what AI and its tools can contribute to the study of ancient Greek and Latin, ancient history, archaeology, and the like. The other is to look at it on a metacognitive level: what do ancient sources actually say about artificial intelligence, robots and androids, and how the relationship between man and machine was perceived in antiquity?

Regarding the first, machine learning is generally actively used in the humanities and has been applied to the study of ancient literature for several decades. In philological fields, developing and using computer software in search mechanisms for vocabulary or syntactic constructions has been particularly productive. This has also led to a revolutionary change in research methods in Classics.[91] Linguistic data processing (*natural language processing*) is applied to Ancient Greek and Latin, using machine learning to accomplish tasks such as tokenisation (breaking down the given text into tokens, the smallest units in a sentence), stemming (finding the root of words), lemmatisation, part-of-speech tagging, and word embed-

---

[89] See above p. 5–10.
[90] Graubard 1988, Boden 1990. See also a useful overview by David Alan Grier in https://www.computer.org/publications/tech-news/closer-than-you-might-think/debating-artificial-intelligence, last accessed February 21st 2023.
[91] Solomon 1993b.

ding.⁹² It is becoming increasingly evident that a significant number of growing projects, spearheaded by scholars such as Gabriel Bodard and Monica Berti, illustrate a potential need for a response from the Classics to the computational challenges we are facing.

As for the second way, ancient literary texts describe at the metacognitive level a kind of artificial intelligence and robotics. Ideas about artificial intelligence were popular in ancient times.⁹³ The relationship between human and machine, and between natural and artificially created individuals, has long been a theme in literature.⁹⁴ The 'androids' of Hephaestus in the *Iliad* or the phenomenon of Pandora in Hesiod have long been considered the earliest examples of a posthuman artificial intelligence.⁹⁵ Hephaestus' machines serve as thinking tools to achieve the god's goals, and can thus be seen as projections of his extended mind.⁹⁶ Most important to Hephaestus' metalworking are his 'automatic' bellows, which expel hot air whenever he needs it (*Il.* 18, 469–473), or his tripods, which reveal their robotic character (οἱ αὐτόματοι) as soon as they are made (*Il.* 18, 372–380).⁹⁷ There may be more to the issue than meets the eye: it seems that in both instances of Hephaestus' machine and the creation of Pandora, the concept of 'artificial intelligence' has been perceived as divine intelligence in the god's creations. The scene depicted on the Attic Chalice Krater, dating from the mid 5th century BCE (Fig. 2), shows the 'roboter' Pandora receiving gifts from the gods (the scene functions also as explanation for her name). This was the first woman ever, formed from earth by Hephaestus, the god of fire, at the behest of Zeus as punishment for the fire stolen from the gods by Prometheus (Hsd. *Theog.* 570–589).

---

92 The bibliography is extensive and growing, as are numerous workshops, congresses and conferences which are held each year on the subject that has now established itself as a discipline: Digital Classics. See Berti 2019. Cf. also Chronopoulos, Maier, Novokhatko 2020, and Chronopoulos, Maier, Novokhatko 2022; Graziosi, Haubold, Cowen-Breen, and Brooks 2023.
93 The landmark study is Mayor 2018. Cf. Part V on AI in the *Routledge Handbook of Classics and Cognitive theory* (Meineck, Short, and Devereaux 2019) on AI in ancient Greece: Lather 2019 and Gerolemou 2019.
94 On the long-term relationship between human and artificial intelligence, see in particular Fuchs 2020, 21–70. On the philosophical background of this process, see also Reinhardt 2020. On dehumanisation in general and on animals, monsters and robots in ancient Greek and Roman literature, see Mayor 2018, Bianchi, Brill, and Holmes 2019, Chesi and Spiegel 2020, and Gerolemou and Kazantzidis 2023. For representations of artificial intelligence in Greek and Roman epic poetry, including the way in which it was received in later literature, see also Bär and Domouzi 2024.
95 Marcinkowski and Wilgaux 2004, Lather 2019, Silverman 2022, see also Clark and Chalmers 1998, Clark 2003, McCorduck 2004.
96 Lather 2019.
97 Translation by A. T. Murray (1925).

In the centre of the painting, Pandora stands en face, rigid and lifeless but looking like a human woman, her feet close together, her hands at her sides, each holding a wreath. Beside her, to the left, Athena with both her hands holds out a wreath to Pandora. Next on the left is Poseidon, looking at Zeus, seated on a chair. To the right of Pandora is Ares, moving to the left and looking back to Hermes, running to the right, looking back and holding his caduceus in his right hand, stretched out towards Ares.[98] The relationship depicted here does not seem to be one of nature versus artifice, or humanity versus machine: it is a complex interplay between the human, divinity and machine. This leads us to the field of contemporary posthuman studies, where this interplay is primarily questioned.

Artificial life and human thinking can be represented on the theatrical stage in the form of sculptures with animated physical accessories and body parts.[99] Natural intelligence consists of mental functions such as learning, feeling, remembering, understanding, and mental habits and patterns of behaviour. It could be argued that AI refers to inanimate artefacts that exhibit traces of natural intelligence, if we are to apply the terms to the ancient world. For example, in Euripides' *Helen*, Teucer is certain that Helen is a "murderous image" and a "copy" of the woman he hates. He is therefore impressed by the reproduction of the body, which is identical to Helen's body. He is unaware that a "phantom" is responsible for his suffering, which he is unable to distinguish from the real Helen (Eur. *Hel.* 71–74). Artificial replicas of mental functions on stage are presented in such a way as to have a psychological and physiological effect on the mimetic body. In other words, here too, the relationship between the human body and a non-human object is questioned.[100]

It seems that discussions about digitalisation and so-called artificial intelligence are characterised by the coexistence of two closely related visions of the future: one utopian, the other dystopian.[101] There is no doubt that public discourse about AI is ambivalent: it is both praised and damned. Indeed, the inevitability of AI in our studies of the future is accompanied by the simultaneous emergence of discourses of world salvation and the decline of the humanities. In this context, the study of Greek and Roman texts with their reflections on human, non-human and

---

98 I owe this detailed description to the British Museum. See also for further bibliography: https://www.britishmuseum.org/collection/object/G_1856-1213-1, last access September 25th 2024.
99 Gerolemou 2019. On the 'embodied view' on stage, see Meineck 2017, 52–58.
100 Gerolemou 2019, 348. On the human body and the object on stage in Greek tragedy, see a recent study by Worman 2021. See the discussion below p. 44–51.
101 Reinhardt 2020.

Fig. 2: *The making of Pandora.* Red-figured calyx-krater, circa 460–450 BCE. London, British Museum 1856,1213.1. © The Trustees of the British Museum.

post-human relationships between objects, machines, robots and the human mind seem surprisingly contemporary.[102]

---

[102] For the historical context and how humanist-post-humanist reasoning relates to ancient

Towards a constructive dialogue?

So what does 'cognitive' actually mean when we use it for so many different subjects – language and linguistic categories, the sensory world, emotions, materiality, geography, archaeology and artificial intelligence? It is an umbrella term used against the strict use of 'cognitive' in the sense of 'first generation'. It no longer refers to the computational-rational mind in the model of a computer programme as a process of symbol manipulation.[103] The term 'cognitive' in today's 'second wave' studies, or perhaps already in 'post-second-wave-studies', implies that experience is not a computational modelling exercise in which we create an internal scale of our environment, but an embodied, judgemental discovery of the world.[104] It emphasises the embodied essence of the mind and the dynamic relationships between the mind and its environment.

The key word 'experience' and the notion of experiential background are perhaps, among other things, a kind of legacy of John Dewey's "art as experience" and Hans Robert Jauß's "aesthetic experience".[105] For the 'school of Constance', the "professional reader" / "ideal reader" is fundamental.[106] This is the 'experienced' reader who has sound literary 'experience' and knowledge and is thus able to recognise the signals and cross-references in the text. It appears that, at the same time as phenomenological frameworks are also becoming increasingly popular as a method of reading classical texts, there is a growing understanding that the 'experience' of the reader is shaped by their bodily engagement with a text or theatrical performance.[107] Here we come close to the concept of experientiality. Reader-response criticism has proved in part to be a continuation of previous interpretive practice that is characterised by the communication model with a (decoding) receiver. Here, however, the meaning of the text is strongly predetermined by the "implied readers", directed by the author's mind. They can unfold meanings that the actual reader has not yet unfolded, namely when it proves what aesthetic experience the sender has conveyed to the recipient. For their part, enactivists claim

---

thought, see Rengakos 2022 and Rengakos 2024. See further Mayor 2018 and Gerolemou 2022. See also various chapters in Chesi and Spiegel 2020 and Gerolemou and Kazantzidis 2023.

103 Kukkonen and Caracciolo 2014, Morgan e.a. 2017. See also Budelmann 2023, 1–3. See above p. 5–6.
104 Caracciolo 2014, 16–19.
105 Dewey 1934, Jauß 1982. On the notion of 'experience' see below p. 106–110.
106 Iser 1971, Iser 1972, Iser 1976. See also Sneis 2018 with further bibliography. Jauß and Iser's ideas are reflected in theory of mind research currently emerging from cognitive studies (see p. 19–21 above) that shed light on the mental activities of audiences in filling gaps and processing complex narratives, see Stockwell 2009, 134–167. See also p. 109–110.
107 See Weiss 2023 for a recent study of Greek theatre and phenomenology.

that these are not mental representations inscribed in the mind, but an engagement with the world determined by the set of values that permeate the human field of experience.[108]

Literary texts deal with the human experience, and "literature plays with the brain", as Paul Armstrong has remarkably stated: through the experience of harmony and dissonance, opposites are brought into motion that are crucial to the underlying neurobiology of mental behaviour.[109] Readers, who are able to enjoy harmonic or dissonant art, can make sense of the texts and use the insights of neuroscience and phenomenology to process their aesthetic experience. This is where Armstrong sees the opportunity for an exchange: for neuroscientists, various fields of research – the neurobiology of seeing and reading, the mind-body interactions that underlie feelings – can be associated with various aesthetic and literary phenomena. For philologists, questions arise about the role and function of aesthetic experience: when we read a work of literature, what actually happens? Is the interpretation of a literary text related to other forms of knowledge?

An evaluative embodied experience is a mental act of imaginative and often physical approach to objects. We do not relate to objects in our environment by building static mental representations, but by perceiving their performances, i.e. by mentally exploring how a body can respond to them (what James Gibson termed affordances).[110]

At this point, the topic of body and environment becomes particularly relevant for scholars of antiquity: while the body as a material object is usually the focus of archaeologists, it is, as already discussed, increasingly also an area of interest for historians and philologists in general.[111] Therefore, many expressive devices, especially metaphor, are engaged in the interaction of embodied experience and representation.[112]

Perhaps the biggest sticking point in applying cognitive studies to the ancient world is the question of how relevant our current data are to a society that existed three or two thousand years ago. The last twenty-five years, dominated by cognitive

---

[108] Caracciolo 2014, 8–11. See also Caracciolo and Kukkonen 2021, 174–195.
[109] "How literature plays with the brain" is in fact the first part of Armstrong's book title, see Armstrong 2013.
[110] Gibson 1979, 127: "The *affordances* of the environment are what it *offers* the animal, what it *provides* or *furnishes*, either for good or ill. The verb to *afford* is found in the dictionary, but the noun affordance is not. I have made it up. I mean by it something that refers to both the environment and the animal in a way that no existing term does. It implies the complementarity of the animal and the environment".
[111] James Porter raised the problem of materiality in ancient studies, cf. Porter 2003, Porter 2010. See also Canevaro 2019 and see p. 44–57 below.
[112] Cairns 2019, 23–24. See below p. 97–104.

approaches in the humanities and ancient studies, have attempted to address this problem.[113] Human existence involves complex and multifaceted relationships between the brain, the body, other people, the external material world, and a wide variety of things and technologies.[114] This means that we can expect the concepts of 'embodiment' and 'distributed cognition' to influence our perception of all the cognitive artefacts left to us by the ancient Greeks and Romans.[115] The ancient ways of thinking that underlie these artefacts, some of which will be presented in various chapters of this book, explicitly reflect points of view that we might in some ways regard as acknowledging this fact. Indeed, many ancient thinkers take into account the connection between the mind and the body with other people and the environment. An understanding of embodiment and distributed cognition should inform much of what we do as researchers of the ancient world in our attempts to understand and illuminate that world.[116]

As mentioned earlier, I have chosen here five basic concepts of cognitive studies applied to ancient sources: 'embodiment and materiality', 'space and cognition', 'visualisation and vision', 'experience', and 'emotion'. These five concepts form the structure of this book. They are closely interwoven and influence each other. People's experiences of seeing, hearing, reading, writing, travelling, visiting, participating, etc. are something that cultural history has difficulty analysing with the resources at its disposal. A person's experience remains subjective and thus difficult to evaluate, which is why this dangerous endeavour has often been avoided. At the same time, the growing number of works on perception, emotion, materiality and, not least, artificial intelligence in various disciplines of ancient studies shows that this is a fundamental question.

Why cognition matters for the humanities in general, and for ancient studies in particular, is explored in the trends and initiatives discussed above and below. Cognition is understood as a distributed process when the mind is seen as something that cannot be reduced to the brain and is fundamentally oriented towards world-encompassing, situational and responsive action, often involving non-neural structures and media.[117] The place and function of embodiment and the embodied organism as a system in the perception of its environment seems, from this perspective, to be fundamental to all the classical disciplines.

---

113 See, for example, Richard Nisbett's many years of work on cross-cultural cognitive studies and his famous statement that "human cognition is not everywhere the same" (Nisbett 2003, xvi).
114 Cairns 2019, 36.
115 Habinek and Reyes 2019.
116 On these issues, see Fagan 2011, especially his very insightful introduction, pp. 1–12.
117 Garratt 2016, 7–10. See also above pp. 6–10.

'Cognitive Classics' should not be understood as a new turn or paradigm shift. On the contrary, the lines of research that are emerging at the intersection of cognitive theory and literature, anthropology, and cultural expressions in general, the arts, are hardly new. The most sustainable interdisciplinary collaborations are based on models and insights that acknowledge the inescapable fact that the mind is embodied.

My aim here has been to explore how far interdisciplinary conversations between cognitive and classical studies have progressed until now, and to get a perspective on the extent to which the increasingly developing field of consciousness studies can benefit from and be helpful to ancient studies. As Alva Noë repeatedly points out, consciousness is a worldwide dynamic process, and only by taking a holistic view of the active life of humans or animals can we truly understand the brain's contribution to conscious experience.[118]

---

[118] Noë 2009, 47–65.

Chapter 1
Objects acting: Ancient sources and 'material turn(s)'

We are surrounded by things, by objects, and we are in constant interaction with them. The most obvious discipline in the study of antiquity that deals with objects is archaeology, and so it is no coincidence that the 'material turn' in Classics is closely linked to the findings of 'cognitive archaeology'. It is therefore perhaps easiest to begin the discussion of how we perceive the material objects around us and in the ancient texts with 'cognitive archaeology'. Cognitive archaeology, like other 'cognitive' disciplines, is the archaeology of the mind and therefore encompasses the full range of activities that skilled people perform, such as making tools, planning and building new social worlds. It is a recognition that the human mind and intellect are grounded in the immediate experience of the physical world and can therefore be studied by exploring the material remains of the past.[119]

Cognitive archaeology emerged in the 1970s as a response to the demand of processual archaeology (or 'New Archaeology') to interpret the past strictly on the basis of material evidence.[120] The pronounced "materialism" limited archaeology to identifying and describing artefacts and excluded further wider ranging readings of their possible cognitive and cultural significance as something outside the reach of deductive reasoning.

However, processual archaeology now made it possible to investigate the lifestyles of the people who produced and utilised material culture. The view emerged that by studying the traditional way of life of contemporary peoples, one could better understand the way of life of the ancient world.[121] Lewis Binford's work helped to advance the idea that material forms can convey information about the way of life and, as the product of intelligence, can reveal how and indeed perhaps what their makers were thinking. Interestingly, archaeologists in the 1960s criticised cognitive archaeology, claiming that only people's deeds and not their minds were preserved in the documentary record.[122] Cognitive archaeology responded to this type

---

119 Cf. Overmann and Coolidge 2019 and Malafouris 2022; cf. now generally Henley, Rossano, and Kardas 2019 and Wynn, Overmann, and Coolidge 2022. On the critique and a certain imbalance of 'psychology' versus 'traditional archaeology' in 'cognitive archaeology', see Apostel 2020.
120 E.g. Willey and Phillips 1958.
121 Binford 1962, Binford and Binford 1968, Binford 1972, Binford 1989.
122 Cf. Overmann and Coolidge 2019 in detail.

of scepticism by pointing out that it does not attempt to understand 'what' ancient people did on the basis of material structures, but rather 'how' they thought.[123] As will be pointed out below, this is a beloved dual opposition in the cognitive classics (and perhaps not only in the classics) more generally to claim that the others emphasise the 'what' while the cognitive approach is interested in the 'how'. This train of thought can perhaps lead to a generally understandable and justified assumption that seems to tend to simplify the reasoning of others in order to defend one's own 'how'.[124] But now back to archaeology.

1.1 General premises

Originally, cognitive archaeology arose from a need of prehistorians: while art historians are concerned with the analysis of the works of art of past societies, or historians with the analysis of the written sources that have come down to us, we are at the service of cognitive archaeology to understand the way of thinking of those populations of whose present only few and indistinct symbolic means have survived. On the basis of the psychobiological model – for example by analysing the cultural remains and bones of humans, which allow conclusions to be drawn about their symbolic ability – an attempt is made to understand the emergence and development of human behaviour in the course of its evolutionary process. Behaviour can be understood as the response that individuals make, through their cognitive or mental processes, to the socio-cultural and environmental stimuli they feel or receive from their surroundings. Human action and thought are closely linked, so knowledge of one can help us analyse the other.[125]

However, the study of cognition presents some problems that are not easy to solve. For example, the lack of objectivity results not only from the difficulty of discarding the implications of existing concepts and ways of thinking, but also from the lack of a method by which this objectivity can be achieved. Faced with the inevitability of subjectivity, archaeologists have abandoned an understanding of cog-

---

[123] A number of early books helped spread the message that ancient thought can be studied and characterised, including, for example, Donald 1991, Mithen 1996, Lewis-Williams 2002.
[124] See below p. 34–44.
[125] The bibliography on cognitive archaeology is extensive. A few seminal publications will be mentioned here, without claiming that others not mentioned here are less important. See Renfrew 1989, Renfrew and Bahn 1991, Renfrew and Zubrow 1994, Rivera Arrizabalaga 1998, Rivera Arrizabalaga 2005, Hernando 2002, Huth 2013, Bruner et al. 2018, Henley, Rossano, and Kardas 2019, Bruner 2023. See also numerous publications by the Center for Cognitive Archaeology, University of Colorado, USA (https://cca.uccs.edu, last access June 3rd 2024).

nition and, in response to the absence of global laws of thought, have limited themselves to interpreting human behaviour in very detailed and specific contexts.

Cognitive archaeology is classically divided into two major areas: "evolutionary cognitive archaeology", which attempts to use material traces to gain a deep insight into the cognitive development of humans, and "ideational cognitive archaeology", which concentrates on the symbolic structures that can be recognised on material objects from past cultures or were derived from them.[126]

'Evolutionary cognitive archaeology' uses archaeological evidence to draw conclusions about changes in the cognition of human ancestors. Sometimes it builds on theories, techniques, and evidence from other disciplines, such as comparative cognition, experimental replication, palaeoneurology and practical involvement in the production and use of traditional technologies. The known use of stone tools, for example, and their longevity is very revealing of how cognitive abilities such as intelligence, spatial and temporal orientation and working memory, as understood, and interpreted by cognitive psychology, change. It also reveals how stone tools are operationalised so that their use in archaeological finds can be traced. In addition, 'evolutionary cognitive archaeology' is concerned with the development of the mind, visual perception and visual-spatial skills, technical thinking, language, and computation.

In particular, the works of Colin Renfrew and Lambros Malafouris pursue a cognitive framework for the study of the ancient mind, borrowing concepts from the philosophy of mind and environmental psychology to explore more profoundly the role of physical objects in human cognition.[127]

Renfrew and Malafouris have coined the term 'neuroarchaeology' to describe their approach.[128] Neuroarchaeology is concerned with how human thought becomes visible in material structures. It is probably this ability to utilise material structures for cognitive purposes that distinguishes human cognition amongst all other forms of behaviour. A characteristic illustration of this concept, which Malafouris frequently uses in his research, is the production of pottery. Malafouris does not view the vessel as a form that the potter has created by imbuing the outer clay with an inner concept of mind.[129] Rather, the potter's brain and body interact with

---

[126] Gowlett 1979, Parker and Gibson 1979, Wynn 1979, Huffman 1986.
[127] E.g. Renfrew 1982, Renfrew 1993, Renfrew 1994, Renfrew 2004, Renfrew 2006, Renfrew 2007, Renfrew, Frith, and Malafouris 2008, Malafouris 2004, Malafouris 2007, Malafouris 2008, Malafouris 2009, Malafouris 2012, Malafouris 2013, Malafouris 2016, Malafouris 2019a, Malafouris 2019b.
[128] Malafouris 2009.
[129] Malafouris 2021. On materiality in recent classical literary studies, which is strongly influenced by the ideas of cognitive archaeology in general and the work of Malafouris in particular, see below p. 44–51.

the material – the clay and the kiln. The shape of the clay is ultimately created through an intricate relationship between the potter's feeling for the feel of the clay, the touch of the fingers, the texture, the moisture content, the colour, the balance, and the potter's reaction to the shape.

Today, 'evolutionary cognitive archaeology' works with interdisciplinary data from neurophysiology, such as the functioning of the nervous system in the brain, spinal cord, nerves, and sensory organs; social anthropology, which looks at the ways people live in diverse social and cultural environments; physical anthropology, which examines biological and behavioural aspects of humans from an evolutionary perspective; comparative cognition and understanding of cognitive abilities and mechanisms in human and non-human species; and a lot of artificial intelligence, such as processing large amounts of data accumulated over years of research and stored in archives. Other topics such as the origin of language, the possibility of inferring intention from the form of artefacts, and the lively interaction of archaeology with the philosophy of mind are discussed as well.[130]

The archaeologist Thomas Huffman described 'ideational cognitive archaeology' as "the study of prehistoric ideology": the values, norms and assumptions that constitute a society's understanding of the world.[131]

'Ideational cognitive archaeology' draws on semiotics, psychology and sociocultural anthropology to examine a wide range of spatial, politically authoritative, religious and material symbols. People act based not only on sensory influences but also on their previous experiences, including their birthplace and background. These experiences reflect a kind of cognitive map that orientates the individuals.[132] Communities of people who live together tend to share a common worldview and develop similar cognitive maps that shape the physical architecture of the community.

This is a fascinating example of how cognitive archaeology and cognitive linguistics, but also theory of mind in general, intersect. For one of the most important linguistic concepts of recent decades, 'common ground', revolves around the same question, but relates to the linguistic abilities of a community. The term 'common ground' was proposed by Herbert H. Clark and Susan E. Brennan in 1991 and then discussed in detail in Clark's 1996 monograph. It is a basic assumption of some discourse models in linguistics and communication theory, which assume a common "knowledge space" between the communication partners.[133] In this

---

130 Overmann and Coolidge 2019.
131 Huffman 1986.
132 Eden 1988, Epstein, Patai, Julian, Spiers 2017. See also below p. 58–76.
133 Clark and Brennan 1991. See also Clark 1996, Colston 2008. See below p. 81, and above 11–16.

case, the common cognitive maps are at the centre of interest of both linguists and archaeologists, only from different perspectives.

The material records contain evidence of behaviours that are the result of human thinking and were shaped by a variety of experiences. Material culture and human deeds are therefore inextricably interwoven with the ideas behind these deeds and the use of the objects.

In this context, the Frankfurt archaeologist Cornelis Bol used cognitive science methods to analyse the late archaic and the early classical period in ancient Greece.[134] Bol approaches early forms of representation using the example of early Greek images and opens up for us both the closeness and the distance to early forms of representation by anchoring them anthropologically and linking them through a continuous development to the perspectival image systems that the modern viewer encounters.

In the spirit of the new image sciences, Bol perceives images in terms of their contribution to social relations and collective cognitive structures either established or once formed in every individual and every collective.[135]

The science journalist and prehistorian Elisabeth Pühringer worked with different material – units of measurement and systems of weight.[136] Using the weight relations of cast cake moulds or parts of them, a weight scheme for the Early Bronze Age was attempted to be proved. For every form of trade, units of measurement are necessary to define the value and countervalue of the traded goods. Pühringer's diagram of the weight ratios of raw metal ingots for cast cakes reveals a lot about the mindset and perception of payment systems and pre-monetary means of payment in Europe several thousand years ago.

The interdisciplinarity of evolutionary biological, neurological, psychological, and sociological studies contribute to understanding the origin and evolution of forms of behaviour.[137] Thinking, behaviour and language thus have to be considered on the same level when asking the question "How did they think?". However, there are doubts that the information from the material evidence and the archaeological record is accurate enough to explain cognitive development. Thanks to ethnological work, we can be sure that thinking and speaking have developed differently throughout history depending on place and time. Language and symbolic language systems explain the difference between the existence of general structures and the existence of special and unique developments. Language is essential

---

134 Bol 2005.
135 On the images and the imagination, see p. 3–4 above and p. 77–105 below.
136 Pühringer 2004.
137 Heyes 2012.

for the transmission of culture among members of society and for binding societies together, but its meanings can vary within one group compared to other groups.[138] However, language is always deeply cognitive: it gives a sense of space and time, contributes to (lack of) self-awareness, articulation of ideas, etc. The interpretative use of archaeological data is therefore embedded in cognitive archaeology, albeit with a psychobiological orientation.

As has become clear in recent years, cognitive archaeology aims to reveal the nature of the categories underlying our understanding of reality such as the way people think about the social construction of the world. In doing so, it is possible to build a cognitive architecture consisting of a deepening of the fundamental axes of reference and order that underpin the different ways of understanding human relationships with their environment.[139]

1.2 Cognitive archaeology and ancient material

In the following, we consider some cases where the findings of cognitive archaeology are particularly promising and significant for interpreting classical sources. For example, rituals, sanctuaries, and the concept of *ekstasis* (being out of the realm of the ordinary) itself were rediscovered recently under the realm of developing post-colonial studies of ecstatic experiences and have benefited greatly from new approaches in archaeological research.[140]

Cognitive theoretical approaches based on context, history and action are crucial for the study of religious experience. Archaeologists are concerned with issues of meaning, experience and embodiment, all of which can be used to better understand physical and emotional elements of religious experience.[141] Possible interactions between modern scientific approaches and ancient data such as the Minoan palaces, the Eleusinian Mysteries and the cult of Asclepius are explored, drawing on an initial body of evidence for ancient ideas of interaction between humans and the gods, and considering how experimental approaches might contribute to historical studies. Thus, cognitive approaches have the potential to breathe new life into religious studies. Scientific research is shedding light on the extent to which processes such as altered states of consciousness are similar or not to today's laboratory reports.

---

138 Barham and Everett 2021.
139 Vaesen 2012, Taylor e.a. 2015. See also below p. 65–70.
140 Stein, Costello and Foster 2022, 2–3. On a cognitive boom in religious studies, see p. 114–121 below.
141 See below p. 117–119.

The methods and performance of ecstatic rituals are often mysterious, the visual and textual cues are often cryptic or abstract, the cultic equipment involved is often broken and unusable, and the universal essence of the experience and its implications for belief systems are often obscured by specific cultural objects and interpretations. Moreover, we cannot ask living participants whether their experience was an ecstasy or a mystical moment, a trance or a hallucination, whether it was positive or negative, what the characteristics of each phase were, or how they saw the final outcome.[142] As a result, cross-cultural studies of ecstatic experiences rarely deal with the ancient world and almost never go back before the advent of writing. The lack of conclusive evidence is often cited as the main reason for this gap, but there are undoubtedly other factors besides the traditional preference for canonical texts.

A new look at the archaeological and textual traditions, as well as recent analytical work, ethnographic projects, and theoretical modelling, can open up new insights in this regard. Again, it is important to remember the interdisciplinarity of approaches: although objects and materiality remain at the centre of research in every respect, other spheres such as ecstatic rituals, the bodily experience of rituals and patterns of communication should also be taken into account. Therefore, sites where ritual alterations of consciousness are likely to have taken place are being explored, along with examples of the materials and techniques most likely to have been used; in this way, new insights can be gained into the visual and verbal expressions of the mind in an altered state of consciousness and consideration of their intellectual and emotional meaning and impact.[143]

Such scholarly research has great potential to deepen our understanding of communication patterns in important aspects of past societies. This process raises a number of questions, such as how the experience was constructed and achieved, who exactly participated, when and where the ritual took place, and what the relationship was between the experience and mythology, religion and politics.

Studies in landscape archaeology (understanding artefacts and sites in terms of the larger spatial domain, both physical and meaningful, of past human experience), symbolic archaeology (the understanding of material culture as organised according to a set of principles that give meaning to the social world, while human actions are meaningfully framed within a cultural setting) and sensory archaeol-

---

[142] On the gap between the experiential accounts of living subjects and the fragmentary evidence from antiquity, cf. Cardeña 2022. For definitions of the specific terms closely related to *ekstasis*, such as altered state of consciousness, hallucination, possession trance or spirit possession, see Stein, Costello, and Foster 2022, 3–4 with further bibliography. On the cognitive science of religion, also see below p. 114–121.

[143] See below in the chapter on experience and the senses p. 106, 110–114.

ogy (sensory perception being a cultural construct, the meanings that individuals ascribe to sensory aspects being based on socially adopted sensory models), to name but a few, are expanding our understanding of the lifeworlds of people in the past and the ways in which archaeologists can access these experiences.

Religious studies – I will return to this area in the chapter on experience and the senses – is a particularly telling example of sensory archaeology (as it is obviously both sensual and material), and cognitive approaches have changed our conception of the human mind and human behaviour, and thus our understanding of ancient religion.[144] Archaeologists are now looking more closely at the field of symbolic thought, and new journals are being published that explore past cognitions and thoughts.[145] For example, the *Handbook of Cognitive Archaeology* includes chapters on the use of psychoactive drugs such as hallucinogens, alcohol, tobacco and cannabis to induce religious experiences.[146] The study of religion as experience is emerging from the side-lines and preparing to take its place in the mainstream of archaeological studies.

1.3 Material engagement and "how things shape the mind"

In recent years, much thought has been given to the way in which people give meaning to things and vice versa, and paradoxically, how things give meaning to people, how they make us who we are as individuals, as societies, and as eras.[147] This is because physical objects constitute human thought and action, and human cognitive processes develop and mature through interaction with them. The broad outlines of the human mind and body, as understood and experienced by authors of different periods and genres, can be gleaned from literary representations of material objects and human interactions with them.

The 'material turn' has its origins in the so-called New Materialisms, a politically engaged field of research that emerged about thirty years ago.[148] Accordingly, investigations from this perspective concentrate on the primacy of matter and ma-

---

[144] Whitley and Hays-Gilpin 2008, 13. See also Costello 2022, and Misic and Graham 2024.
[145] E.g. *Cambridge Archaeological Journal*, founded 1991. On 'cognitive history' and 'cognitive historiography', see below p. 63–65, and 158 f. 472.
[146] Hagen and Tushingham 2019.
[147] On the application of 'materialisms' and material studies in classical studies, see also below, p. 45–51. On the 'material turn' among classicists, see Canevaro 2019.
[148] Coole and Frost 2010 and Lemke 2021. The bibliography is extensive. See below p. 41. See also for history the summary by Schouwenburg 2015, for archaeology Knappett and Malafouris 2008, Malafouris and Renfrew 2010, and Hodder 2012. See also Boivin 2008.

terial action and seek a new investigation of the entanglement of matter and discourses. Matter is conceived as an active force and an agent and is involved in the creation and facilitation of social worlds and forms of expression and experience. New Materialisms are not 'cognitive' in the sense of contemporary cognitive studies, and they notoriously advertise their preference for material reality and corporeality over "language, consciousness, subjectivity, agency, mind, soul; also imagination, emotions, values, meaning and so on".[149] However, in the general posthuman wave of interest in objects and their agency that has been emphasised in recent decades, New Materialisms are a necessary precursor and interlocutor of 'material engagement theory' or 'actor network theory'.

Led by thinkers such as Manuel DeLanda, Elizabeth Grosz, Vicki Kirby, Karen Barad, Rosi Braidotti and Jane Bennett, the New Materialisms have emerged primarily from feminism, philosophy and science studies and remain prolific for both the humanities and the sciences.[150] As will be discussed below, material agency was fuelled by a productive confrontation with linguistic studies (the concept of 'embodiment'), social constructivist and in particular New Historicism frameworks that critically questioned their boundaries derived from the meaning of language, culture and representation.[151] Much attention has been given to material culture approaches. These approaches express the role of things in shaping human practices and beliefs. We experience things, we like or dislike things, we are attached to certain things. Modern European philologies have also made a 'material turn' in the vein of Bill Brown's 'thing theory'.[152] With a delay of perhaps a decade, this development reached the field of ancient classical authors.

The important difference to earlier approaches is that it is no longer just the fact that we encounter ancient culture in tangible material remains such as archaeological sites, artefacts, papyri, and manuscripts. It is also not about seeing the text as an object or searching for the objects in the text. Rather, the objects act, hence the crucial term 'agency', they do not simply 'speak' or 'communicate',

---

[149] E.g. Coole and Frost 2010, 2 and Nooter 2019a: "a taste of the great variety of modern materialisms and also a sharp sense of what these movements disavow: explorations of the soul, the spirit, transcendence, language as a transparent or logical system, transparency or logic, human agency, consciousness, intentionality, or authorship". On this debate see also Devellennes and Dillet 2018. For a good epistemological overview of material approaches and cognitive thinking, see Noel 2023b and Noel's introduction "Prologue: the objects' debate" in Noel (forthcoming).

[150] See e.g. DeLanda 1991, Grosz 1994, Kirby 1997, Barad 2001, Braidotti 2002, Barad 2007, Bennett 2001, Bennett 2010, Grosz 2017, DeLanda 2021.

[151] See below p. 52–57. For an overview of constructivist and New Historicist models from the 'material' perspective, see Folkers 2013.

[152] Brown 2001. See numerous publications such as Perry 2001 and Hawkes 2011. For an excellent analysis of the recent debates on the materialist focus of Shakespeare studies, see Knapp 2014.

as was the core of the semiotic view. The previous view of matter as a uniform and indifferent entity or as a fact constructed by society is being revised and new ideas of its active power, its associative character, its creative impulse, and its capacity for self-organisation are being brought to the fore.[153]

It seems that phenomenological insights into the renewed interest in materiality from the point of view of distributed cognition and the New Materialisms "not interested in consciousness" have changed the way we understand the physical world. And this, in turn, led to the important question of whether and how it could be applied to ancient societies.[154] The potential applications of material agency in ancient studies are enormous and give us a new perspective on ancient texts and artefacts, but above all on ways of thinking.[155]

The linking of material agency with the human mind – in a sense the 1960s computational theory of mind issue discussed above! – stimulated a rethinking of the human-non-human-posthuman relationship.[156] The various theories of '4E cognition' attempt to decipher the way in which the brain responds to and interacts with external influences, and the question of cognitive materiality is now to link '4E cognition' to material agency.[157] It is a willingness to challenge the Cartesian dualism that juxtaposes material things and mental operations that 'material turn' and embodied cognition share.[158] Mental activity is linked to the functioning of the body and depends on the body's interactions with its physical environment, including the material entities within it.

Because '4E cognition' sees the mind as embodied, extended and enacted rather than brain bound, this shift in thinking opens up important new questions about the connection between humans, cognition and physical objects. In his *How things shape the mind*, Lambros Malafouris proposes an interdisciplinary framework of analysis to explore the extent to which objects have become cognitive projections of the human body.[159] Malafouris' *Material Engagement Theory* not only challenges traditional beliefs about the limits and place of the human mind, but also inspires the reader to rethink classical archaeological insights into human cognitive development.

The content of a state of mind is partly conditioned by external elements, and cognition cannot therefore be studied in isolation from the external (social or tech-

---

[153] Alaimo and Hekman 2008, Bennett and Joyce 2010, Grusin 2015.
[154] See below p. 44–57.
[155] A good overview can be found in Canevaro 2019.
[156] See above p. 23–27, anf especially f. 102.
[157] Newen, De Bruin and Gallagher 2018. See also p. 6–10 above.
[158] Cf. above p. 4–5, 7–10.
[159] Malafouris 2013.

nical) world.¹⁶⁰ Using the example of the Mycenaean Linear B tablets, Malafouris is less concerned with deciphering and translating the writing system than with depicting human and material interactions. The idea of 'material engagement' helps to discover and know more about ancient work, social practices and verbal forms of communication that indicate the exchange of information between cultural traditions. The exchange between people, artefacts, environment, and time must therefore be taken into account in research.

Malafouris describes this methodology as a shift from communicating to acting, from semantics to practice. Mycenaean Linear script B is seen not as an abstract code, but as a constituted and located technology involving reciprocal and culturally staged and enacted interactions between people, situations, tool use and space.¹⁶¹ Malafouris suggests that we avoid the tendency to interpret the content of Mycenaean thought as it may have been encoded on the tablets, and instead look at the course of Mycenaean thought and the role that Linear B may have played in shaping that process.¹⁶² In other words, we use the example of tablets to ask 'how', not 'what', the Mycenaeans were thinking. This requires an understanding of the Linear B system as a cognitive asset and artefact of trade relations, family relations, symbolic thinking, property ownership and storage (cf. the Linear B tablets from Knossos recording textile workers, chariot wheels listed according to their shape and the type of material used, women and their sons and daughters, and such like).¹⁶³

Descriptions of objects and their contemplation have always been an important part of good textual commentary. What material engagement theory brings in is the question: to what extent can we judge what was intended in the minds of the recipients, or whether there was a difference in the cognitive impact of a physical object compared to what was mentioned but not shown. There are many examples of this type of activity: pottery or stone cutting and polishing. Making a clay pot requires not only the artist's imagination, but also the embodied process itself, as the artist's hands and body are involved in making the vessel, and the mind is at the same time mobilised to imagine how the form should look.¹⁶⁴

Similarly, the diversity of activities and abilities that make up the elemental form of a skilled stonemason's work with the material implies the creative approach to stone artefacts and what fundamentally distinguishes humans from an-

---

160 Malafouris 2013, 67.
161 Malafouris 2013, 79.
162 Malafouris 2013, 69.
163 Malafouris 2013, 70, fig. 4,3.
164 E.g. Malafouris 2008, Malafouris 2021.

imals. It is crucial to understand the material's origin, value, quarrying or mining methods, and the relationships involved in order to fully comprehend the object's function. If one considers the cognitive processes involved in tool making, the cognitive skills required by the body to make and use these types of tools, and if one considers the range of techniques (e. g. the nature of the surface, the position of the workpiece, or the angle of impact) that a blacksmith must master to make a hand axe, one can conclude that tools are the product of a mind capable of having intentions to make or use tools, and a body capable of externalising or executing those intentions.[165]

As recent publications show, specific sensorimotor approaches, such as focusing on the temporal qualities of touch and the haptic properties of making, can help us to decipher the dialogue between maker and material.[166] With growing skills, haptic awareness plays an effective role in transforming a purely physical exchange, in which sculptor and stone, potter and clay, blacksmith and metal are causally linked, into a multimodal kinaesthetic process in which the artist is sensitive and aware of the expressive possibilities of his material, and the material responds recursively to the creative potential of the artist's touch. The connections and relationships between touch and mindful participation in the making of a material object are thus foregrounded, as is the dialogic nature of creative interaction with the physical, in other words, an anthropological *homo faber* concept (or what Andy Clark designated *Natural-Born Cyborgs* in 2003!) of how humans cannot exist without tools or fire. It is a human need to process food to feed their hungry brains, and it is a human need to integrate tools and supportive cultural practices into their existence.

The most fascinating aspect of this process is the exploration of the relationship between the creation of material objects and thought, with particular emphasis on the entanglement of mind and matter. Essential here are the distributed and 4E theory of cognition, as well as the enactivist approaches that follow them.[167] Focusing on hands as part of the body, rather than human hands and material tools, does not lead to a view of hands in isolation. The becoming of the human being, in which craft marks the transition from the primate to the human being, is examined at the point where the brain, the body and culture meet. As Alva Noë has argued, thinking is not the way in which the brain represents things in our heads, but the way in which the brain and the body deal with things in the world.[168] Malafouris has turned this postulate into a fine play on words: *thinking is thinging.*[169]

---

165 Malafouris 2020, 110–112.
166 Malafouris and Koukouti 2022.
167 See above p. 6–10 and below p. 146–147, 151–153.
168 Noë 2009, 5–7, 67–95.

According to Malafouris, human cognitive becoming is captured in terms of creative material engagements.[170] The malleability of the forms we make is also inseparable from the human. Hands and tools therefore trans-act in an attentive engagement with matter, and this same attentiveness is in turn a prerequisite for becoming human. To understand knowledge and embodied culture is to understand their unity in shaping human beings. To explore this situated entanglement of brain, body and things, the experienced space between the human hand and tools offers a distinctive anthropological angle. Of course, many other forms of material engagement, such as painting, hunting, or farming, also offer valuable insights into the changing ways in which people's bodily worlds touch and are touched. However, the interactive use of hands and tools provides an arena for exploring how human gestures are integrated into a coherent evolutionary, historical, and cultural process of making. Just as hands are made and used by tools, material tools are made and used by human hands. In this case, the function and the meaning of the hand are determined by the tool itself. The term 'human becoming' in material engagement theory refers to the process of constant change that characterises the uncertain, incomplete, and constantly changing human ambience.

1.4 "Material turn" and the interpretation of texts

These approaches have shown outstanding results in recent years, offering new ways of thinking about ancient sources in both literary criticism and cognitive archaeology. The essays in Mario Telò's and Melissa Mueller's volume on materiality in Greek tragedy, for example, have shifted our view of the people and things in it, but also revealed promising opening for further analysis.[171] Passages from Sophocles' *Philoctetes* serve the editors as an example of what the theories of 'material turn' can do. The figure of Philoctetes, with its representation of a bow, a foot, a wound, a voice, all embedded in a social experiment of absolute human loneliness, invites such an examination of persons and things. The Attic terracotta oil jar shows Philoktetes sitting under a leafless tree, holding his bandaged foot, suffering from a nasty and foul-smelling wound caused by a snakebite (Fig. 3).[172]

---

[169] Malafouris 2014, Malafouris 2019a, Malafouris 2021.
[170] Malafouris 2021.
[171] Telò and Mueller 2018a. See also the detailed review of the volume by Sarah Nooter in https://bmcr.brynmawr.edu/2019/2019.11.03/ (Nooter 2019a), last access June 3rd 2024.
[172] Cf. in particular Telò and Mueller 2018b, 3–10. On the cognitive function of props in tragedy, see also Chaston 2010.

1.4 "Material turn" and the interpretation of texts — 45

Fig. 3: *Philoktetes on Lemnos.* Terracotta squat lekythos, circa 420 BCE. New York, Metropolitan Museum of Art 56.171.58. © OA Public domain https://www.metmuseum.org/art/collection/search/254917, last access June 11th 2024.

Furthermore, Mario Telò, in a separate essay in this volume, also interprets Philoctetes' interaction with others as a form of "cannibal friendship" (p. 135) that is threatened with diminishment.[173] In this sense, Neoptolemos and the bow become "homologous prosthetic objects" (p. 140), until Heracles appears and "cannibalises" Philoctetes with his voice (p. 151). The use of "affect theory" is meant to modify the classical reading of the play: here the characters are addressed but not blended,

---

[173] Telò 2018.

and the external is involved but not fully assimilated, which can lead to a 'responsible affect', which Telò equates with a tragic affect (p. 152).

In the same vein, Nancy Worman's 2021 monograph argues for a new reading of Greek tragedy, attentive to how bodies on stage oscillate between human and object.[174] This book deals with tragic enactment in the human body, building on and developing recent interactions between posthumanism and materialism in relation to classical texts. Departing from semiotic assumptions, Worman opens up cognitive approaches and explores the limits of the body offered by tragic representation, how bodies register at the intersections of tragedy, where directive and figurative language come together to emphasise visual, haptic and acoustic details. Her study covers most of the extant tragedies and concentrates on four areas – Oedipus and his family, especially in Sophocles and Euripides; the house of Atreus, in all three playwrights; the heroes Ajax, Philoctetes and Heracles; and female characters in distress. Applying the insights of New Materialisms, Worman sees tragic "bodies as strange objects or materials" and argues that the 'post-bodies' of the New Materialist approach "re-inhabit and revise contemporary understandings of tragic imagination and enactment at the margins of the human".[175]

Amy Lather-Mars has also published a monograph on materiality in Archaic Greek thought: an in-depth examination of cloth, armour and textiles in vase painting and poetic texts by Homer, Hesiod and Pindar.[176] Lather-Mars explores the material and cognitive dimensions of the quality *poikilia* ("colourfulness, embroidery, adornment") and how the entities denoted by *poikilia* participate in an enactive interaction between mind, body, and objects. She argues that *poikilia* is in fact an enactive process in which the mind, body and physical objects are equally involved in building and shaping the *poikilia* experience. The decoration of the Acropolis Korai and the black figures depicted in the vase painting shape how they are perceived. The visual details make the viewing experience more complex and extended.[177]

In addition, literary representations of women's weaving (Helen in *Il.* 3, 125–128 and Andromache in *Il.* 22, 440–441) are analysed. These women and the texts that describe them construct *poikilia* and illustrate 'material engagement' as an interaction between people and material.[178] Weaving is an embodied cognitive proc-

---

174 Worman 2021. See also above p. 23–27.
175 Worman 2021, 248.
176 Lather 2021. For a thorough analysis of 'material' theories, their quibbles, and their application to Homeric poetry, see also Grethlein 2019.
177 Lather 2021, 29–54.
178 Lather 2021, 58–60.

ess. Textiles are extensions and projections of the minds and physical bodies of those who weave them (cf. Fig. 4).

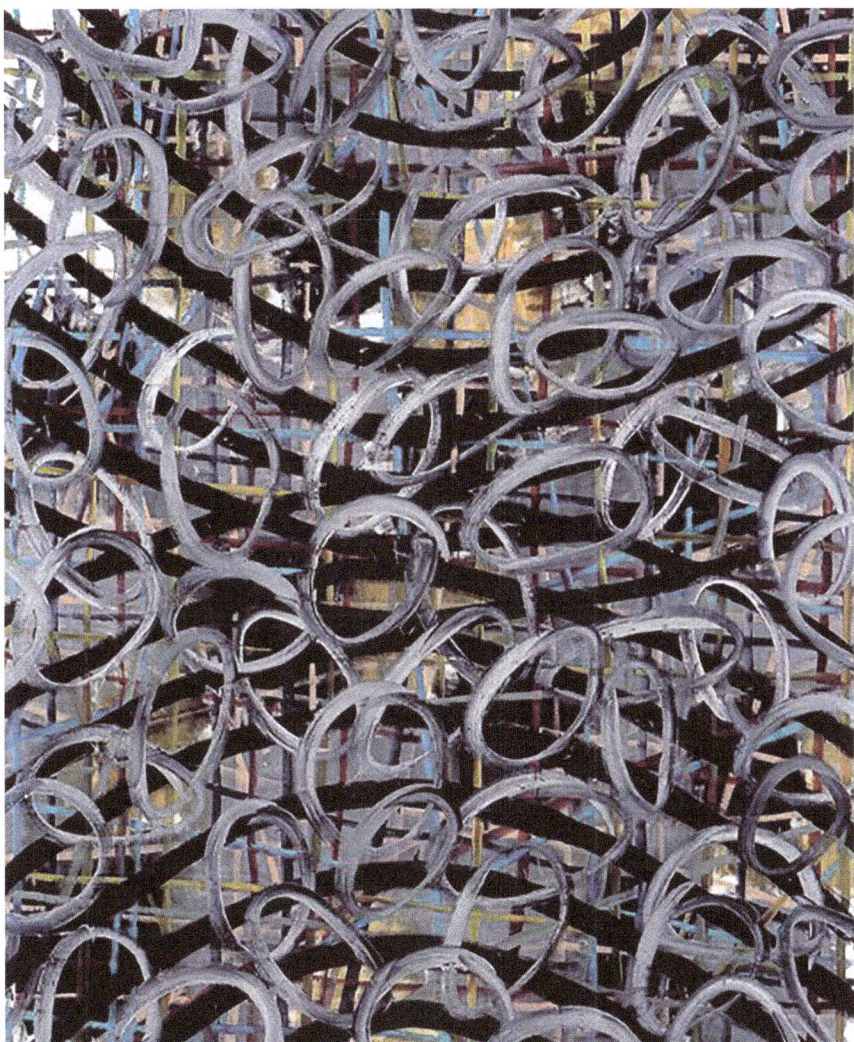

Fig. 4: Gela Samsonidse, untitled, 2003, oil on canvas, 240x200 cm. © Gela Samsonidse.

The author also shows that the combination of armour and the wearer creates sensory effects.[179] Homeric passages dealing with the interaction between the body, the emotions and the warrior's armour (e.g. *Il.* 13, 130–135 and *Il.* 18, 599–601) as well as the dynamic aspect of the imagery in Alcaeus' characterisation of the helmets (fr. 140, 3–10 Voigt) demonstrate that the coupling of the armour with the body creates a form of artefact, something distinct from both the body and the armour.[180] Whereas in Sappho ("a decorated headband", fr. 98a-b), Alcman ("a scintillating serpent", *Parth.* 1, 66) and Anacreon ("a richly hued ball", PMG 358), as Lather-Mars shows, the congruence between the mutability of the meaning of the term *poikilos* and the dazzling substances it depicts, in a kind of perceptual imitation, illustrates the shimmering, ephemeral attraction of the figures represented, Pindar emphasises a two-way mode of perception, in which both the phenomenon represented and the process of imagining it are brought to life (e.g. "an elaborate ornament", fr. 194, "a gleaming dragon", *Pyth.* 8, 46, "her shimmering head", *Pyth.* 10, 46, "titillating lies", *Ol.* 1, 29, "my decorated song", *Ol.* 6, 87, "her shifty designs", *Nem.* 5, 28, "playing animatedly on the kithara", *Nem.* 4, 14).[181]

Following 'material theories' but with an eye to the study of emotions, neuroscience, psychology, artificial intelligence, mental health, and cognitive archaeology, as well as research in music, theatricality and acting – theatre director and classicist Peter Meineck considers the main performative features of Greek theatre. From the point of view of cognitive science, they are conceived as embodied, living, staged experiences. He pays particular attention to the significance of the mask as "material agent" and "mind tool", an object he has been working with for years, as reflected in numerous publications.[182] The mask was an enactive element in the overall experience of the theatre, as was the open-air environment in which it operated. Rather than creating distance between the audience and the performance, Meineck says, it effectively expands the performer's field of attention and emotion. The early Greek theatre space, a frontal wooden tribune, was designed for an enactive spatial engagement and was "a grandstand for a view that expanded the mind".[183] Meineck addresses the question of the dual nature of the mask as a

---

[179] Lather 2021, 18–94.
[180] Lather 2021, 91–93.
[181] Lather 2021, 132–153.
[182] Meineck 2011, Meineck 2012, Meineck 2017, Meineck 2019. On the exchange of neuroscience and performance, see also Falletti, Sofia, and Jacono 2016, Ciesielski 2017, and Kemp and McConachie 2018.
[183] Meineck 2019, 74.

face and object and claims that the mask can be more expressive than the face (Fig. 5a and 5b, contemporary version of the 5th century BCE mask type).[184]

In an arena of some five to six thousand spectators, as in the classical theatre of Dionysus, the body rather than the face was intended to convey affective states, and the mask was particularly useful in intensifying and emphasising the spectator's perception of bodily movement. Drawing on his own experience of working in contemporary theatre and contemporary experimentation, face recognition, and emotion studies, Meineck demonstrates that the very act of wearing a mask in front of an audience has a transformative effect on the environment in which it is worn, triggering a vibrant, extended mental bond and cognitive interface between artist and viewer. In addition, the mask required a frontal vocal performance and direct frontal engagement with the audience, appealing to the natural human instinct to follow the direction of the mask's gaze and thus an emotional response.

Meineck's studies, based in part on the insights of the 'material turn', thus generally offer a new understanding of how classical Greek drama functioned on stage and how it became such an effective social, ritual, cultural, and political force and agent.

A very recent study by Lilah Grace Canevaro looks at material agency and a variety of human and non-human characters in Theocritus' *Idylls* and contributes to the theoretical field of material ecocriticism.[185] Women, landscapes, non-humans and various undervalued actors and agents practice being read and heard from the text of Theocritus' poems. Material ecocriticism, which applies ecology to literary studies, examines how material forms such as landscapes, objects, bodies, fabrics, chemical, organic and inorganic materials, biological forms and organisms interact with each other and with humans to produce and convey meanings and discourses that can be accessed and interpreted by recipients.[186] Theocritus' *Idyll* 1, 32–38 features a scene on the cup offering a detailed description of a woman (all translations are by Canevaro):

Inside is fashioned a woman, with godlike artistry,
dressed with cloak and headband…[187]

---

184 On the relationship between mask and face, see the seminal work of Frontisi-Ducroux 1995.
185 Canevaro 2023. On dehumanisation and animals, see also Bianchi, Brill, and Holmes 2019, and Chesi and Spiegel 2020, and above p. 23–27.
186 See Iovino and Oppermann 2014, Clark 2019, 111–136.
187 Canevaro 2023, 48–66.

Fig. 5a and 5b: Masks. Courtesy of Peter Meineck, Aquila Theatre, photography by Richard Termine.

To fully comprehend the physicality of this scene, it is necessary to think of the cup as a being with material properties, and the implications this has for our interpretation. The cup has a round shape, is tangible and present, the woman depicted on it, who is the focus of the male gaze, remains untouched and withdrawn. The whole is not only a pictorial scene but also a material.

Idyll 7, set in a bucolic context similar to *Idyll* 1, focuses on a broader theme: imagined landscapes (vv. 39–48). Simichidas, who is introduced as the first-person narrator and thus also the poet himself, is told that all the stones fall on his feet as he walks "as they sing against his boots" (*Id.* 7, 25–26). From the point of view of material ecocriticism, as Canevaro points out, the interpretation of these lines can be broadened. Through a stone (λίθος), a thing, a non-human subject, something happens to the human character. The stone trips over the feet and thus comes to the fore and becomes an active agent: the moment when, like a broken hammer that no longer strikes or an empty jug, the material world exercises its physical power and makes us aware of it, as observed in Martin Heidegger's 1951 essay "Das Ding".[188]

The verses 45–48 further read:

*I very much dislike the builder who strives to
build a house as high as mount Oromedon,
and those birds of the Muses who, crowing,
labour in vain against the Chian singer.*

The metaphorical link between the construction, which is as high as a mountain, and the epic poem is emphasised by the merging of the singers with the animals and the reduction of the text to a dissonant tone.[189]

'Material theories' thus bring new readings and new ways of looking at literary plots, such as the functioning of matter, the interaction of humans and non-humans in complex diffuse interactions, and the dynamics of communication with objects, things, non-human elements, in other words anything that can be called matter. They have profoundly influenced concepts of agency, narrative and text.[190] Things are capable of producing their own meanings, and material forms are 'storytellers' and seek to explore the interplay of story, material relations and discourse.

---

188 Canevaro 2023, 112, referring to Heidegger. See Heidegger 1951.
189 Canevaro 2023, 91–99.
190 Iovino and Oppermann 2012, 79.

1.5 Embodied perception

The main result of the interaction between 'material studies' and linguistics seems to be the notion of embodiment, which can also be described as 'embodied language'.[191] In essence, it views the two worlds of the corporeal and the mind (or culture, which are seen as intentional objects and phenomena) as a unity, thus standing in contrast to duality, as postulated by Descartes.[192] The physical is not understood as a 'vessel' but as the being itself. Mind and spirit are not refinements of biology, but integral parts. Thus, body and mind are fused into a single being – the only difference between matter and being is the way the being is viewed. The concept of embodiment is broadly understood as the physical underpinning of phenomena such as cognition, mind, and language. According to this theory, the structures that make up our conceptual systems develop and acquire meaning on the basis of bodily experience. The nature of conceptual systems is firmly rooted in perception, physical activity, and physical and social experience.[193]

The role of embodiment determines the semantic meanings of different linguistic practices, including verbal affordances, lexical items, discourse particles, prepositional phrases and the semantics of tenses.[194] Embodiment studies in linguistics are particularly indebted to the idea of embodied meaning pioneered in cognitive semantics. According to this theory, people's ability to understand and communicate their experiences is based on cognitive structures and procedures that arise from people's bodily interaction with the particular social and physical environments in which we live or have lived in the past.[195]

Such cognitive structures and processes operate in ancient languages at different levels of meaning-making: lexical, syntactic, textual. These shape the entire spectrum of conventional and imaginative forms of expression in Greek and Latin. To cite a few examples: Douglas Cairns has examined emotion terms such as αἰδώς ("shame" and "respect"), φρίκη ("shudder"), ψυχή ("breath/soul", and in specific contexts also "courage/desire") and θυμός ("spirit/anger") in the light of conceptual metaphor theory.[196] Cristóbal Pagán Cánovas analysed the ancient

---

[191] See p. 98, 109. See Gibbs 2005, Alexiadou 2013, 65–66, Gibbs 2017, Bergen 2019. See also Short 2016. See also p. 97–105 below.
[192] See various contributions in Scarinzi 2015.
[193] Cf. Lakoff, 1987b: xiv.
[194] On cognitive linguistics see also above p. 11–16.
[195] Wachsmuth, Lenzen, and Knoblich 2008, Lakoff 2012, Johnson 2015, Stocker 2015.
[196] E.g. Cairns 1993 (the detailed analysis of *aidōs* in Greek without applying the conceptual metaphor theory, but metaphors for *aidōs* are discussed in Cairns 2016c), Cairns 2008, Cairns 2009, Cairns 2013, Cairns 2014, Cairns 2015, Cairns 2016a. See below p. 97–105.

Greek poetic imagery of love expressions in terms of conceptual integration theory.[197] An edited volume by Mihailo Antović and Cristóbal Pagán Cánovas focuses on how recent findings in language and cognition can advance the study of orality. It describes how studying the art of language in its native, spoken environment can provide new understanding of issues such as semantics, communicative pragmatics or multimodal communication.[198] Oral poetry has produced insights that are important for the analysis of classical poetry, as well as for our broader sense of language and cognition: for example, the formulaic style as a result of practised spontaneity, the structuring of traditional narratives into themes, or the use of everyday language in poetry, and much more.

The Lacoffian approach to metaphor has been applied by Francisco García Jurado to the comedy of Plautus. The so-called orientation metaphors, which cognitive linguists identify as an elementary way of thinking ('GOOD IS UP', 'BAD IS DOWN', etc.), are also to be found in archaic Latin.[199]

In his volume *Embodiment in Latin Semantics*, William Short brings theories of embodied meaning from cognitive science to the study of Latin semantics, explaining the profound role that embodied cognitive patterns and procedures play in the construction of conventional Latin phrases at all lexical and syntactic levels.[200] This study demonstrates the extent to which human embodiment is universal in Latin semantics, and the ways in which Latin speakers express imaginative and culturally distinctive modes of meaning making through embodied understanding.

More generally, Short shows how the thought, speech and behaviour of Latin speakers, even in seemingly disjointed contexts of social practice, were perceived by the recipients as unified and interconnected – and thus meaningful – within a coherent worldview characterised by its own distinctive metaphorical 'themes'.[201] He explores, from an anthropological and culturally comparative perspective, how aspects of the metaphorically structured model are implemented in Roman social practice, and suggests that the Latin conceptualisation of the mental domain in spatial terms underpins Roman understanding and behaviour in relation to literary tradition. In idiomatic expressions, such *as nihil ad rem pertinere, ad rem esse, in rem esse* and *res est (alicui) cum*, for example, *res* means a "subject", "concern", or "interest", this mental representation is lexically encoded as a thing – in the same way that *reri* ("think, assume, calculate") interprets mental activity as a

---

197 Cánovas 2011, Cánovas and Antović 2016a, Cánovas and Antović 2016b.
198 Antović and Cánovas 2016.
199 García Jurado 2000. See also Caracciolo and Kukkonen 2021, 23–43. On conceptual theory of metaphor applied to classical texts, see also below p. 97–105.
200 Short 2016a.
201 Short 2012, Short 2014, Short 2019a.

kind of mental "thingifying".²⁰² Short extends theories of embodiment into anthropological analysis, drawing on metaphorical speech patterns in Latin to reconstruct concepts common to the entire Roman world.

Kiki Nikiforidou, on the other hand, analyses the function of conceptual metaphor in mediating semantic change in ancient Greek from a diachronic perspective.²⁰³ And Chiara Fedriani examines the orientational constructions that underlie the coding of emotions in Latin.²⁰⁴

As discussed above, cognitive linguistics is increasingly being applied to ancient Greek and Roman texts, and several volumes in recent years have provided an overview of current work in this relatively new subfield of ancient studies.²⁰⁵ In this chapter only issues related to material studies and the concept of embodiment are relevant. For example, cognitive semantics can provide a valuable corollary to the current semantic perspectives of classical philology. They offer a psychologically realistic and neuro-appealing theory of the representation of meaning and a consistent, coherent system of principles for analysing the meaning of linguistic expressions, both diachronically and synchronically.²⁰⁶ Where approaches to literary criticism have focused too much on the local dimension of meaning in particular social groups, cognitive semantics can help to illuminate those widespread patterns of conceptualisation that shape the meaning of language for members of social groups.

From a cognitive perspective, constructions are seen as semantic in themselves, that is, as having meanings that arise independently of the individual words of which they are composed. In a construction grammar, however, linguistics patterns, like morphemes, lexemes, or idioms, can be combined independently of semantic patterns.²⁰⁷

For this reason, the perspective used for the study of language should be 'constructive'. A constructionist approach to the nature of language treats the use of language as a conventionalised coupling of structure and (semantic or discursive) function, the aggregate meaning of which cannot be deduced from its components

---

202 Short 2012, 113.
203 Nikiforidou 1991.
204 Fedriani 2011, Fedriani 2014, Fedriani 2016, Fedriani 2019, Fedriani 2020, Fedriani and Unceta Gómez 2021.
205 See above p. 11–16.
206 Antović and Cánovas 2016, Short and Duffy 2016, Mocciaro and Short 2019a, Meineck, Short and Devereaux 2019a, 19–106.
207 Mocciaro and Short 2019b, 6. Cf. also Langacker, 1987, Langacker 1991, Langacker 2005; Wierzbicka, 1988; Goldberg, 2003.

but is perceived, acquired and remembered as an independent unit.[208] This notion of 'construction' is closer to Saussure's concept of the 'linguistic sign' than to other recent theories of grammar, particularly the various strands of generativism, which assume that human beings have an innate capacity for language and that this language is shaped by some basic principles that are part of the human brain. This comprehensive view is a crucial aspect of cognitive approaches to language analysis, closely linked to other theoretical assumptions and to the suggestion that linguistic texture is deeply embedded in, and bounded by, the use of language and the physical embodiment of speakers.[209]

It is clear from this brief description that this semantic approach can be applied to ancient languages at all levels of analysis, from lexical semantics to the use of grammatical classes traditionally regarded as unimportant, such as nominal-only 'containers' for the semantic meanings of constituent lexical items. Cognitive linguistics rejects the assumption that the rules of grammar are empty and meaningless structures, arguing instead that structures are themselves driven and shaped by meaning. It is seen as a form of embodiment because an individual's aims, desires, insights and beliefs are inevitably shaped and influenced by personal experience, and in so far as they influence language, this would suggest that language is contingent on personal experience of the world.[210] In this view, the different stages of language analysis (morphological, lexical, syntactic) are in a sense built from the same material: there is no clear distinction between the stages, which are rather seen as separate areas within a continuous range from vocabulary to grammar. A telling example of this, as Jennifer Devereaux has argued, is the metaphor that Cicero uses in relation to Antony in his *Philippics*.[211] In the context in which he calls Antony Charybdis, there are a number of words that mean consumption or pouring out (e. g. *effuderit, absorbere, potabatur, devorare, Phil.* 2, 25 and 2, 67). Wealth spilled out like bodily fluids, engulfing furniture, clothing, and other objects; fine wines are drunk, and cities, kingdoms, houses and gardens are devoured. Most of the 'physical' verbs associated with this metaphor are intended to evoke a negative emotional response in those receiving the message.

More recently, Anna Novokhatko's monograph on the embodiment of scholarly discourse in ancient Greek comedy builds on Lambros Malafouris' 'thinging theory' and Peter Meineck's study of Greek theatre and cognition, arguing that cognitive approaches, and in particular the 'material turn', can offer a new perspec-

---

208 Cf. Goldberg, 2006: 4–6.
209 Mocciaro and Short 2019b, 2–3.
210 Bergen 2015: 14.
211 See the discussion in Devereaux 2016, 248–249.

tive on the interplay of comedy with early Greek proto-philological approaches.²¹² The role of drama, due to the corporeality of theatre in its essence, is particularly spectacular when it comes to the adaptation of society to certain discourses. People perceive the environment through the somatic experience of interacting with other similar bodies, and this bodily relatedness helps to determine the metaphors we use.²¹³ In the fifth century BCE, archaic poetics was gradually replaced by the tendency to think in abstract categories behind the sensual interplay of ideas and to explain mythical images rationally. Drama conceptually concretised ideas by creating metaphors and equipping them with various sensorimotor tools on stage, thus "thingifying" abstract categories.

The embodiment of discourse in drama is a way of paying attention to detail that heightens sensory awareness of the distinctiveness of things, affective engagement with ordinary acts and objects, and a sharp critical eye for ways of thinking about everyday behaviour.²¹⁴ By confronting audiences with the problems and dilemmas facing society and attacking celebrities by name, theatre, and comedy in particular, is designed to be consumed in an experiential context.²¹⁵

Physical behaviour, facial expressions and actions are crucial to understanding the complex and varied ways in which we engage with our environment. The presence and influence of embodied forms of perception and reception, such as sensory awareness, memory, inspiration, intuition, and affective sensitivity, are particularly expressed in the physical body. Environmental theories were applied to the performative moment of Greek theatre, which saw cognition as a composite of the environment and the way we interact with it, thus providing a new appreciation of the individual's experience. The stage emphasised the reciprocal relationship between the world visible to the audience and the world evoked by the imagination, between the physical world of the theatre structure and the natural world and the fictional environment.

Theatre demands a response from the audience. It presents concrete physical actions on stage and the process is linked to the physical experience of the audience, unlike theoretical texts written to be read alone or speeches written to persuade an audience at a conference. In parallel with the cerebral stimuli associated

---

[212] Novokhatko 2023, 29–33. See in particular Rehm 2002 and Meineck 2017. See also above p. 39–44 and 48–51.
[213] Lakoff and Johnson 1980, 14–21, 87–96; Gibbs 2006.
[214] On aesthetic embodiment, see Mascia-Lees 2011.
[215] On comedy as being "from its origins a theatre of the body" and on "comic somatisation", see Hubbard 2021, 179.

with the narrative of the text and its linguistic dimension, theatre productions also trigger physical sensitivity and physical engagement in actors and audiences. This overcomes resistance, prejudice and fear and often opens up new possibilities for communication and deep emotional learning.[216]

The role of materiality in human cognition is therefore a hotly debated topic, with a growing body of research into what is now referred to as the 'posthuman'.[217] Whether one tends to separate strictly cognitive approaches to materiality from other areas of the material turn in which emotions, senses, rituals and communication are intertwined, or whether one considers the whole wave of the last thirty years in which Edmund Husserl's *Zurück zu den Sachen selbst!* has been revived in '4E cognition' oriented approaches, it is clear that objects are currently at the centre of many transdisciplinary studies. The anchoring of materiality and mind in the ancient sources can lead to innovative approaches – from archaeological investigations to the analysis of literary forms and linguistic units. Brain activity can vary in response to engagement with the physical world, and the properties of the physical world can vary brain activity, so that thinking through materiality is contrasted with thinking about materiality. A kind of cognitive map, to recall the term from cognitive archaeology, is reflected in people's previous experience, which gives them guidance in dealing with the material world, and in particular ancient sources that deal with materiality, thus opening up new horizons and perspectives of analysis.

---

216 On the theory of embodied cognition applied to performative studies, see Lutterbie 2011. On the concept of 'trust' in theatre and its connection with the physical, mental, and emotional state, see Rokotnitz 2011, 12–17 and 129–132. See also below p. 65–70.
217 E.g. Küchler 2005 and Overmann and Wynn 2019. See also Vint 2020.

Chapter 2
Spatial perception and ancient sources

Another important direction of research in recent decades, which has influenced classical studies, can be described as the 'spatial turn'. Again, as with 'material studies', this is not necessarily linked to cognitive science, and much work has been done in this area without a direct cognitive perspective. However, if space is relevant in the sense of "how it is perceived as space" and "how a mind perceives space", then, as recent results show, new insights are opening up in the field of cognitive geography and in the field of cognition, emotion and space.

Space is conceived as a cognitive entity capable of agency, rather than a static external domain. The importance of bodily sensory-motor experience in a feedback cycle with the world around us tends to be emphasised in theories of cognitive embodiment. The real environment in which we live must be a layering of many inactive sceneries, each containing its own elements for producing predictions and attracting interest.

Modern theorists distinguish between 'landscape', 'place' and 'space', the three categories that could be grouped under the umbrella term 'environment' from a cognitive perspective. The concept of 'landscape' is charged with historical, cultural and, above all, aesthetic significance.[218] Landscape encompasses aspects of multilayered cultural settings that are familiar to us, such as the theatre and temple precincts of Athens, but also Panhellenic sanctuaries of fame such as Nemea, Isthmia, Delphi, and Olympia, or distant lands and regions of the world such as Sicily, Phoenicia, and Egypt. Landscape as a cultural medium plays a double role when it comes to abstract things like ideology. On the one hand, it is a cultural and social construction that is taken for granted by presenting an artificial world as if it were self-evident and inescapable. On the other hand, it orientates this representation by placing the viewer in a more or less certain relationship to its givenness as sight and place. Landscapes oscillate as a means of exchange, a locus of image acquisition and a site of identity making. Such conceptualisations suggest contestation and struggle, not only for the territory itself, but also for how it is seen.

People organise their beliefs and knowledge in relation to the places they visit. In the study of landscape perception, a distinction is made between four paradigms: the expert-led paradigm (based on experts' judgments about the visual quality of landscapes, ignoring the opinions of non-experts), the psychophysical paradigm (the visual quality of landscapes is judged by non-experts such as the

---

[218] See also Mitchell 1994 (2002), 2, and Zube, Sell, and Taylor 1982.

lay public), the cognitive paradigm (analysing the reasons why people prefer certain landscapes, which have meaning and influence aesthetic judgments), and the experiential paradigm (human experiences influence the perceived value of the landscape).[219] In addition, factors such as gender, race, nationality, age, leisure time, educational background, work experience and religion play a role in the perception and experience of landscape.[220] So it is not just the landscape or a particular place itself, but the multi-layered web of memories, opinions, actions and relationships that closely connects the complex of the viewer to the architectural site, the building itself and/or the landscape. The Greeks were aware of this complex of memories, relationships, opinions, expectations, and actions, as the earliest testimonies show.

'Place' is a personal and experience-oriented social construct that involves attitudes and issues of status and identity.[221] Place includes the meanings constructed by experience, as it is known not only through the eyes and the mind, but through all the senses, and modes of experience.[222] Getting to know a place means both understanding it in the abstract and getting to know it personally by visiting it. When we visit, we remember that we are part of the whole, with the whole range of visual, auditory, and olfactory associations associated with the place. There is also an emphasis on perspective, as the viewer is in fact the creator of the spatial dimension. Looking at place reveals the relationships between features of topography, identities, and the physical body, while exploring the angle through which place is viewed suggests the ways in which scenarios can be designed and manipulated by ideas to promote authority and status.

Finally, 'space' is the most abstract, inclusive, and fluid term. Generally speaking, 'space' is more abstract, global, framing and theoretical. 'Place' is value-laden, felt, experienced, lived, and embodied.[223] As Yi-Fu Tuan points out in his work on space, what begins as an indistinct space is transformed into a place as we know it.[224] The opposition between space and place dissolves with the fluid relationship between the two. Space can be an opposition between inside and outside, it can contain both symbolic and factual and material dimensions, and it can encompass domains as diverse as those defined by topographical attributes. Unlike the concept of place, however, space is not necessarily about individual identities, but about

---

[219] Zube, Sell, and Taylor 1982.
[220] Aoki 1999.
[221] Tuan 1975, Tuan 1977, Harvey 1996, 293–294.
[222] Tuan 1977, 136–148.
[223] Tuan 1977, 3–7, and Cresswell 2015, 15–17.
[224] Tuan 1977 and Casey 1997. Cf. Cresswell 2015, 1–18.

ontological categories in a broad and symbolic sense, such as borderlands inhabited by monsters and other hybrid figures.

2.1 Space and social cognition

Sanctuaries, theatres, stadiums, and the like can be considered from the perspective of spatial and site analysis. The design and form of perimeters around and within ancient monuments, and the influence of these perimeters on the nature of the experience of the athletic, ritual or performative practices that took place within them, are of particular interest in relation to cognitive research.[225] The active influence of these walls, particularly on the visual and sonic environment with which participants engaged, was critical to the power, emotion, impact and persuasiveness with which participants experienced the building.[226]

The architectural forms interacted with the experiences of the participants to produce, enhance, and expand their awareness, perception, experience, imagination and memory of the practice carried out in the architectural complex.[227] Much evidence of ancient sporting or religious practices is not preserved textually, but in material form. New methods from the neurocognitive sciences that complement traditional archaeological and historiographical methods could offer an approach to experience from material culture. Here, experience is identified with the modulations of historically detectable measures of everyday sensation through the concentration of attention. Techniques that bring about such modulations are often preserved in material evidence and allow for a traceable history at the neurocognitive level. The walls, the building complex itself and the effect of light or shadow all combined to change the listening process, both in terms of the depth of the experience and the sense that the group had entered a world of its own. Thus, Hesiod's poem *Works and Days* describes the relationship between man and the earth, the idea of *oikos*, cultivating the earth and following the rhythms of nature.[228] Texts encourage readers to imagine vivid images and allow us to ex-

---

[225] Cf. Tuan 1977, Tuan 1990, Holloway and Hubbard 2001, Montello 2018, Portugali 2018, Agarwal 2018.
[226] On sensory studies see below p. 110–114. See also p. 65–70.
[227] For studies on feelings and attachments to a place, see especially Hornstein 2011, Norberg-Schulz 2000, Dovey 2010, Kreider 2014.
[228] Canevaro 2023 traces the pastoral poet Theocritus back to Hesiod and interrogates the multilayered imagined landscapes and stone narratives. She illustrates this study with two excursions to Sardinia and Marsden Bay on the north-east coast of England (Canevaro 2023, 140–145 and 202–210). See also p. 49–51 above.

ercise our ability to guess what other people feel and think. Ancient Greek and Latin texts have much to offer to critical debate today, for as long as people create texts, they are thinking critically about their place in nature, which is far beyond them in its scope and duration.[229]

Other traditionally rather separate academic fields where interdisciplinary activities can form fruitful overlaps are communication and geography.[230] For example, Henri Lefebvre argued in his *La Production de l'espace* (1974) that there are different modes of spatial production, ranging from physical space ('absolute space') to more complicated spatial flows where meaning is generated by events in society (e.g. 'social space'). Each mode of history is defined by Lefebvre as a tripartite interplay of daily habits and sensations (*le perçu*, 'the perceived'), narratives or conceptions of space (*le conçu*, 'the conceived'), and the imagined space of time (*le vécu*, 'the lived').[231] Space is thus seen as a social product or complex social construction that influences spatial practices and perceptions. It is also an instrument of action and reflection, not only of productivity, but also of power, control, and authority.

Particularly important for our understanding of the ancient perception of a stadium, theatre, agora or forum, circus, etc. is the concept of 'representation of space' proposed by human geographers.[232] Social space is represented and shaped by communication. It is taken up by artists, authors, politicians, athletes, and thinkers. The distinction between place and space at this point is usually that 'place' represents a multi-layered subjective experience based on local discourses (in the sense of Michel Foucault as based on the totality of statements on a subject, independent of author, time and place of appearance) and conditions, while 'space', on the other hand, is a reflection of the current and future flow of entities, objects, data and information, and all communication.[233]

Landscapes, places, and spaces, generally called 'environment', can be considered in relation to how they are seen and experienced. Is it possible to look at a space without also physically interacting with it? This is as crucial for our understanding of ancient texts as it is for any textual perception in general. This is about different capacities of the body: simply looking and observing, engaging other

---

229 On the dialogue between contemporary environmental theories and classical texts, see Schliephake 2016.
230 The first crossovers between geography and communication theory were formulated by scholars working on toponyms and dialects in the early 20th century. See Adams and Jansson 2012, Sharag-Eldin et al. 2019.
231 On the spatial triad see Dünne and Günzel 2006, 333–336, cf. Schmid 2010, 191–245.
232 Aase 1994.
233 Cf. Tuan 1977, Cresswell 2015, 1–18, Agarwal 2018.

senses, and moving. The act of movement itself, whether into, out of or through a space, contributes to its shaping, just as the direction in which one moves – whether forward, backward, or sideways – adds further personal coordinates to the experienced space (Fig. 6).

Fig. 6: The Temple of Zeus at Stratos, Agrinio, circa 321 BCE. Photography by © Georges Salameh.

The analysis of texts that illustrate environmental concerns and the study of environmental issues in literature and environmental studies in general are collectively referred to as 'ecocriticism' (a term coined by William Rueckert in 1978).[234] Also known as green (cultural) studies, ecopoetics and environmental literary criticism, ecocriticism is a deliberately expansive field.[235]

The cultural environment consists of living and complex constructions that are created and negotiated in different ways. Geographical and topographical indica-

---

[234] Rueckert 1978. See also Janowski and Ingold 2012, Cohen 2015. On ecocentrism and ecology in ancient texts, see Schliephake 2016. See below p. 77–86.
[235] Gander and Kinsella 2012.

tions can be linked to social and anthropological practices and to the dynamic, multi-layered perspective of the recipient. In other words, geography and communication are two traditionally separate disciplines. However, they share commonalities and intersect at specific boundaries where multidisciplinary practices offer fruitful intersections, as discussed above.[236]

2.2 Theoretical preconditions

The perception of space and place is intimately linked to what has been called 'cognitive history'.[237] Understanding people's thoughts, motivations and purposes requires bringing together biologists, philosophers, historians, and cognitive scientists – as we shall see, this combination has led to very fruitful results in the history of religion. This is already a crucial difference between philological and historical approaches: In most 'cognitive' philological interpretations of ancient texts, cognitive scientists and philologists are not in dialogue, but philologists try to think 'cognitively' and apply modern theories from cognitive science to classical texts. In contrast, the aim of such approaches among historians is to make current historical data available for analysis by cognitive scientists. At the same time, conversely, current theories of cognition are made available to historians. By bringing together these two (traditionally rather separate) topics, the two disciplines can discuss their respective contributions, which mainly overlap in the area of spatial perception.[238]

American religious scholar Ann Taves has long worked in the field of scientific worldview research, on experience and mind.[239] Her distinction between neurophysiological, immutable and culturally determined different processes has proved important for their application.[240] It offers a new way of looking at the attachment of religious meaning to particular occasions and focuses on experiences that are considered religious, and thus on different things that are considered specific, rather than on 'religious experiences'. Taves uses 'top-down' and 'bottom-up' approaches from information processing and knowledge organisation.[241] A top-down strategy is basically breaking down a structure to understand its substruc-

---

[236] Sharag-Eldin e.a. 2019. See also p. 37–39 and 114–121.
[237] E.g. Dunér and Ahlberger 2019, and p. 158 f. 472 below.
[238] See especially Dasgupta 2016. See also Pachis 2019.
[239] See Taves 1999 and Taves 2009; see also their approach, summarised, and discussed in detail, in Larsson, Svensson, and Nordin 2020.
[240] Taves 2009, 99. Cf. Eidinow, Geertz, Deeley, and North 2022a, 2–3.
[241] Wolfe, Butcher, Lee, and Hyle 2003.

tures. It is a kind of reverse engineering. Thus, an overview of the whole is formulated in which all first-level subsystems are specified but not described in detail. The 'top-down' strategy takes the big vision and breaks it down into smaller pieces.

A 'bottom-up' strategy, on the other hand, assembles systems into more complex elements, turning the original ones into subsystems of the emerging whole. 'Bottom-up' information processing, relies on data coming in from the environment to build perceptual awareness. From the point of view of cognitive psychology, input information reaches the eyes ('bottom' or sensory input) and is transformed in the brain into an image that can be identified and recognised as a perception ('top', which is 'built up' between processing and final perception). The key elements of the system are first outlined in great detail in a 'bottom-up' approach. These components are interconnected to form larger systems, and further components are often interconnected at multiple levels to form a fully-fledged top-level system.

The 'top-down' or deductive processes vary according to culture and context. Through these processes, thoughts trigger feelings, or thoughts and feelings trigger perceptions. In contrast, 'bottom-up' or induction processes, also called automatic neurophysiological processes, are fixed and independent of culture and context; thoughts and feelings are triggered by physiological processes or perceptions.

From the perspective of cognitive neuroscience, what is essential in these studies is the concept of 'experience', which can be understood as the conscious perception of neurophysiological states. These states deviate from the everyday levels of sensation, in other words, from the normal basic processes.[242] 'Experience' is in fact any deviation from an everyday level of physiological or cognitive sensation that is under the influence of institutionalised practices and is therefore interpreted as institutional in this framework. Indeed, claims about 'experience' seem to offer an authoritative indication of subjectivity and authenticity. All experience is seen as material, neurophysiological. 'Experience' emerges from the emotional, sensory, and mental dimensions, with both space and the design of space and material culture playing a generative role.

In historiography, the use of objects that seem to describe direct experience in this sense can be contrasted with objective or empirical interpretations. Material culture is seen as a living and active agent of an embodied, extended, and distributed mind. Cognition occurs on the basis of 'mappings' configured by past experiences, brain and body processes, and cultural and social models of behaviour that

---

[242] On 'experience' as a key concept in second-generation cognitive science, see above p. 28 and below p. 106–110.

are constantly updated throughout life.²⁴³ While we as social beings construct social and cultural worlds, our brains and bodies construct them as well.

2.3 Ancient theatre as place and space: a case study

Consider, for example, the Greek theatre as an architectural complex and an important social institution from the perspective of the 'spatial turn'.²⁴⁴ Theatrical space has been an object of scholarly interest for some time. Peter Brook's 1968 seminal work discussed the bodily activation of space in the theatre.²⁴⁵ Gay McAuley has divided theatrical space into five categories: physical space, presentational space or the actors' bodily engagement with space, fictional space on and off stage, thematic space, and textual space.²⁴⁶ In her recent study of the phenomenology of Ancient Greek drama, Naomi Weiss discusses the category of 'dramatic space'.²⁴⁷

Theatre, θέατρον, is a place of viewing, both emotionally and architecturally. It can also refer metonymically to the audience itself. First of all, the Greek theatre is a 'representation of space' from the earliest sources. These sources thus treat the theatre building on the one hand as part of the urban landscape and at the same time as an instrument of thought and action. The examples of the fusion of human action, movement, affect, and vitality are numerous and range from the earliest evidence in Herodotus ("the whole theatre burst into tears", Hdt. 6, 21, 2) and Plato ("that the consciousness of the high expectations which the theatre attached to my speech upset me", Pl. *Smp.* 194a-b, "for the true judge should not make his judgments according to the dictates of the theatre.... but it has also spoiled the pleasure of the theatre", Pl. *Leg.* 2, 659a-c, "so the theatre-goers became loud instead of quiet, as if they knew the difference between good and bad music, and a kind of low theatrocracy took the place of a musical aristocracy", Pl. *Leg.* 3, 701a), to Amphis ("while the city is a theatre of clear misfortune", *Erithoi* fr. 17, 4 PCG). The other component, theatre as a place and event that evokes and generates emotions, may be explained in terms of cognitive geography and 'place attachment theory'.

---

243 On 'cognitive mapping' see Eden 1988, Buzan and Buzan 1993.
244 On the theatre as a spatial parameter and container of emotions as perceived by the Greeks of the Classical period, see Novokhatko (2025a, forthcoming).
245 Brook 1968.
246 McAuley 1999.
247 Weiss 2023, 41–77.

Greek theatre, in fact, evokes a 'place attachment' from the earliest sources.[248] Place attachment refers to an individual's emotional connection to a place and the memories, emotions, associations and perceptions that the place evokes. Attachment to place is multidimensional, based on the interplay between doing and feeling, behaving and experiencing. It results from the maintenance of meanings and artefacts associated with created places. For individuals, places often acquire meaning through experiences, life stages and events of individual development. For a society – and in the case of theatre this is a society with a collective attachment to place – places take on religious, historical, or other cultural meanings. The shared exploration and processing of emotional experiences associated with a place lead to a sense of belonging, connection, and engagement with the community. The behaviour of a community – a theatre community, for example – contributes to the attachment to place felt not only by the citizens of that community as a collective, but also by individuals. This concept of connectedness has been used to explain why people develop preferences for certain types of buildings.[249]

Theatre is the subject of many literary texts from the classical period. Originally, the building in which theatre took place was an auditorium, an environmental site construed for the performance of tragedies and comedies. However, it is at the same time such a powerful geographical, ecological, economic, and social 'place' that it is also staged and alive from the beginning (Fig. 7).

Theatre is alive in the physiological sense and can feel, see, hear, taste, and move. It is socialised and symbolised, constructed by society through its interaction with the biophysical environment in which that society develops its existence. As the examples above reveal, theatre has a strong inherent collective identification (cf. Plato's *theatrokratia*) that defines its identity through its objective spatial characteristics.[250] The process of collective identification is conditioned by material reality, but its expression is symbolic and based on a representative model of that reality. The sense of place and belonging to a community on which collective identity is built can be seen as key to clarifying the role played by the social dimension of theatre for the Greeks of the fifth and fourth centuries BCE.

The authors use theatre as a means of experiencing the world. It is not only a conceptual tool of historians, geographers, philosophers, orators, and playwrights, but appears daily in discourse and in the social world surrounding them. It has an extraordinary influence on the way Greeks represent and treat themselves and the

---

248 Low and Altman 1992, Smith 2018b, Manzo and Devine-Wright 2021.
249 On the connection of memories and feelings with space and place, see Tuan 1975, Casey 2009, Lewicka 2011, Trigg 2012. On architectural perception, see Conroy Dalton, Krukar and Hölscher 2018.
250 See f. 254 p. 68.

Fig. 7: The Theatre of Thorikos, north of Lavrio, circa 525–480 BCE. Photography by © Georges Salameh.

world around them. From the joy of the tired peasant to the way an old intellectual philosopher imagines the universe, theatre has the power to affect us all in different ways.

For example, the oldest surviving accounts, on the one hand, treat the theatre environmental complex as part of the urban landscape and at the same time as an instrument of thought and action. For example, Greek historians and rhetoricians, from their earliest times, explicitly refer to the theatre as a geographical site. To be more precise, it may be the case that our "earliest" sources are not as early as we think. It is possible that the first theatres were actually not architectural until at least the mid to late fifth century BCE. It seems that they were more akin to a slope overlooking a sanctuary with wooden niches and the concept of the theatre was not necessarily linked to the idea of an architectural structure. The idea of the theatre was more closely associated with the idea of a space where performances could be watched. For example, there are several references in the sources to the theatre of Dionysus in Mounichia, in the Athenian deme Peiraeus. At the time of the oligarchic revolutions in 411 and 404 BCE, meetings of the assembly were held there. The theatre once stood at the foot of the hill of Kastella, behind the small port of Mikrolimano, and is now lost.[251] The otherwise probably rather insignificant municipal theatre of Mounichia functioned not only as a topographical site in a military context, but also – in an unusual setting and given the existence of a new kind of power in Athens – as an ideological landmark. For example, the assembly passed a resolution calling for condemnation after hearing the formal charges against the generals and officers.

Furthermore, the site of the Dionysus theatre in Mounichia was now highly visible to the Spartan occupiers and was still important for assemblies later on: Demosthenes may have alluded to assemblies here in 346 BCE, although he did not explicitly mention the construction of a theatre. It may be the case that this is because the space and sanctuary at this point resembled the Pnyx more than a building (Dem. 19, 60 and 19, 209, cf. 19, 125). It is not known whether this was an unusual or regular practice when naval matters were on the agenda. Meetings were also held here in the third and second centuries BCE, as shown by a series of inscriptions, each referring to the location of the Dionysus theatre.[252]

How is all of this relevant to cognitive studies and the 'spatial turn'? Theatre-goers and assembly-goers should be seen as part of their environment. Their agency merges with the lithic agency, with the stone walls and the material architecture of the theatre ensemble. Cognitive geography examines place as an event that evokes and generates emotions. As mentioned above, place attachment involves an individual's emotional connection to a place and the thoughts, feelings, memories, and interpretations that the place evokes.[253] The landscapes, spaces, and locations of theatrical sites in the ancient world invite such a perspective, in order to see their meaning in terms of the rituals and emotions involved in the process of going to the theatre.

Furthermore, comedy, with its famous self-referentiality, uses the word *theatron* from the beginning, and it always includes the whole notion of the place filled with people, that is, the people sitting in a certain place and the actors who address this entity. The *theatron* is alive, personified, it is the audience that the chorus addresses in the parabasis.[254] In Plato then, the theatre is a personified architectural place, a huge enactive monster that can feel, see, hear, teach and rule: "Thus the theatre-goers became loud instead of quiet, as if they knew the difference between

---

[251] Thuc. 8, 93, Xen. *Hell.* 2, 4, 32, Lys. *In Agoratum* (=13) 32 and 55.
[252] MacDowell 2000, 232–233, and Garland 1987, 81–82.
[253] Montello 2018, Agarwal 2018, Smith 2018a, Manzo and Devine-Wright 2021.
[254] Ar. *Ach.* 628–629, Ar. *Eq.* 507–508, Ar. *Pax* 734–735, Eupolis *Marikas* fr. 192, 157 PCG, Metagenes *Philothytes* fr. 15 PCG, Amphis *Erithoi* fr. 17 PCG, Adesp. fr. 206 PCG. Cf. also Hdt. 6, 21, 2.

good and bad music, and an aristocracy in music was replaced by a kind of low rule by spectators (θεατροκρατία τις πονηρὰ γέγονεν). For if in music, and in music alone, had arisen a democracy of free men, such a result would not have been so very disquieting; but as it was, in music arose the general conceit of common wisdom and contempt of law, and on the heels of these came liberty. For since men thought themselves knowing, they became fearless, and from boldness arose impudence", Pl. *Leg.* 3, 701a).[255] The theatre could be considered an architectural complex in Plato's time. However, it is also the case that the perception of this landscape, place, and space is merged with the spectators' emotions, which allows them to experience this place bodily and sensually.

In terms of place attachment theory, theatre can be seen as people's cognitive and emotional connection to a particular scenario and environment. It is the experience of a long-term affective attachment to a particular geographical and architectural entity. The meanings attributed to such an attachment change over time and develop in people a sense of belonging that makes a particular place an anchor of their identity and community. The collective identity of the theatre audience in classical Athens is the result of a continuous process of symbolic construction based on and simultaneously generating a sense of belonging. The audience and the performers are aware that they form a group that is distinguished from other groups by the development of shared feelings of belonging and attachment to a particular place and space.

The behaviour of a community – a theatre community, for example – contributes to the sense of place felt not only by the citizens of that group, but also by individuals. When the thoughts, feelings and deeds associated with belonging to a place are experienced and shared, it creates a sense of unity, solidarity, and commitment to the community. It could be argued that the community can be understood in a number of different ways. Some messages of the chorus are addressed to the Athenian citizens only, which could potentially lead to jokes perhaps being misinterpreted or misunderstood by a foreigner. Some messages, however, clearly have a broader, imperial dimension and concern allied states. It is possible that these messages might be of particular interest to the fifth or so of the audience who were not Athenians, but allied.

Taking the emergence of the institution of theatre in Greece from the fifth century BCE as an example, it is possible to explore how novel cognitive landscapes are formed, and their implications more generally, by looking at the connections and interplay between identity and materiality, between personal engagement and the challenge of innovation. The ancient Greek landscape that defined the lo-

---

[255] See also Pl. *Smp.* 194a-b, Pl. *Criti.* 108b-d, Pl. *Leg.* 2, 659a-c. See also p. 66.

cation of the theatre through its objective spatial features is both familiar and alien to us, and it produced powerful new senses of connectedness that shaped lives for at least a thousand years.

Human engagement with the world provides the ground for an intelligent understanding of it. It is not piecemeal. It follows a set of principles, as work in one area is taken up and extended in others. Human interaction with the environment in all areas of life, whether secular, pragmatic or sacred, leads to profound transformations in the flow of life, challenging such distinctions.[256]

Since concepts can and usually do develop differently in each human group, cultural developments follow different and diversified paths, so that the development of cognitive abilities differs in an infinite number of populations.[257] Since material evidence usually reflects human behaviour, cognitive archaeology also uses archaeological sites; here this methodological basis is used to interpret human behaviour in the archaeological record through the considerations of the psychobiological model. For example, low cognitive development, as non-symbolic thinking, means that the influence of environmental factors is much greater than high cognitive development, as symbolic thinking, which has more social, technological, or cultural skills and adapts and develops much better to the environment in which it lives, a consequence that is manifested and recorded in the archaeological evidence.[258]

2.4 Literary sources and the perception of space and place

More generally, a greater sensitivity to spatial dimensions opens up studies of ancient texts by revealing the ways in which authors construct the action and plot, allowing the audience to experience general space independently of the lived space, i.e. their real environment.[259] Furthermore, authors often manipulate the ideological requirements of contemporary discourses.[260] The tension between

---

[256] Cf. a detailed analysis of the formation of the early medieval village and parish in England from the perspective of material engagement with the world by Gosden 2014.
[257] Gauvain e.a. 2011, Gauvain and Munroe 2012.
[258] Gauvain and Munroe 2012, Heyes 2012, Dasen 2022.
[259] On 'spatial turn' in literary studies in general, see Hallet and Neumann 2009. For ancient studies in particular, see Rehm 2002 (space in Greek tragedy), Gilhuly and Worman 2014 ('spatial turn' and ancient Greek texts), Skempis and Ziogas 2014 ('spatial turn' and Greek and Roman epic), Cole 2005 and Hawes 2017 (landscapes), De Jong 2012 (narratological space), and Heirman and Klooster 2013 (the 'lived space' in texts), Schliephake 2016 (ecocentrism and ecology).
[260] On theatre buildings and their locations, as well as human relations with them, see Carlson 1989.

real and imagined landscapes, the relationship between human bodies and territory, the cognitive connections between places and their (human-given) names, and the role of place in relation to power and identity are just some of the themes associated with contemporary space studies.[261]

The metatheatrical dimension of theatrical landscapes such as the sanctuary of Dionysus in ancient Athens makes the theatre a place where all participants engage with the environment in a way that is perhaps unique. If we recollect that dramatic productions take place at the Sanctuary of Dionysus on the Akropolis, with a retaining wall to the north and slightly further up the hill a circular terrace that would have been the first orchestra of the theatre, we might consider the possibility that the natural amphitheatre of the hill serves as a *theatron*. It is natural as well that this environment may have influenced the way in which each theatrical event was perceived. When the audience sees dramatical plays and dithyrambic choruses on stage, they experience a holistic theatrical environment, and this influences their perception of the play.

The meaning of place is linked to several levels: the real place in the geographical sense where the audience gathers, the imagined place as represented by the characters in the play, and the 'lived place' in the sense of urban theorist Edward Soja, i.e. all kinds of political, social, biological and cultural connotations evoked by the recipients' experience. Soja proposed a theory of three interconnected urban spaces: *Firstspace* (the physical, built environment "in the real world", perceived space and spatial practice), *Secondspace* (the space conceived in the minds of its inhabitants) and *Thirdspace* (the lived space, the way people experience this space).[262] Finally, there is the theatre space itself with the stage, the seats and the atmosphere of the performance in progress.[263]

Cognitive approaches to space can be informative for various Greek and Latin texts, but the 'spatial turn' in literary studies is particularly helpful when reading fragmentary texts. The representation of places with meaning is important in the dramatic fragment as a key to interpretation: even in a short fragment, geographical and topographical indications can be linked to social and anthropological practices and to the dynamic, multi-layered perspective of the audience.

The setting can be imagined and vividly reconstructed, either in the imagination of the author and reader or of the audience, becoming part of the action and events. This category offers the potential to understand how and where the 'imaginary' interacts with 'real' places and practices. The social and place are interde-

---

[261] See a case study of Delphi in Pindar's work in Eckermann 2014.
[262] Soja 1996, 74–82. On the space typology in Lefebvre, see above p. 61.
[263] See also Soja 1996, 8–12 and 26–52.

pendent because place is a facet of our concept of identity. The social can only be manifested in and through place. The construction of place involves identity and its coordinates such as gender, race, and sexuality.

A place is inextricably linked to human behaviour, feelings, sensations, thoughts, and interactions. In the fourth century BCE, the playwright Alexis wrote a comedy called "Men of Tarentum" (Ταραντῖνοι). A remarkable fragment has survived: *Because that's the way it is here in your beautiful Athens* (τοῦτο γὰρ νῦν ἐcτί coι ἐν ταῖc Ἀθήναιc ταῖc καλαῖc ἐπιχώριον): *people start dancing as soon as they see a smell of wine* (Alexis fr. 224, 1–4 PCG).[264] The smell of wine is known to be one of the favourite smells of the Athenians, and the title of the comedy could suggest a certain spatial interpretation here. If the speaker, who is explicitly a non-Athenian, "at your place in Athens" clearly indicating his otherness, belongs to the "men of Tarentum", this could mean that a certain tension between Tarentum and Athens is meant. In any case, wherever he comes from, the speaker refers to a specific Athenian custom to dance a smell, synaesthetically blending seeing, smelling, touching, and tasting into a sensory perception of place.

In his satyr play *Cyclops*, Euripides echoes Odysseus' Homeric 'ethnographic excursus' (*Od.* 9, 181–193, 213–223), but updates his account to reflect fifth-century audiences' geographical and political expectations (especially vv. 113–129).[265] Euripides' Odysseus asks Silenus many questions about Sicily ("What is this land and who lives here?" v.113), its landscapes, its inhabitants, its government, its food, and its politics. Space is blurred on stage: to be in Sicily and to speak about Sicily is actually to engage the minds of the Athenian audience. He asks the satyrs about 'demo-cracy' in Sicily (δεδήμευται κράτοc;) and whether political power is distributed among the people ("Who do they follow? Or has power been divided among the people?" v.119). Sicily is characterised further by drinking milk and cheese, as Sicily is known for its delicious cheese, which is brought to Athens (γάλακτι καὶ τυροῖcι, v. 122). 'Athenised' Sicily as a place is here a communicative concept that plays a key role in Odysseus' quest. The identification of Sicily through the Athenian horizon is a cognitive act. The Athenian audience for whom Euripides writes perceives Sicily and, through Odysseus' and Silenus' questions, establishes a different relationship with Sicily than would be the case with those of other cultural or political systems. Again, the details presented by the performers on stage are complemented by the recipients' knowledge of the context and their emotions and attachment to Sicily.[266]

---

[264] Arnott 1996, 641–642.
[265] Hunter and Laemmle 2020, 121.
[266] On the meanings of place framed by human behavioural patterns, see Agarwal 2018.

A common, crucial feature that unites Alexis' representation of Athens and Euripides' representation of Sicily is an enacted and embodied place that appeals to the minds and senses of the spectators. Athens, seen through the eyes of the 'other', is characterised by dancing, seeing, smelling, tasting, and drinking. Sicily, also seen through the eyes of the 'other', is characterised by its tasty goods, its people, its political structure, in other words by an active and enactive interaction with the place.

I wonder if it might be helpful to revisit an appropriate term that was coined in 1989 by Christiane Sourvinou-Inwood, namely 'zooming devices'. She suggests that the relationship between the world of the audience and that of the play was never constant and inert, but rather created by the performance and manipulated in different ways throughout its course. It might be suggested that these devices had the effect of distancing the action from the world of the fifth-century Athenian polis, differentiating the two. Similarly, it could be suggested that they had the effect of bringing the world of the play nearer, prompting the audience to relate their experiences and assumptions directly to the play.[267] Ancient Greek drama makes use of these 'zooming devices' in particular when choruses zoom the audience in and out of the space and back again.[268]

Human mind and behaviour – what we think, feel, do with our bodies, how we move, whether alone or in groups – always occur in the context of physical and socio-cultural environments.[269] Products, artefacts, plants are thus active agents that make the place and are in fact the place. Space and place are often staged in journeys with goods from all over the world. Catalogues of goods brought to a particular place from other places are also enactive representations of those places, with the full range of ideological, mental, and emotional coding.[270]

For example, Hermippus' fr. 63 PCG from the play *Basket-bearers* (428–425 BCE) contains a catalogue of goods as an example of multifaceted geography; cities, regions and countries are thrown together as part of his list.[271] The content of the fragment reveals a complex relationship between place, the human brain, the

---

267 Sourvinou-Inwood 1989, 136.
268 For further insight into the manipulation of choruses and their relationship to what we watch, see Weiss 2023 (such as the Oceanids in the *Prometheus Bound* or the Birds in the *Birds*). Weiss also makes a reference to the distinctive aspect of the *Birds*, where the entire play is centred around the concept of skyspace and the open-air theatre, thus creating a blend between the theatrical space and the imaginative space (Weiss 2023, 68–70).
269 Montello 2018, 3.
270 Cf. also Ar. frs. 428–431 PCG. On the representation of space in theatre, see Rehm 2002 and Meineck 2017, 52–78.
271 On the date and the content of the fragment see Storey 2011, 306–309, Comentale 2017, 242–243, 249–275.

body, and artefactual forms, which are mutually shaped by the human imagination. The Mediterranean space is embodied and enacted on stage, vividly and materially, and at the same time highly ideologically. Dionysus sailed the sea as a merchant, bringing various goods to Athens. On one level, the interaction with the environment is translated into material form, with objects acting and enacting the space. A silphium stalk and ox hides (καυλὸν καὶ δέρμα βόειον, v. 4) from Cyrene, mackerel and salted fish (σκόμβρους καὶ πάντα ταρίχη, v. 5) from the Hellespont, barley meal and beef offal (χόνδρον καὶ πλευρὰ βόεια, v. 6) from Thessaly, pigs and cheese (σῦς καὶ τυρὸν, v. 9) from Syracuse, hanging gear, sails and papyrus (τὰ κρεμαστὰ ἱστία καὶ βύβλους, v. 12–13), from Egypt, incense, also known as olibanum (λιβανωτόν, v. 13), from Syria, cypress wood (κυπάριττον, v. 14) from Crete, ivory (ἐλέφαντα, v. 15) from Libya, raisins and dried figs (ἀσταφίδας τε καὶ ἰσχάδας, v. 16) from Rhodes, pears and apples (ἀπίους καὶ ἴφια μῆλα, v. 17) from Euboea, slaves (ἀνδράποδ', v. 18) from Phrygia and mercenaries (ἐπικούρους, v. 18) from Arcadia, servants and tattooed men (v. 19) from the Thessalian city of Pagasae – Thessaly is thus mentioned again, whose barley and cattle have already been mentioned above,[272] – nuts (τὰς δὲ Διὸς βαλάνους καὶ ἀμύγδαλα, v. 20) from Paphlagonia, dates and hard wheat (καρπὸν φοίνικος καὶ σεμίδαλιν, v. 22) from Phoenicia, blankets and embroidered pillows (δάπιδας καὶ ποικίλα προσκεφάλαια, v. 23) from Carthage.

The places and landscapes on the Panhellenic Mediterranean map are perceived materially and emotionally at the visual, auditory, tactile, olfactory, and gustatory levels. The interaction of the mind with the material is underlined not only by the name of the raw product, but by the whole process of dealing with the material, such as the making of the statues of the gods from cypress wood (κυπάριττον τοῖσι θεοῖσιν, v. 14) or the sale of ivory (ἐλέφαντα πολὺν παρέχει κατὰ πρᾶσιν, v. 15).

Whoever the speaker of this monologue may have been, he was clearly not passive, but active in gathering and processing information. He evaluates and makes behavioural choices in space and place. Intriguingly, Hermippus includes some general features of a 'behaviour and cognition' approach to space and place: he focuses on the individual person and their experience; behavioural activity is based on the world as perceived and imagined rather than as it objectively exists; and finally, the interrelationships between the individual and the environ-

---

[272] Thessaly is a more appropriate location here. The reading Θετταλίας χόνδρον ("barley meal from Thessaly", v. 6) is preferable although it has a variant Ἰταλίας χόνδρον ("barley meal from Italy") in the text transmission. Ἰταλίας is the reading in the manuscripts C and E. See the discussion in Comentale 2017, 255.

2.4 Literary sources and the perception of space and place — 75

ment are bidirectional, each affecting the other. Internal mental states and processes mediate spatial behaviour.

Spatial behaviour and interaction involve movement, travel, communication, land use and the exchange and distribution of goods – all issues addressed by the so-called 'behavioural approach' to geography, which emerged in the 1960s and incorporates realistic models of human psychology.[273] The exchange and distribution of goods narrated on stage as a constituent of playwrights' engagement with the environment serves as a lens through which to interpret fragmentary catalogues.

Drama, perhaps more than any other genre, is full of references to place. What makes it special and unique is the theatrical environment itself. On the one hand, places are embodied and enacted on stage; they can act as characters, as in the *Cities* (*Poleis*) of Eupolis, when the subject states of the Athenian Empire – Tenos, Chios and Cyzicus – move, dance and are agents (frs. 245–247 PCG). Some titles that refer to places such as countries (e.g. Plato's *Hellas ē Nēsoi*), islands (e.g. Epicharmus' *Nasoi*, Aristophanes' or Archippus' *Nēsoi*, Timocles' *Dēlos*, Amphis' *Leukas*), regions (e.g. Demetrius' *Sikilia*) and the like also suggest that the place was important in the play.

Unfortunately, there is no surviving play with such an explicit title. However, we can enjoy Aristophanes' *Acharnians* (425 BCE), in which the chorus of a mob of old charcoal burners and peasants from the Athenian deme Acharnae could be read as standing for the place Acharnae itself. On the other hand, the theatrical environment itself is a material agent, an enacted and extended space that affects the perception of the play in a unique way: the weather conditions in the open-air theatre, the sky, the landscapes, the hills, the trees, the movement and breathing of other spectators – all this makes the dramatic genre very specific in terms of space and place. One should mention the sacred nature of the space, the division created by masks, the kinesthetic relationships created and the inactive elements of what is being perceived in the open air. The combination of these elements affects the way in which spaces in theatre are perceived, whether they are perceived as real, staged or imaginative.

To conclude. Cognitive studies of space and spatial perception contribute to a deeper understanding of how space was perceived in antiquity, and also prompt further inquiries. Things, thoughts, and memories accumulate in certain configurations associated with the practices of daily life.[274] The agora, for example, is informed by actual ritual and legal practices. A focus on place has the potential to

---

273 See Cox and Colledge 1969.
274 Escobar 2001, 143. See also Malpas 1999, 36.

encourage an approach to an embedded form of meaning, the shared realm of experience of all participants in the performance. This experience is a holistic one: the mind, the body and the environment are joined together in a stream of sensations, ideas, images, and implications.

The act of movement itself, whether into, out of or through a space, contributes to its design, just as the direction in which one moves – whether forward, backward, or sideways – lends further personal coordinates to experienced space. Different capacities of the body and mind are involved: simply looking and observing, using other senses, creating imaginary scenes in the mind, or movement.[275]

The authors not only create a vivid geographical and political unity through the evocation of its visual and acoustic qualities, but also align it with ideological – personal, regional, national, and ethnic – interests. Places are not static but dynamic and subject to change in relation to the people who experience them. Places only count if they are perceived to be there. The engagement of human beings with the world forms the basis of their understanding of it, and the elements of everyday life have an influence on the place. In addition to the dimension of seeing, recognising, and understanding the world, the environment has an epistemological dimension.

Cognitive geography and cognitive approaches to archaeology influence our understandings of what any place actually meant to its inhabitants and visitors. In literary texts, too, space is not just a place where things happen, but an active participant, an agent. The enacted and embodied space and place in the text, with the full range of sensations, intentions and emotions involved in the process, is therefore fundamental to the act of experiencing the ancient world.

---

[275] Purves 2014, 96.

Chapter 3
Imaginations, visions, and perception

When we communicate with the outside world, we not only use sensory perception, but also embed what we perceive in memory and imagination. Imagination, which helps us transform texts into mental images, is crucial for perception and can be described as a complex set of processes involving the relationship between impression and memory.[276]

In the following, I will first discuss the visual perception and spectating in theatre, and then present some recent findings on metacognitive considerations in Greek and Roman texts, especially those dealing with visualisation and image-making. The second part thus shows that ancient authors themselves dealt with visual imagination and consciousness, while the third part discusses some recent work in classics in which modern theories, especially the conceptual theory of metaphor, have been applied to ancient texts.

3.1 Cognitive approaches to viewing in ancient dramaturgy and theatre

As has been discussed above in the context of place attachment and ecocriticism, theatre played a central role in the ancient world, and especially in Greece. It is thus no coincidence that a large part of cognitive literary studies is linked to theatre studies. The cognitive dimensions of performance and spectatorship have been explored outside the classical world in numerous studies of Shakespearean and modern theatre.[277]

Theatrical performance and spectacle were at the heart of all facets of everyday life: court and assembly, cultic and religious ritual, arts and education.[278] Various aspects such as gaze and vision, vividness, attention, *ekphrasis* (a rhetorical form through which an object, an act or landscape is described in a vivid and pictorial manner, thus imaginatively 'placed before the eyes' of the viewer), theatre

---

276 Klein, Damm, and Giebeler 1983.
277 See Blair and Cook 2016b, 11–13. For Shakespeare see e.g. Tribble 2011 and p. 40 f. 152.
278 The gaze and visuality in the ancient world have been at the centre of research for a number of decades now, enjoying a wealth of relevant discussions and bibliographies. See e.g. the seminal book of Simon (1988), Villard (2002) and Villard (2005), Bartsch and Elsner 2007, Blundell et al. 2013, Squire 2015, Hölscher 2018, Kampakoglou and Novokhatko 2018, Thein 2022.

and performance were examined from the point of view of seeing and imagining something.

In a free democratic society where people are expected to participate in voting on state issues, the idea of theatre as a social, cultural, and political force was crucial. To this end, theatre provided a detached and immersive experience that increased empathy, broadened perceptions, and encouraged sensitivity. The key performative elements of theatre are fully explored from a cognitive science perspective as embodied, living and staged events, including new approaches to storytelling, physical space, masks, movement, music, language, intention and emotion.[279] In the ancient world, the theatre was also a place of otherness and diversity, where audiences were confronted with different points of view and critical perspectives.

Anne-Sophie Noel, for example, has a long-standing interest in the diversity of spectatorship and audience response in fifth-century BCE Athens, in order to better understand how spectators accumulate, juxtapose or divide their experiences of different performance settings.[280] For example, theatregoers, in their respective roles in public or private life, were members of a variety of socio-cultural groups and subcultures, and as spectators were confronted with a variety of audience reactions and situations.[281] They can be studied in terms of gender, race, citizenship, age, social status: they brought their experiences of their previous lives and performances to the theatre.[282]

It can be assumed that the Athenian citizens were continually thinking and feeling their political role and opinion. We also need to consider the extent to which the role of spectator is used in contexts other than theatre performance, as in theatre playwrights may assign different 'functions', 'identities' or 'roles' to audiences. The dramatic characters are an explicit appeal to the citizens, but at the same time, the playwrights do not neglect the presence of 'the other' in the audience. The theatregoers also assume different roles in other contexts of social life, such as actors and spectators of the 'court spectacle' that took place in the courts of

---

[279] See Falletti, Sofia and Jacono 2016; Blair and Cook 2016a; Shepherd-Barr 2020.
[280] Noel 2013, Noel 2019, Noel 2023a, Noel 2023b, and various forthcoming. See also the activities and publications of Noel's project *InSpectA* (https://inspecta.hypotheses.org, last access June 3rd 2024), which aims to assess the extent to which the idea of the performative experience of spectators can be documented for antiquity, and which explores the interrelationship between the multisensory stimulation that a theatrical performance provides (the embodied "senses") and the emotional and cognitive responses it evokes (the "intelligences" of the spectators).
[281] See e.g. Gruber 1986, Roselli 2011, Robson 2017.
[282] Budelmann and Power 2015, Revermann 2006. See also Meineck 2016.

the city.²⁸³ It is difficult to determine the composition of the Athenian audience with any certainty. It seems reasonable to suggest that they may have participated in religious rituals and celebrations in both public and private settings, as family members, friends, neighbours, colleagues and so on. In this way, they experienced the performance as part of a living space whose social functions and effects were defined by society.

The interplay between the senses, made possible by the combination of acoustic cues and visual effects, and the cognitive processes that take place in the imagination of the viewer/recipient is also being researched today on the basis of multisensory integration in neuroscience and brain theory.²⁸⁴ To this end, research on embodied cognition and the processing of emotions has been applied in theatre studies for a few decades. The main thrust of Bruce McConachie and Rhonda Blair's work is an exploration of the function of the *mirror neuron system* (engaged when one performs a motor action or views another person perform the same action: this could potentially provide a neural mechanism by which we might gain a deeper understanding of other people's action goals), empathy, and embodiment in the shaping of the actor/audience relationship and the audience experience in the theatre more generally.²⁸⁵ Neither multisensory interactions nor the interplay between the senses and the imagination have yet taken centre stage in this still nascent field. However, several volumes have been published on the topic of how the findings of neuroscience can impact acting pedagogy, acting technique and applied theatre.²⁸⁶

Another approach has been provided by *functional Magnetic Resonance Imaging* (measures the flow of blood in areas of the brain). Much research has been done in multisensory studies to gain a better understanding of our everyday real-life actions, which often stimulate multiple senses simultaneously.²⁸⁷ This includes studying the spatial organisation of multisensory brain regions: for example, the *bimodal superior temporal cortex* (bSTC) has been identified as a part of the brain that is sensitive to both sight and sound, and whose responses are en-

---

283 On the role of spectators in the Athenian polis in the theatre, the agora, the assembly, and the court, see Villacèque 2013. For a much-discussed theme of the merging of the role of spectator on the theatrical and political stage, in theatre and assembly, see Weiss 2023, 55–65, with extensive bibliography.
284 Ladda, Wallwork, and Lotze 2020; Jola and Hansen 2021; Greaves e. a. 2022. Cf. also Martin and Sauter 1995 and Carlson 1990.
285 McConachie 2008, McConachie 2013, McConachie 2015, Blair 2007, Blair 2009, Blair 2020. See also Garner 2018, 145–184, and Ciesielski 2017.
286 See f. 182 p. 48 above.
287 Huettel, Song, and McCarthy 2014. Cf. Olsen 2019.

hanced when the input is multisensory (auditory-visual).[288] However, researchers in this field are still struggling with important methodological issues: some acknowledge that most experiences based on processing abstract stimulus material such as button press, dot and sound do not reach the complexity of integrating audiovisual inputs in a real-world context. There are also certain temporal, regional and cultural limitations that should be taken into account. Nevertheless, a number of convergent experiences have indicated that the multisensory system is capable of considerable flexibility. Multisensory integration is now well recognised and essential to contemporary sensorimotor neuroscience, defined as the range of mechanisms by which sensory information from some modalities, such as vision, hearing, touch, and smell, cooperates with information from other modalities.[289]

In the field of brain theory and philosophy of mind, the conceptual view of perception as a constructive process provides a useful framework for examination of the viewer's experience. Perceiving is not a passive process of receiving sensations, but a continuous activity in which the mind optimises the information between sensory signals and a few neuronal representations.[290] It's based on the idea of the Bayesian brain (derives from Thomas Bayes' theorem), which posits that the brain acts like an inference machine, with an internal representation of the world that is not only formed by sensory input, but also reshaped to fit that representation. This is also called 'predictive processing': In our perception of the external world, we constantly make predictions about sensory impressions according to the represented model that we have internalised.[291] When one hears a pounding sound, one will spontaneously draw conclusions about all possible sources of this potentially alarming signal and then select the sensory impressions that are relevant for an efficient identification of this signal under the given circumstances. Building on this, Andy Clark articulates the fact that perception requires imagination: perceiving human beings are therefore also imaginative beings, beings who discover and live their world not only through physical perception and action, but also through imagination, dreaming and often consciously created mental simulations.[292] The engagement of perception and imagination is significant here above all.

This neuroscientific research and theoretical modelling allow us to rethink what it means for a spectator to experience a simultaneous multisensory input in a theatre performance. Meineck's experimental research on masks, discussed

---

[288] Rolls 2021; Chuanji Gao e. a. 2022.
[289] Van Dam, Parise, and Ernst 2014.
[290] Moutoussis 2016; Anderson 2015, especially 1–40 and 179–205.
[291] Kirchhoff 2018; Bottemanne, Longuet, and Gauld 2021. See also below p. 119–120.
[292] Clark 2009, Clark 2015, 84–108.

above, convincingly supports the idea that ancient spectators may have been more receptive to the multimodal and sensorimotor facets of language processing and movement because masquerading requires the combination of highly coordinated movement, gesture and heightened poetic language for effective communication.[293] Noel develops Meineck's thesis further by also highlighting the acoustic effects and citing excerpts from tragedy that comment on the interactions between visual and acoustic effects.[294]

Greek drama is replete with examples of a character on stage stimulating the audience's brain to combine its prior shared knowledge, common ground, and internal representation of a particular event with the incoming sensory impressions to create an auditory and visual image of it. Since the real cannot be depicted per se, the represented event is always an imaginary event. But an act of performance, in which the resemblance or mimesis is strong and effective, is created by the imagination of the audience, the actors and the author.[295]

In the parodos of Aeschylus' *The Seven Against Thebes*, for example, the women of the chorus rush onto the stage clutching the statues of the gods to express their fear of the impending war. This famous passage underlines the visual construction of sound and, conversely, the auditory construction of sight (Aesch. *Septem* 100–103). Above all, "I see the clash" (κτύπον δέδορκα, v. 103) suggests a complete synaesthetic fusion of the heard and the visual, which the poet purportedly evokes here.[296]

The primary function of the fusion of sound and image in drama is to represent patterns of thought about various dynamic processes common to human experience, particularly in relation to the regulation of emotions and the movement of bodies through space.[297] Physical expressive movements generate the same kind of felt experience in the viewer, regardless of whether they accompany speech. In this way, expressive movements provide the experiential basis for the creation and construction of mental images.[298] People's understanding of musical movement is

---

[293] Meineck 2011 and Meineck 2019. See above p. 48–50.
[294] Noel 2019 and Noel 2023a.
[295] Aristotle discusses this very topic of child development within his mimetic theory in similar terms (e.g. Arist. *Poet.* 1448b4–8). Cf. also Merlin Donald's concept of "mimetic culture" as a fundamental stage in human evolution which developed the ability to imitate, which was applicable in rituals and crafts. This stage predated the development of verbal communication and contributed to the increase in brain volume and the complexity of social life forms (Donald 1991).
[296] The passage is discussed in Marinis 2012 and Noel 2019, 299–300. On synesthetic fusion in Aeschylus, see more generally Weiss 2018.
[297] Gibbs 2017, 245. See also p. 48–50 above and the analysis of blending in tragedy by Golab 2023. On Aristophanes see recently Angelopoulou 2024.
[298] Forceville 2009b.

also based on physical experience. Music moves slowly, abruptly, gently or powerfully in 'passages'. The recipient, from the perspective of the observer, can imagine the whole piece of music at once, as if it were an object to be viewed from a distance.

In classical Athenian theatre, music and song were an important part of dramatic performance. This included songs for the choruses only, for the chorus and for one or more actors, solo songs (*monodiai*) especially in tragedies, recited passages with musical accompaniment and short instrumental compositions. The outstanding musical instrument of the theatre was the flute (*aulos*). The *aulos*-player had an enormous influence, because during the performance he drove the plot forward to a greater extent than the playwright.[299] The Greek audience experienced the musical form of the choruses as a natural and necessary reality and as a form of interaction.[300]

This juxtaposition and synaesthesia of seeing and hearing is particularly important. In Aristophanes, many choral passages are full of auditory constructions, and two examples of these will be considered here. In Aristophanes' *Frogs*, the ferryman Charon informs Dionysus that they will soon hear the glorious songs of the frog-swans (βατράχων κύκνων θαυμαστά, v. 207): "for you will hear the most beautiful songs (ἀκούσει γὰρ μέλη κάλλιστ') as soon as you bow to the oar" (Ar. *Ra.* 205–206). "You will hear" is an explicit reference in the text for the listeners. A chorus of frogs is indeed heard without any testimony in the text that it is also seen. It has been argued that the chorus remains audible but invisible throughout the scene.[301] The chorus sings nonsensical words like croaking (the repeated βρεκεκεξ κοαξ κοαξ, vv. 209–210, 220, 223, 225, 235, 239, 250, 256, 260, 267), a song they once sang to Dionysus, the son of Zeus, in the marshes (212–217). It is assumed that one group sang "brekekex" and the other "koax koax" to imitate the antiphonal croaking of frogs.[302] Dionysus, who rows in the boat disguised as Heracles, mocks them. The frogs retort that after all the Muses, Pan and Apollo appreciate them (Ar. *Ra.* 229–234). Dionysus says his bottom hurts and he wants them to stop (v. 241), but they sing even louder about hopping and swimming (Ar. *Ra.* 257–259). Finally, Dionysus roars along with them in the spirit of competition to drown them out (v. 261). As the frogs retreat, he shouts to them that they will

---

[299] Bundrick 2005, 175–178.
[300] Bacon 1994/1995, 6.
[301] Allison 1983. For the song of the frogs, see Nooter 2019b, 203–205. On sound studies applied to classical texts, see below p. 113–114. Cf. the discussion of this passage in the context of multimodal metaphors in comedy, Novokhatko 2025b (forthcoming).
[302] D'Angour 2020.

never beat him and that he will defeat them musically, while in fact joining them in their song (Ar. *Ra.* 263–268).

The text of the repeated *koax* itself sometimes makes little sense, and the reader has the impression that he is reading a transcription of notes in a lesson at the music conservatory. This changes as soon as the recipient imagines that the whole scene is sung and perceived acoustically. In recent decades, various ideas have been expressed about what the chorus of frogs stands for.[303] In particular, Armand D'Angour's argued that the frogs capitulate to the theatre god Dionysus at the level of the moving power of music and metre, and that this capitulation is particularly important for the development of the character of Dionysus in the play.[304] The musical exchange of melodies between Dionysus and the frogs is indeed a multimodal auditory metaphor for the literary contest that the second half of the *Frogs* has as its central theme and for which preparations are already being made here.

In a similar way, Aristophanes uses the musical and physical possibilities of the bird chorus in his *Birds*.[305] The chorus begins with the aria of the king of the birds, with which he calls the flock of birds together, accompanied by the playing of the flute and the song of the nightingale. In the piece, the king of the birds, the hoopoe Tereus, calls his wife, the nightingale, with his song from the bushes (Ar. *Av.* 209–222). No sooner has he fallen silent than the flute sounds behind the scene, imitating the nightingale's chirping. A figure on stage underlines the acoustic effect of the flute playing as the nightingale's song: "By Zeus, the voice of this bird! How it fills the whole of the bush with its honey!" (Ar. *Av.* 223–224). As the play progresses, the audience's imagination is also called upon to create the necessary auditory bridges, linking the frenzied running and screeching of the birds to contemporary events in Athenian political life: "For an old man has come, a wise head, with new ideas, inventor of new projects, so now all come for consultation, come, come, come!" (Ar. *Av.* 223–224). "Toro toro torotix! Kikkabau! Kikkabau! Toro toro torolililix!" (Ar. *Av.* 255–262). The birds' appearance corresponds to their nature: twittering and screeching, fluttering excitedly, they run wildly and without order through the orchestra (Ar. *Av* 305–307). In the case of the hoopoe mentioned earlier, the song only gradually changes from birdcalls to human language.

While the staging may be comic, it is important to note that the underlying narrative is one of horror. The hoopoe is a rapist and a potential wife murderer,

---

[303] E.g. Aristophanes' rivals, criminals of Hades, fake musicians, a parody of contemporary poetry are the main options. See Campbell 1984.
[304] D'Angour 2020.
[305] On the sounds on stage in Aristophanes' *Birds*, see Nooter 2019b, 200–203, and Nooter 2024. In the rich scenic potential of the bird as an image, see Weiss 2023, 104–121 with further bibliography.

while the nightingale is a woman who is responsible for the death of their own child Itys (cf. v. 212: τὸν ἐμὸν καὶ σὸν πολύδακρυν Ἴτυν "my and your much-bewailed Itys"). The audience perceives the sweet ἰὼ ἰὼ ἰτὼ ἰτὼ ἰτὼ ἰτώ (v. 228) and τιὸ τιὸ τιὸ τιὸ τιὸ τιὸ τιὸ τιό (v. 237) and the prior knowledge about the murdered Itys necessarily colours the acoustic beauty of the sounds.

The singing animal chorus of the Aristophanic comedy has also been handed down to us (rarely) via vase painting. For example, the so-called Naples birds krater (c. 425 BCE) contains an acoustic construct visually fixed on the vase (Fig. 8). This scene might be related to a comic performance. It shows an *aulos*-player with his face turned frontally, standing in the middle, flanked by two actors in comic rooster costumes.[306] The central placement of the *aulos*-player visually reflects his role in the plot and symbolises the sound itself. As a viewer of the chalice, one is directly opposite the face of the aulos player; it almost seems as if one is part of the theatre audience. As the cognitive studies have shown, we feel more connected to the persons portrayed when they are shown in eye contact and from a frontal point of view.[307] This is based on our bodily experiences and real-life situations in which we face the person we want to interact with and look at them or turn away when we do not want to interact. One should mention the fascinating audiovisual fusion present here. It appears that the vase may contain a representation of a sound construct, while the aulos player depicted may represent chirping birds. As Naomi Weiss describes this figure: "His fingers are spread across the two pipes of the aulos; his cheeks are bulging from the circular breathing required to play them".[308] The sound is thus embodied on the vase, while the scene is further enhanced by the bird costumes worn by the two actors, which contribute to the overall performative context.

Audiovisual fusions are dynamic forms of meaning making. They are affectively embedded and rooted in the sensory experience of physical action. Our experience of fusion in multimodal contexts arises in many sensory domains and is deeply felt. We do not simply interpret the visuality of sound but experience it with our bodies. Thus, words and music can offer different resources for structuring thought: Words capture objects, events and the relationships between them, while music represents dynamic processes, mimicking objects, events and relationships.[309]

---

[306] See Csapo 2014, 102–104, fig. 5,7, and Weiss 2023, 196–203, fig. 22. For few scenes in Athenian vase painting in which an *aulos*-player appears together with the comic chorus members indicate his importance in theatrical production, see Bundrick 2005, 175–178.
[307] Feng and O'Halloran 2013, 330; El Refaie 2017, 153.
[308] Weiss 2023, 198.
[309] Zbikowski 2009.

Fig. 8: Naples birds krater. © Museo Archeologico Nazionale di Napoli 205239, formerly Malibu 82.AE.83, courtesy of the Italian Ministry of Culture, photography by Giorgio Albano.

Multisensory studies in neuroscience seem to offer new insights into understanding Greek theatre. Greek drama, and perhaps tragedy in particular, attracted such approaches early on, and visual perception and audience behaviour became essential areas of analysis. By harnessing the cognitive mechanisms of seeing, invitations to see enriched the experience of Greek drama by engaging theatregoers more closely with the affective and thematic issues addressed in the productions.[310]

3.2 Cognitive vision in ancient sources

I have already mentioned in the introduction that what is now called cognitive approach to vision and imagination actually has roots in ancient Greek and Roman thought. The example of Fronto's treatment of images was used to support this suggestion.[311] Some considerations at the interface of linguistics, cognitive science and philosophy of mind are indeed close to contemporary neuroscientific findings. There have been several attempts in recent years to rethink ancient theories of perception, especially Aristotelian approaches.[312]

Ancient intellectuals were concerned with the processes of communication and the relationship between language and cognition, as evidenced by Greek and Latin theoretical texts on mental vision and conceptual thought. It is fair to mention the particularly rich collection of texts we find in Roman times, both in Greek and Latin. Unfortunately, there are not many examples of Greek texts surviving from the Hellenistic period. However, there are indications, such as Theophrastus' and Philodemus' fragments on metaphor, that there may have been lively debates in this area. It seems that Rome became a centre of such intellectual discussions, and we can gain insights on vision, imagination and perception from Late Republican and Imperial texts.

In order to understand and interpret the use and meaning of the concepts and ideas of Roman vision, 'Longinus' and Plutarch provide important background. They show that the interaction between speech and meaning, between language and knowledge, was of paramount importance in Roman thought, which was influenced by Stoic theories. Greek writers constituted a necessary part of the development and crystallisation of both Greek and Latin linguistic concepts, since they also lived in Rome and participated in Roman intellectual discourses.

---

[310] On the effect of joint attention and calls to 'see together', see Duncan 2023.
[311] See p. 3–4 above.
[312] On certain caveats in applying cognitive approaches to Aristotle's worldviews, see especially Silk 2003 and Wood 2017.

Theoretical views on cognition and vision in later Greek and Latin ancient sources have been re-examined in recent years.[313] The semantic and cognitive value of the *imaginatio* is central to their analysis. 'Longinus', Plutarch, Seneca and Fronto reflect contemporary debates about the relationship between objects and their names. These debates first emerged in early Greek philosophy of language and continued in Greek and Roman linguistic thought through Plato, Aristotle and the Stoics.

In Letter 9, Seneca quotes Epicurus and argues that what matters is not the exact words but their meanings: "Or if the following formulation seems better to you, for one should proceed in such a way that we use meanings and not words" (*id enim agendum est ut non verbis serviamus sed sensibus*, Sen. *epist*. 9, 20).[314] The Stoic opposition *non verbis sed sensibus* (σημαῖνον/word for *verbum* versus σημαινόμενον/λεκτόν/meaning for *sensus* in Stoic terminology) recalls the discussions among the Sophists at the time of the first linguistic exercises and experiments in the analysis of language. Socrates at the beginning of Plato's *Ion*, emphasizes the necessity to deal with Homer and to examine not only his words but also his thought and his meaning (τὴν τούτου διάνοιαν ἐκμανθάνειν, μὴ μόνον τὰ ἔπη, Plat. *Ion* 530b). The contrast καὶ τὴν διάνοιαν vs. τὰ ἔπη, which the rhapsode was to investigate in the Homeric text, corresponds to Seneca's *non verbis serviamus sed sensibus* and Quintilian's *non ad nomen sed ad vim significandi* (Quint. Inst. 8, 2, 6) and suggests the essential duality in language in general and in the theory of *imaginatio* in particular, that of content and expression.[315]

Seneca deals with metacognitive considerations elsewhere: "When the mind has become accustomed to despise the commonplace and to think the ordinary vulgar, it looks for the new in speech (*in oratione quod novum est quaerit*); at one time it conjures up and displays old and old-fashioned words, at another time it coins the †unknown and† defaces it, at another time – which has become common of late – a bold and frequently used metaphor (*audax translatio ac frequens*) is employed" (Sen. *Epist.* 114, 10). By contrasting the creation of a new meaning and the fiction (*fingit*) with the reuse of a familiar vocabulary (*antiqua verba atque exoleta revocat*), Seneca again reflects on the nature of meaning and image. The char-

---

313 The material used below on the treatment of *imagines* and *imaginatio* in Roman theory can be found in various publications of mine, such as Novokhatko 2016 (*Ad Herennium* and Cicero), Novokhatko 2017 (Quintilian), Novokhatko 2019 (Seneca and Quintilian), Novokhatko 2021b ('Longinus', Plutarch, Quintilian), Novokhatko 2024 (Fronto).
314 See the discussion in Novokhatko 2019, 389–396.
315 Cf. also Sen. *Epist.* 89, 17.

acterisation of metaphor as "bold and frequently used" underlines Seneca's acquaintance with the traditional theoretical discussions of imagery. According to Aristotle and Theophrastus, metaphor should not be "audacious" but "apologetic".[316]

Seneca's letters are a kind of theoretical background to this feature of the *imaginatio*, which is used several times in theoretical texts of the first century BCE.[317]

In what may be an indication of the importance of this topic for contemporary theorists, Seneca comes close to discussing the theory of language and thought on several occasions. In book 4, chapter 12 of his treatise *On benefits*, Seneca discusses the meaning of the term *beneficium:* "You say, he said, a favour is a loan that cannot be repaid, but a loan is not something that is desirable for its own sake. We use a mental image and metaphor when we say 'loan' (*imagine et translatione utimur*, Sen. *Benef.* 4, 12, 1). Here Seneca uses the concrete and structured vocabulary of finance ('source domain') while speaking about the abstract and unstructured topic of favour ('target domain'), returning to the metaphor he dealt with in the same work (*Benef.* 2, 18, 5).[318]

He sees favour as a loan. The parable compares favour to money.[319] Seneca's *beneficium creditum insolubile* is thus an example of what is now known as conceptual mapping in the sense of Lakoff and Johnson, where one concept is understood in terms of another concept. It is important to note, however, that in Sen. *Benef.* 4, 12, 1 Seneca marks and comments on this conceptual shift: "When we say *creditum* we use a mental image and a metaphor".

The term *imago*, a complex and somewhat ambiguous term that has already been mentioned in the introduction in relation to Fronto, is here understood to mean something like 'mental image'. Let us consider again how Fronto uses the term *imago* in his teaching, returning to our earlier discussion that we previously had. This may assist in grasping the term in the writings of other Roman theoreticians, and in discerning the Romans' perceptions of the concepts that are today actively employed in the interplay between cognitive theories and classical sources.

The *imago* is used in Fronto to embellish, discredit, compare, devalue, reinforce or transform a less credible thing into a credible thing (εἰκόνα *ei rei adsumi ut aut ornet quid aut deturpet aut aequiperet aut deminuat aut ampliet aut ex minus*

---

[316] Theophr. frs. 689 A–690 FHSG. Guidorizzi and Beta 2000, 70–73, 163–164, Novokhatko 2014, 416, Novokhatko 2019, 390–391.
[317] See Zanker 2016, 171. Cf. e.g. Philod. *Rh.* 1, 174; *Eloc.* 80; Ps.-Long. *Subl.* 32.
[318] For the concepts of 'source domain' and 'target domain' in conceptual metaphor theory, see above, p. 4f., 11.
[319] Novokhatko 2019.

credibili credibile efficiat, Front. *Ad Marc.* 3.8.2). These functions of the *imago* are in fact very similar to the functions of metaphor in the classical manuals. The author of the *Rhetorica ad Herennium* (first century BCE) famously highlights six functions of metaphor: that of vividness (*rei ante oculos ponendae causa*), brevity (*breuitatis causa*), avoidance of obscenity (*obscenitatis uitandae causa*), expansion (*augendi causa*), devaluation (*minuendi causa*) and embellishment (*ornandi causa*).[320]

In Fronto, the spatial dimension of the cognitive metaphor is used: If none of the enumerated things is needed, there is also no place for an image (*locus* εἰκόνος *non erit*). Now here the question arises: where will there be "no place for an image"? In the imagination of the participants? In their minds? In their communication? The physical experience of the participants, the situational, discursive and conceptual-cognitive context are all involved in the metaphorical process in which the images are created.[321]

When designing an image for a proposed subject (*ubi rei propositae imaginem scribes*), Fronto continues, one should also take into account the characteristics of the subject one is painting (*insignia animadverteres eius rei cuius imaginem pingeres*, Front. *Ad Marc.* 3.8.2), and likewise when writing, as one would do as a painter. The actual working method of how the metaphorical image is created is presented: Making image can be taken up from various points of view (*multis modis*), such as the resemblances of kind (τὰ ὁμογενῆ), the resemblances of form (τὰ ὁμοειδῆ), the whole (τὰ ὅλα), the parts (τὰ μέρη), the individual characteristics (τὰ ἴδια), the differences (τὰ διάφορα), the opposites (τὰ ἀντικείμενα), the consequences and the resultants (τὰ ἑπόμενα καὶ παρακολουθοῦντα), the names (τὰ ὀνόματα), the accidents (τὰ συμβεβηκότα), the elements (τὰ στοιχεῖα) and in general everything from which arguments are drawn (*fere omnia, ex quibus argumenta sumuntur*, Front. *Ad Marc.* 3.8.2).[322] Transference-imagery is constantly present, and the coexistence of two or more mental spaces is actually presupposed in all the features listed.

Fronto's discussion is in fact a precursor of contemporary theories of metaphor and mapping as a mental and imaginative force. In fact, conceptual transferring or mapping is a crucial part of the conceptual metaphor theory, where metaphor is conceived as a process and an act in which images are transported or 'mapped' from one domain to another.[323] This 'transportation', which is particular-

---

[320] *Rhet. Her.* 4.45, Cic. *De orat.* 3, 161. Cf. also Arist. *Rhet.* 3, 11, 1 1411b24–25. The connection of metaphor with mental imagery is first discussed by Aristotle in *Rhet.* 3, 2–11 1405b12–1411b25, later also in the scholia. See Novokhatko 2016, 398–399. Cf. also Schmitt 1934, 20–22.
[321] On the context that gives rise to metaphors, see Kövecses 2015.
[322] On the possible sources of Fronto, see Van den Hout 1999, 111. See also Schmitt 1934, 23–25.
[323] E.g. Fauconnier 1997.

ly important for Fronto, has become a technical term in psychological and communication studies over the last few decades, referring to the whole realm of 'imaginability' concepts such as 'immersion', 'engagement', 'make-belief', 'absorption', 'vividness', and 'presence'.[324]

In his treatment of the *imago*, Fronto displays a great deal of interest in what is today called experientiality and experience.[325] Fronto's aim is to come as close as possible to reality. As already mentioned, his method originally consisted of "capturing" (*conprehendundas*) ideas like the "island" from reality in order to "adapt" them into an imaginary world (*adcommodandasque*).[326] The image that the mind makes of an object must be transferred to other things, because the human mind needs this transfer in order to be able to represent them, to match two domains. Herein lies a profound principle of experientiality: the art of images can only attempt to make the world real, *imagines quasdam rerum*, he says. The image thus materialises and embodies that which is too fleeting and too difficult to analyse in the movements of the mind. Fronto illustrates this with the example from his own experience: because of a phrase at the beginning of his letter, he thought Marcus was seriously ill and was deeply touched by it; in reality, however, it was not his student Marcus but Marcus' daughter Faustina who was ill.[327] Therefore, Fronto is reassured that the child's illness is not serious and will soon pass. He is also relieved to learn that his student's health is not in danger.

Fronto's *imagines* are based on the substrate of common ground and are intended to facilitate the understanding of abstract phenomena and intellectual questions by training the imagination of his students. The *imagines* do not embellish the discourse but clarify the subject and give support to the narratee. The most original aspect of the Fronto's approach lies in the enactivist method of experientiality in the process of metaphorical action and image-making that creates a syn-

---

324 See in particular Bortolussi and Dixon 2015, but also van Laer, de Ruyter, Visconti and Wetzels 2014, and various contributions in Hakemulder, Kuijpers, Tan, Bálint and Doicaru 2017. Long before this, see Gerrig 1993, who conceived of 'transportation' as a complex of interacting processes and sensations, including mental imagery.
325 The term 'experientiality' was proposed by Monika Fludernik as a term for the "quasi-mimetic evocation of real experiences" through narratives and was subsequently much discussed. See in particular Fludernik 1996, 12 and Fludernik 2010. Marco Caracciolo built on this concept and developed it further for literary narration and the author's and reader's reaction to the narrated text. However, Fludernik's definition remains very illustrative for Fronto's exercises. See also below p. 106–110.
326 On the Stoic background of the cognitive process, which is only conceivable from a rigorously exact 'grasping' of reality, see Collin 2010, 223–227.
327 Novokhatko 2024, 572–575.

thesis between mind, body, and the surrounding world.³²⁸ Thus, these are not static mental images, but active agents. The participants experience all imaginary states "as if" they were there themselves, with the scenes from the participants' everyday life being acted out vividly and emotionally. It has already been noted that ancient (and even more so medieval!) thought, particularly in psychology, is far less Cartesian and separative of body and mind than modern European thought, and in this sense it has much in common with contemporary research into enactivism.³²⁹ Fronto's theory of images confirms this view.

The Greek term that Seneca or his Latin source are translating here is difficult to determine. Various terms such as εἴδωλον, εἰκών, φάντασμα, φαντασία could stand for 'mental image' in this context.³³⁰ The word *imago* is also attested by Quintilian when he discusses the variants of *enargeia*, but without the close connection with 'meaning' that we find in Seneca.

> Quint. *Inst.* 8, 3, 63–64:
> *There is a kind [of enargeia] in which the whole picture of things* (rerum imago) *is somehow painted in words [...] The most outstanding representative of this kind, as well as of the others, is Cicero: could anyone be so far from perceiving mental images of things that he does not appear to see the people, the place, and the clothes, and add something that was not said for himself?*³³¹

Imagination, image-making and mental image are juxtaposed here and discussed together. Interestingly enough, ancient discussions of visualisation (or mental imagery) outlined above have proved fertile material for debates among contemporary philosophers in recent years. The question of whether mental images really function like a kind of picture in the brain or more like a text is fiercely contested. Pictorialists advocate the idea that visualisation is about the formation of images in the mind against propositionalists and enactivists.³³² Propositionalists suggest that the visual work is not done by images but by propositions. In recent years,

---

328 On enactivism see above p. 6–10.
329 See especially Ostenfeld 2018. See also Gill 2019. On the 'concrete' character of earlier Greek perception and the shift from materialisation to abstraction in Archaic Greek, from 'symbolic' thinking to 'conceptual' thinking, see already Finley 1955, 3–22.
330 See below p. 93–96.
331 Novokhatko 2019, 392–393. On *enargeia* and the enactivist components of the concept, see Huitink 2019 and Huitink 2020. See also Steiner 2021, See also the discussion of *enargeia* in the interview with Douglas Cairns below p. 150–152.
332 See an overview in Thomas 2016. For a recent perspective from cognitive scientists, see Keogh, Pearson, and Zeman 2021. For the pictorialist view, see e.g. Kosslyn (1980), Kosslyn, Thompson and Ganis (2005), for the propositionalist view, see Pylyshyn (2003a), and Pylyshyn (2003b). For enactivist position see Thomas (1999), O' Regan and Noë (2001), Bartolomeo (2002).

the enactivist position, discussed above, has increased in popularity.³³³ According to enactivists, cognition is embodied and context-dependent, and they therefore assume that we do not create detailed internal representations but look for the concrete information we need when we need to make a behavioural decision. Luik Huitink, in particular, has argued for the enactivist position in a number of publications on classical texts. Huitink consciously counters the dominant pictorialist approach to vividness and imagery in narrative with an embodied perspective, drawing on the cognitive studies of the 'second generation'.³³⁴ He claims that *enargeia* provides a sensorial, emotional, and experiential sense of what is happening, rather than an intellectual understanding. For instance, 'Longinus', the anonymous author of the Greek treatise *On the Sublime*, suggests that listeners and readers may experience a certain "disturbance and co-movement (συγκίνησις) of the mind" (*Subl.* 20, 2). Huitink draws attention to a particular strength of the term συγκίνησις, which in fact echoes Cicero's aims of the orator (*docere, delectare, movere*): "In my view the term συγκίνησις is suggestive of how readers may imaginatively follow the virtual blows, encoded in the text, with their eyes in an effort to duck the blow; the addition 'of the mind' refers only to the fact that readers do not actually start turning left and right, but in all other respects what they feel is physical (reliant on sensorimotor resonances)".³³⁵

It is evident, then, that Roman intellectuals were aware that imagination and visualisation is a creative on-going process that concerns the relationship between form and meaning in language and their bodily perception.³³⁶ It is based on facts of experience and implies similarities whose perception depends on cultural codes. Seneca's *creditum insolubile* is culturally determined, the Roman reader sharing a cultural ground with Seneca's work perceives this "cognitive instrument" perfectly.³³⁷ Seneca's theoretical statement that when we use a metaphor we are "borrowing" a mental image and a metaphor is very close to Lakoff's "metaphorical language makes use of conceptual metaphors".³³⁸

'Longinus' shows that discourses on the interplay of language and imagination were common in first century CE Rome. 'Longinus' states that images are associated with both language and affect: They produce language and move the recipient

---

333 See above p. 6–10.
334 E.g. Huitink 2019, Huitink 2020. See also f. 345 below.
335 Huitink 2019, 181. On this passage, see also Halliwell 2022, 284.
336 On the 'iconic' character of metaphor based on Charles Sanders Peirce's semiotics, see Henle (1958: 177–181) and Gumpel (1984), Danesi (1995: 266). On the iconicity of metaphor see Nöth (1985); Nöth (1990: 131–133); Eco et al. (1994).
337 Nöth (1990: 133).
338 Lakoff (2008: 24).

to see these images mentally. The following passage is paradigmatic for discussing the concept of imagination in ancient thought.

> Long. *Subl.* 15, 1:
> *The images/visualisations* (αἱ φαντασίαι), *my friend, are very adept at offering weight, size and competition. This is what we call it, others call it the "production of images"* (εἰδωλοποιίας). *For generally speaking, image/visualisation is anything that in any way suggests a concept* (in the mind), *which gives birth to language* (καλεῖται μὲν γὰρ κοινῶς φαντασία πᾶν τὸ ὁπωσοῦν ἐννόημα γεννητικὸν λόγου παριστάμενον); *but at present this term is chiefly used when you think you see by inspiration and emotion* (ὑπ' ἐνθουσιασμοῦ καὶ πάθους), *what you describe and bring before your recipients* (ἃ λέγεις βλέπειν δοκῇς καὶ ὑπ' ὄψιν τιθῇς τοῖς ἀκούουσιν).

The term φαντασία is difficult to translate (e.g. "visualisation", "fantasy", "vision", "imagination").[339] It seems that for 'Longinus' it is an active creative and begetting (γεννητικὸν λόγου) mental power (ἐννόημα) that produces speech. Further, the author points out that φαντασία in speech requires emotion, stimulation, and sympathetic effect (τὸ συγκεκινημένον, *Subl.* 15, 2). The image is defined as a mental act, which means that the cognitive and emotional components of language are interactive and interrelated at the basic lexical level. To emphasise the cognitive background of the process, 'Longinus' has to refer to areas beyond rhetoric and use Platonic and Epicurean terms for the creation of mental images εἰδωλοποιία.[340] The visual image of the speaker is conveyed to the receiver through language, which creates a visual image in the mind of the recipient.

At the same time, Quintilian drew on contemporary discourses on images to reflect on the process by which language and image can interact in the minds of speakers and recipients and wrote his *Institutio* as a reference work for the everyday use of language and the creation and reception of living language.[341] Language evokes coherent visual images in the mind. In presenting his paradigmatic fourfold typology of metaphor (animate to animate, inanimate to inanimate, animate to inanimate, inanimate to animate), Quintilian recalls the Aristotelian ἐνέργεια by pointing out that in culmination a "marvellous sublime" (*mira sublimitas*) emerges from subjects exalted by a bold and dangerous metaphor (*audaci et proxime periculum tralatione*). This happens when we give the senseless objects a kind of action/actuality and feeling (*actum quendam et animos*, Quint. *Inst. or.* 8.6.11), in

---

339 See Halliwell 2022, 232–255, 284, with bibliography. See also Russell (1964: 120) and Novokhatko 2021b, 152–153. On curiosity about the notion of the mental image in early modern European thought, see also Cassin 2014: 245–249, esp. 248–249.
340 Pl. *Soph.* 235b8, 236c6, 239d3, 260d9, 264c4, 266a10, 266d4, 268d1; *Tim.* 46a3; *Crit.* 107b7; *Resp.* 605c2; Epic. fr. 253 Us. Cf. also Porter (2016: 454).
341 See the discussion in Novokhatko 2021b, 153–158.

other words, when we animate the inanimate. Again, *actum quendam* functions as a translation or paraphrase of the Greek ἐνέργεια. The metaphor provides movement, and actuality itself is movement. The creative and cognitive power of the imagination to create active mental images is crucial for Quintilian.

In order to successfully convey a message to the receiver, the speaker must force himself to experience the emotions (*adfectibus*) he wants to impose on the receiver (*qualem facere iudici uolet*), the receiver in Quintilian's case being a judge in court (Quint. *Inst. or.* 6, 2, 27). How can the speaker evoke the emotions? Quintilian's answer is that language has a property that engages the imagination of the recipient, and that this property is crucial to the production of emotion through the act of speaking.

> Quint. *Inst. or.* 6, 2, 27 and 32:
> What the Greeks call phantasiai *(we call them* visiones*), whereby the images of absent things are presented to our minds, so that we seem to see them with our eyes and they are present to us. The one who can use this technique well will reveal the greatest power in relation to the feelings ... What then follows is the enargeia, which Cicero calls* illustratio *and* evidentia, *which does not so much appear to us to narrate as to show the actual scene, while our emotions arise no less than if we were present at the event itself.*

Modern cognitive linguistics uses the term 'image schema' to describe a structure that motivates conceptual image associations.[342] Mark Johnson postulates: "An image schema is a recurring dynamic pattern of our perceptual interactions and motor programmes that gives coherence and structure to our experience. ... 'Experience' ... is to be understood in a very comprehensive, broad sense that includes basic perceptual, motor programme, emotional, historical, social, and linguistic dimensions."[343] The image schema is experiential and meaningful; it integrates information from different modalities; it is flexible and undergoes numerous transformations in different contexts of experience.[344]

As an example of ἐνάργεια, Quintilian describes such an image schema, a pattern that gives structure to the 'common' experience of a murder case in court.[345] Quintilian obviously does not elaborate on the relationship between mind and

---

[342] See below p. 97–99.
[343] Johnson (1987: xiv, xvi). See also p. 106.
[344] Hampe (2005: 1–2). Cf. also Lakoff (1987b: 459–461).
[345] On a thorough analysis of this passage and the term *enargeia* as "the ability to visualise a scene" (Webb 2009: 105), see Webb (2009: 88–105) in detail, and for further additions Huitink 2019 who treats *enargeia* not from a pictorialist but from an enactivist perspective, the events are thus not statically 'depicted' but dynamically 'enacted' in the mind.

brain, but he nevertheless presents a murder scene as a mental process with questions full of visual and auditory details, emphasising 'iconicity'.

> Quint. *Inst. or.* 6, 2, 31:
> *I mourn for a murdered man: shall I not have before my eyes all the circumstances that could plausibly have occurred in this case? Will not the assailant suddenly burst forth, will not the victim tremble when he sees himself surrounded, and cry out, or plead for mercy, or run away? Will I not see a man strike and the victim fall to the ground? Will not his blood, his pallor, his dying groan be etched in my mind?*

The scene described is part of the routine experience of court proceedings in a "very rich, broad sense that includes basic perceptions, motor programmes, emotional, historical, social and linguistic dimensions", as Johnson says. The ἐνάργεια/ *inlustratio/evidentia* ("vividness, clarity") appeals to the active imagination, and language is used as a means by which a mental image (*imagines rerum absentium*) is transmitted from speaker to receiver.

Quintilian's analysis of the term ἐνάργεια is crucial to the cognitive nature of imagination. To illustrate his argument, Quintilian draws examples from Cicero's *Verrines* (Cic. *Verr.* 5, 86).

> Quint. *Inst. or.* 8, 3, 64:
> *Is anyone so weak in imagining mental pictures* (concipiendis imaginibus) *that he does not think he sees not only the persons and the place and the clothes, but adds other details which are not mentioned to himself, when he reads the text against Verres, which reads, "There stood the praetor of the Roman people in his sandals, with a purple cloak and a long tunic, leaning on one of his wives on the beach"?*

Quintilian uses *concipiendis imaginibus* for "thinking/conceiving/forming images in the mind", a term that occurs several times in his work and always refers to mental images: φαντασία *in concipiendis uisionibus* 8, 3, 88; *Quare capiendae sunt illae de quibus dixi rerum imagines, quas uocari* φαντασίας *indicauimus* 10, 7, 15; *concipiendis uisionibus quas* φαντασίας *uocant* 12, 10, 6.[346] How can a speaker achieve this goal of forming images in the mind of the receiver? Quintilian gives an answer to this question that is of crucial importance for today's modern psycholinguistic theory.

> Quint. *Inst. or.* 8, 3, 71
> *The way to this great virtue is, in my opinion, very simple: we should observe nature and follow it* (naturam intueamur, hanc sequamur). *All eloquence is about the activities of life* (circa

---

[346] Watson (1994: 4774–4775).

opera uitae est), *everyone applies what he hears to his own experience, and the mind accepts in the simplest way what it recognises* (et id facillime accipiunt animi quod agnoscunt).

As has been repeatedly noted in recent decades, effective communication depends on "common ground management". According to the much-cited definition of psycholinguistic common ground theory, the "common ground between two people is the sum of their mutual or shared knowledge, beliefs, and assumptions".[347] Quintilian's *id facillime accipiunt animi quod agnoscunt* presupposes a "common ground" based on cultural and communal experiences.[348] The speaker and the receiver should share certain attitudes to life and activities (*circa opera uitae*), the speaker should refer to the receiver's knowledge because the receiver can then apply it to his own horizon (*ad se refert quisque quae audit*). This notion of horizon may refer to cultural rather than political or personal experience. The speaker for example at a Roman court does not necessarily share personal experience with every member of his audience. But they do share cultural commonalities, attitudes, and role models, and it is these role models to which, according to Quintilian, the orator should appeal. Quintilian's psycholinguistic reference is noteworthy because it underlines his awareness of the cognitive power of the imagination.

The passages discussed above from different periods and cultures show the active metacognitive engagement of ancient authors with the question of how mental and imaginative power relates to perception. The cognitive faculty of metacognition monitors and selects what to attend to and learn, and is essential in the selection, transmission, use and expansion of knowledge and in the stabilisation of practices that together constitute a culture.[349]

Furthermore, the examples of Quintilian's training of an orator or Fronto's method reveal that ancient considerations of language and cognition are by no means cut off from contemporary thought. On the contrary, it can be productive to consider ancient theories of thought, mind and imagination in the context of cognitive studies, not only because the now intensively developed approaches open up new perspectives for interpreting the known ancient material, but – no less valuable – because they give a sense of the many ways in which distributed cognition left its mark on the culture and thought of the classics. Ancient theories serve larger epistemological purposes about human thought in general, and provide us with further models and methods by which ancient sources can be challenged, examined and explained.

---

347 Clark (1996: 92). See also p. 35–36 above.
348 Colston 2008.
349 Proust and Fortier 2018, 2.

Instead of making images of what we see or imagine, we experience the world by interacting with it. Vision and imagination are closely related, both in the processes our brains go through when we respond to an imaginary world, and in the language we use to describe such an experience. And again, the ancient discussions show that they were actually quite interested in this, and *mutatis mutandis*, the ancient analysis of imagination and vision is still very relevant to contemporary experiments.

3.3 Conceptual theory of metaphor and ancient texts

One of the most important mechanisms for abstracting from perception to imagination is metaphor. By extrapolating cognitive skeletons – image schemata – that record repetitive aspects and properties of bodily experience onto the understanding of concepts that are not immediately anchored in one's sensory-motor account of the world, metaphor establishes a transfer from a more concrete realm of experience (such as space) to a more abstract realm (such as time).

The main trends in linguistic cognitive research have grown up around the idea of 'schema' as a consequence of cogitative abstraction from actual experience.

Almost the entire range of terminology in cognitive linguistics is based on the notion of 'schema', from the early 'experiential gestalt' to 'idealised cognitive models' and 'pictorial schemata' – i.e. 'dynamic patterns that function in some way like the abstract structure of a picture, linking a wide range of different experiences that share the same recurrent structure', or 'cognitive archetypes', which can refer to any complex holistic schema that forms the basis of a particular construction.[350] Many conceptual archetypes are relevant to sentence structure, some integrated as constituents of others. A group of related archetypes includes the idea of a material object holding a place in space, and the idea of an object traversing space, e.g. moving through time.[351]

Metaphor has been a central theme of cognitive linguistics and philosophy since its inception. Viewing metaphor no longer as a stylistic trope but as a crucial mechanism of language and thought brought a revolutionary turn to phenomenology and cognitive studies.[352] Metaphors are essential to the formation of abstract concepts as they shape and inform the way we perceive the world. In fact, embodi-

---

[350] See Lakoff and Johnson 1980, Lakoff 1987a, Johnson 1987: 2, Langacker 1991.
[351] Langacker 1993: 485.
[352] For a very good overview of metaphor theories in philosophical rather than rhetorical frameworks in recent decades, see Theodorou 2013. On the "cognitive reality" of conceptual metaphors, see Grady 2007. Cf. also Gibbs and Stehen 1999.

ment is a limitation of (or even corresponds to) the directionality of metaphorical mappings. As Lakoff and Johnson pointed out, we assume first that metaphor has directionality, that is, that we understand one concept from another concept.[353] Typically, we have a tendency to organise less concrete and inherently ambiguous concepts (such as the concepts of emotions) into more concrete concepts that have clearer boundaries in our experience.[354] Cognitive metaphor and embodiment were indeed inextricably linked.[355]

It is now *communis opinio* that far more than a rhetorical device, metaphor is a vital aspect of human thought, cognition, and language. The term 'cognitive metaphor' (or 'conceptual metaphor') has been coined for cases in which not only individual conceptual items are transferred from different conceptual domains, but entire conceptual domains are related to each other by metaphorical transfer. [356]

Metaphor studies applied to ancient texts are an important part of cognitive narratology, poetics, and linguistics.[357] Always closely linked to cognitive approaches, they have helped to blur the traditional disciplinary boundaries between literary criticism and linguistics.[358]

The cognitive theory of metaphor has been applied to classical texts for some time, and it is impossible to list all the relevant publications here. Douglas Cairns, Andreas Zanker and Fabian Horn have explored cognitive metaphor for ancient Greek literature, while William Short and Chiara Fedriani have done so for Latin literature, but this list is far from exhaustive.[359] A variety of metaphors

---

[353] See above p. 4 f. 11.
[354] Lakoff and Johnson 1980: 132. On the current state of research in the field of the theory of cognitive metaphor and its application to the analysis of texts, as well as on a fruitful and mutually enriching communication between linguistic cognitive metaphor theory and literary analysis, see a detailed introduction by Monika Fludernik in Fludernik 2011.
[355] Rohrer 2007: 32.
[356] The bibliography is extensive. Among the seminal studies are Lakoff and Johnson 1980, Gibbs 1994, especially 120–264, and Gibbs 1996. According to cognitive-linguistic metaphor theory, individual linguistic metaphors that occur in concrete texts are usually (but not always) instantiations of underlying ideas called "conceptual metaphors" (Lakoff and Turner 1989, Lakoff 1993, 202–251, and the summaries in Evans 2007, esp. 33–35, and Kövecses 2010, 3–14). For a recent review of the theory, see Steen 2011 and Dancygier and Sweetser 2014.
[357] For one of the pioneering monographs on the theory of metaphor applied to Ancient Greek texts, see Stanford 1936. For a review see Novokhatko 2021a (the text in this section is a repetition of some parts of that review).
[358] See the discussion in Allan 2020. Specifically on metaphor, see, among others, Cairns 2003 and Cairns 2014, and Horn 2016a and Horn 2016b, Cairns 2019, 23–24, Short 2019a, Short 2019b, Devereaux 2019 and Horn 2025 (forthcoming).
[359] Cairns 2003, Cairns 2014, Cairns 2016a, Cairns 2016b, Cairns 2016c, Cairns 2017a, Cairns 2017b, Cairns 2018, Zanker 2016, Zanker 2018, Zanker 2019, Zanker 2020, Horn 2015a, Horn 2015b, Horn

from more concrete and experientially accessible domains shaped and structured abstract concepts in Greek and Roman life and thought. Describing the source-destination projections of cognitive metaphor theory as static, Cánovas argues for a more dynamic and flexible model in which humanity's early mastery of spatial primitives leads to image schemata into which these primitives are integrated and which form the first conceptual structures.[360] Image schemata of this kind were available to create new conceptual blends from different aspects. In his studies of emotional metaphor, Cánovas applies blending theory to ancient Greek poetry.[361]

Another publication on the subject makes it strikingly clear that the use of metaphor is an intentional act that reveals the poet's ability to make connections between disparate concepts.[362] Andreas T. Zanker explores the ways in which epic diction is generally structured on a conceptual rather than stylistic level by underlying folk models and assumptions. Metaphor is usually seen as an intervention between the perceiver and reality in modern philosophical and critical thought.[363] However, as Zanker argues, the idea that much of language and thought is metaphorical does not undermine the possibility of mutual understanding; on the contrary, metaphor serves communication and is unavoidable given the mismatch between the vast diversity of the world and our extremely limited vocabulary to describe it.

Zanker discusses Homeric metaphor in the light of Lakoff and Johnson's work on conceptual metaphor, and considers concepts of time, language and mind in Homeric poetry.[364] He argues that the potential for abstraction is present in the Homeric grammar itself. Homeric descriptions of time reflect a number of metaphorical inferences, such as time as a vessel with boundaries, time as a substance, and

---

2016a, Horn 2016b, Horn 2018, Horn 2020, Horn 2021, Horn 2025, Horn and Breytenbach 2016, Short 2008, Short 2009, Short 2012, Short 2013a, Short 2013b, Short 2014, Short 2016, Short and Duffy 2016, Short 2017, Short 2018a, Short 2018b, Fedriani 2020, Fedriani e.a. 2021. See also recently for Aeschylus, Carroll 2023.
360 Cánovas 2016.
361 Cf. Cánovas 2014. On blending theory, see Fauconnier and Turner 2002; on its application and its interaction between linguistics and literary criticism, see especially Fludernik 2011. On emotions see chapter 5 below.
362 Zanker 2019. In the following, I will use the analysis that I published in Novokhatko 2021a.
363 See Jakobson 1956, 243–244 and Derrida 1974. See a stimulating discussion of attitudes to poetic translation in Matzner 2016, 182–191.
364 On Lakoff and Johnson's theory see above p. 4. Harald Weinrich, whose theoretical approach has many similarities with the theory of metaphor of Lakoff and Johnson, used the terms, *Bildspenderbereich* "image donor domain" and *Bildempfängerbereich* "image receiver domain", cf. Weinrich 1976, 295–316.

time as a self-contained, ontologically independent entity. The conceptual metaphor 'time is a person moving along a path' is also present. However, this is so conventional that the Homeric storyteller may not even be aware of the connection between the domains.

The perception of day and night as controlled by beings who can come and go, be near and far, may have led to a conception of time as one in which the observer is a static being in the midst of a whirlpool of movement. The observer is a static being in the midst of a whirlpool of movement, and around them things move in the change of time, such as the passing of age, divine intervention, time as vertical progression, completion as fullness, death as departure into the underworld, time sometimes as a living being, as money or an infinite resource, as a moving object, as spinning or weaving, human life as a growing plant.

In his analysis of Homeric metaphors to describe language, Zanker invokes Reddy's much-cited *conduit metaphor*[365] both to the systematic character of conceptual metaphor in everyday language, as well as its role in our descriptions of language itself. The Homeric and Hesiodic epics mark the beginning of an unbroken Western tradition of engagement with language. Homeric formulae and epithets, as vernacular models of communication, contain 'fossilised' metaphors that give us clues as to how language was implicitly conceptualised in the past.

The Homeric version of the 'conduit metaphor' structures communication as a quick and uncomplicated process in which speech acts can either be immediately implemented by the receiver or safely stored in the mind. A speech is made up of elements that the listener must collect in order to put the whole together. It is particularly important that the process of comprehension should not be seen as passive but as active: When the words arrive in the listener's mind, they must be incorporated into a meaningful pattern.

To describe the abstract phenomena of language and communication, the singer resorted to terms for very physical and concrete objects. The metaphor of the container, for example, which conceives of the mind as a closed space, implies that thoughts are private and that one cannot know what is in another's mind until they reveal it: As we have seen, the mind itself can 'hide' things, or people can hide one thing and say another. Similarly, in the cultural context in which the Homeric epics were written, the natural elements would have been an important area of knowledge that the singer could use to describe the workings of the mind. Thought is often characterised as a movement in a particular direction, or as a physical process in the chest area involving the movement of air into the lungs. Viewed through the lens of conceptual metaphor theory, these expressions

---

[365] Reddy 1979.

are reminiscent of the way in which abstract entities such as mind and thought are structured in terms of realms accessible through experience.

Even certain persistent puzzles in the text, such as the concepts of mind and self, prove less problematic when viewed in the light of metaphorical concepts. Overall, Zanker's book shows that there are many conceptual metaphors that are common to different languages and cultures. Zanker also argues that if the peculiarities of Homeric language are difficult to explain, this is because cultural changes also bring about changes in the underlying concepts of metaphor, as was the case with certain formulations of the mind and human nature. Zanker successfully demonstrates that the theory of conceptual metaphor can help us to interpret seemingly alien elements in Homeric style, and that Homer's texts support some of the principles of the theory of conceptual metaphor, particularly its reliance on embodied experience to bring abstract concepts to mind. Homeric diction is therefore not as alien to modern thought as it might have been thought.

This analysis allows us to attain a more accurate picture of the cognitive processes behind language processing, i.e. the role that connections at the level of thought play in determining Homeric diction. One of the great advantages of studying the systematic nature of conceptual metaphor in the Homeric style is that it goes beyond the question of whether formulae and epithets have semantic weight in their respective contexts or whether they are used out of metrical necessity. By focusing on the metaphors themselves and treating them holistically, we can build a model of communication within the epics that goes back to the terminology itself.

Zanker concludes by discussing how metonymy is used in the conceptual study of metaphor.[366] Metonymy could serve as a way to select appropriate words: For example, the functional synonymy between the organs of the so-called 'mind group' (θυμός ("spirit"), κραδίη ("heart"), κῆρ ("heart"), ἦτορ ("heart"), φρένες ("mind"), πραπίδες ("abdominal cavity, diaphragm"); all body parts named as the seat of emotional movements) suggests that these terms could serve as equivalents for each other, depending on metrical necessity.[367]

A growing interest in the possible functions of metaphor in ancient Greek and Latin texts is also evident in Fabian Horn and Cilliers Breytenbach's 2016 collected

---

[366] Cf. Allan 2008 on the cognitive mechanisms and cultural factors that enable metaphorical and metonymic mappings. On the close relationship between metonymy and metaphor, and on 'metonymic associations' in conceptual metaphor clusters, see Nagy 2015 and Matzner 2016.
[367] For a thorough analysis of the synaesthetic functions of the organs in Homer and Pindar, see Pelliccia 1995. For his critical evaluation of the conceptual metaphor, however, see Pelliccia 1995, 27–37.

volume.³⁶⁸ The editors emphasise that the linguistic view of cognitive metaphor is rejected by many philologists. Unconscious metaphors and the concepts associated with them can illuminate the cognitive structures that enable a coherent and meaningful reading of experience and the construction of abstract concepts in language.

Using a theory of semantics that is not based on a specific text or corpus of texts, Wolfgang Raible argues that our ability to interpret the world is largely based on metaphor and metonymy. Metaphor and metonymy allow us to identify relationships between different concepts through similarity and contiguity.³⁶⁹ Raible uses examples from the interpretation of the Bible to science and technology to show how widespread these models of thought are. In an overview of ideas on metaphor since Greek antiquity, Raible focuses on the interaction between metaphor and metonymy. He notes that both had already been understood as concepts and not just words by the French phonetician Léonce Roudet (1861–1935). Raible explains the function of metaphors as models of thought using a doctrine of natural science developed by the atomist Leucippus of Abdera and his successor Democritus in the fifth century BCE, based on the concept of alphabetic writing (AN vs. NA etc., Arist. *Met.* A4 985b4).

The atomists were thus the forerunners of a number of scientific disciplines that still use this model today. One of these is molecular biology. Raible mentions that, since 1953, nucleotides, abbreviated as A, T, G and C, have been regarded as the letters of the genetic alphabet. But molecular biologists are generally unaware of the metaphor at the heart of their work.³⁷⁰ Our thinking is therefore essentially either metaphorical or metonymic: while the vocabulary of historical languages is always limited, the number of states or objects to be described is unlimited. The natural consequence of this is polysemy, since words have different meanings depending on how they are used. Léonce Roudet also points to this kind of change in meaning: a term applied to a different cognitive space generates either a contiguity/metonymy or a similarity/metaphor.

This principle can be found in the oldest written sources. Wisdom texts are a popular genre in ancient Egyptian literature, offering advice on how to behave. Camilla Di Biase-Dyson's compelling study examines spatial metaphors (especially path metaphors) and their pedagogical and evocative functions in Egyptian wisdom texts of the New Kingdom and the Third Intermediate Period (1550–712

---

368 Horn and Breytenbach 2016. See Novokhatko 2021a where both Zanker 2019 and Horn and Breytenbach 2016 are discussed.
369 Raible 2016.
370 Raible 2016, 27–29.

BCE).³⁷¹ She focuses on the development of metaphor within and between texts to demonstrate the role of metaphor in shaping the wisdom genre.

Di Beers-Dyson argues that spatial metaphors, especially those involving movement along a path, are a fundamental element of this pedagogical genre. This is because the path metaphor refers to life choices (LIFE AS A JOURNEY), especially actions and behaviour. These metaphors appear both explicitly when we talk about a 'journey' and implicitly when we talk about movement in space. The hypothesis to be tested is that the explicitness of spatial metaphors (and here road-related metaphors) increases with the argumentativeness of the text. In other words, as the prescriptive (but more neutral) genre of wisdom texts becomes increasingly influenced by the more straightforward reminders of written school texts. This approach is applied to a number of genres in the ancient Egyptian text corpus, leading to a qualitative and quantitative analysis of metaphors for ancient Egyptian.³⁷²

Fabian Horn deals with conceptual orientation metaphors in ancient Greek.³⁷³ He advocates the conceptual orientation metaphor 'ACTIVE IS UP' (with a corresponding opposite conceptualisation 'PASSIVE/DESTROYED/DEAD IS DOWN'). There are many single-language instances of this concept, most of them in the form of prepositions or prefixes (ἀνά/ἀνα-, ἐπί/ἐπι-; κατά/κατα-), but also in words conveying the direction up or down such as αἴρω. Horn continues to propose the conceptualisation active is up for metaphor in Lycophron. The cognitive-linguistic formulation of the metaphor of conceptual orientation would therefore be 'ACTIVE IS UP'. It must be admitted that this metaphor of orientation is rather vague, but this is due to the status of the metaphor as a primary metaphor based on physical human experience.³⁷⁴ As people get up and stand to move and become active, the bodily experiential basis of this concept is obvious. Tools and instruments need to be learned before they can be used effectively, so there is a cultural basis as well.

---

371 Di Biase-Dyson 2016.
372 A multi-level analysis incorporating two approaches from contemporary metaphor research is applied to the explicitly 'conscious' metaphors. The first is a word-based study (Steen 2007, also Pragglejaz Group 2007) based on the *Metaphor Identification Procedure* VU University Amsterdam (MIPVU) method by Gerard Steen and colleagues. To provide an empirical basis for identifying metaphors, the 'basic sense' and 'contextual sense' of a metaphorical lexical unit are determined. On the other hand, a text-based analysis developed by Elena Semino will be used to identify specific patterns of metaphorical language in a cross-textual perspective (Semino 2008).
373 Horn 2016a, Horn 2016b.
374 Dancygier and Sweetser 2014, 25–30.

Following the methodology and terminology elaborated in cognitive linguistic theory of metaphor, Horn posits that the use of αἴρω can be explained and traced back to a metaphor of conceptual orientation 'ACTIVE IS UP' (with a corresponding counterpart 'PASSIVE IS DOWN'). The concept is both ubiquitous and highly productive, the metaphorical use of αἴρω being widespread and common in Ancient Greek. It is clear that none of the examples can be taken literally, although none of them is specifically marked as figurative. But the context of αἴρω in these passages is clearly understandable from the root meaning, and the metaphorical use goes back to the same general concept of direction and space described as 'ACTIVE IS UP'.

Ancient writers placed their readers in imaginary scenes so that they became actors, rather than simply describing spaces. Because the experience of the spatial dimension is deeply rooted in the human body, authors allow their audience to play a role in metaphorical spaces, even if they only imagine them. By developing a sense of these environments, they can engage with them. For the effects of this technique to be felt, it is important that the audience becomes an active participant and not just a distant observer.

Recent cognitive science claims that engagement with metaphorical scenarios triggers embodied simulation because the interpreter of metaphors recreates the bodily experience of the imaginary space.[375] When people interpret embodied metaphors, they imagine what it means to carry out the physical actions that are described by the verbal metaphors. The key mechanism in this imaginative process is simulation, the mental realisation of the action referred to in the metaphor. We do not have access to the cognitive response of ancient readers to the spaces in the text, but it may be suggested that readers were stimulated to immerse themselves in these spaces and to imagine themselves to be in action within them. Processing metaphor contributed to the task.

Visualisation and cognition in ancient sources is a growing and promising field in which there are still more questions than answers, and this chapter is only a brief and modest overview of what has been researched and analysed in this area in recent years. I have outlined three directions in which studies are most prominent. Theatre, a genre in itself in which seeing, looking, feeling and knowing collide and produce new meanings, is a particularly productive field. A number of innovative results have also emerged from studies of cognitive metaphor in rela-

---

375 Metaphorical language induces a partial simulation of perceptual experiences associated with the output domain of the metaphor. For this hypothesis, based on the embodied cognition model, see Gibbs 2006 and Ritchie 2008, who argue for the simulation of the listener's imagination of the performance of bodily actions expressed through language. See also Barsalou 2008, esp. 623 and 628–629.

tion to ancient material on mental imagery and mental vision. In between, I have tried to sketch out what some important ancient texts say about seeing and imagination, and how cognitive approaches shed light on these considerations.

Chapter 4
Experience and the senses

Experience is one of the central concepts in cognitive studies, and it is no coincidence that it has played a prominent role in the analysis of classical sources in recent years.[376] I deliberately use the term 'sources' again here because we are not only talking about literary texts, but also archaeological finds, sites, and the whole range of sources with which people have interacted. This chapter discusses the state of research in the classics in relation to two types of 'experientiality': narrative experientiality as the ability of a narrative to evoke experiential states and responses in the recipient, and ritual experientiality, which refers to human experience in religious, sympotic, theatrical and other activities.

4.1 Experientiality and evidentiality in language

The concept of experience in literary textual analysis is concerned with categories of time and consciousness, and is linked to interpretation as our fundamental mode of bringing our minds into contact with the natural, cultural and social world.[377] In classical studies, Jonas Grethlein is probably the scholar who has most applied this concept to the narratological discussions of ancient texts.[378] In his latest book on new approaches to ancient narratives, he underlines his own understanding of experience: "experience grasps not only the interior lives of characters, as the notion of mind, but also the sequential aspect of plot. It conveys the temporal dynamics that the notion of mind does not necessarily embrace".[379]

Let us consider what has happened in recent years in terms of the analysis of experience and experientiality in the classics, and then come back to this statement.

Firstly, some important studies have been done in the field of cognitive linguistics. By describing their sensory experiences, narrators reproduce their lived reality for their listeners. To make this possible, they use linguistically evidential markers. In narratology, this inclusion of the author's perception is called 'experientiality'.[380]

---

[376] See above p. 28–29.
[377] Leidhold 2022.
[378] Grethlein 2013, Grethlein 2015, Grethlein 2017, Grethlein 2018, Grethlein, Huitink, and Tagliabue 2019, Grethlein 2023a, Grethlein 2023b, 111–114.
[379] Grethlein 2023b, 112.
[380] See Fludernik 1996, 12. See also p. 28–29 and 90–91.

The emphasis on perception can serve a dual narrative and evidentiary purpose: it can be used as a means of narrative persuasion by vividly highlighting the narrator's experience. At the same time, it can serve to strengthen the credibility of the story by emphasising the narrator's position as a witness.

Topics include the use of evidentiality markers, expressions that refer specifically to the sensory experiences of their authors, semantic embodiment, deictics, and spatial metaphors.

Evidentiality, as a close linguistic counterpart of experientiality, is not directly related to the speaker's responsibility, awareness, or position towards the utterance. Evidentiality is not a subcategory of tense or modality. Non-evidential categories can develop meanings related to the source of information, such as the perfect, past tense, conditional and other modalities, and complements. A paradigmatic example of evidentiality comes from Turkish, where it is emphasised in morphological form (*-di* or *-mis*): "the girl danced" can be expressed with one morpheme when "I myself saw the girl dancing" and with "other people say the girl danced". The experiments on the use of these morphemes and the characteristic mistakes children make when using them are fascinating.[381] Unfortunately, none of these experiments on evidentiality can be done for ancient languages.

The main significance of evidentiality lies in the source of information – whether the speaker saw the event or only heard it, whether he drew his conclusion on the basis of visual evidence or common knowledge, or whether he was informed about it.[382] Languages may vary depending on whether the information is first-hand or has a specific marker of reported evidence. In larger evidentiality systems, a distinction may be made between visual and non-visual evidence, inferred, suspected, and reported evidence.[383]

In contrast, 'experientiality' refers to the way in which the narrative exploits the reader's familiarity with the experience by activating several 'natural' cognitive parameters, such as embedding cognitive skills, understanding intentional acts, awareness of temporality, and affective evaluation and appraisal of the experience.[384] Underlying Fludernik's definition of narrative is this cognitive relationship between human experience and representations of that experience: a text that brings the above parameters to the fore is considered narrative; a text that ignores these parameters has weak narrative or no narrative at all, because it removes the experiential drive.[385]

---

381 Ünal and Papafragou 2018 with further bibliography.
382 Aikhenvald 2004, 1–19.
383 Aikhenvald 2004, 23–66.
384 Fludernik 1996, 12. See also Fludernik 2003 and Fludernik 2010.
385 Fludernik 1996, 28.

For Fludernik, then, 'experience' and 'narrativity' are quasi-interchangeable terms. Marco Caracciolo argued decidedly against some points of this definition, stressing that in Fludernik's presentation it remains unclear whether experience is meant as an inherent and identifiable feature of narrative or as a psychic operation induced in the interaction between text and reader.[386] This vagueness of definition is also the reason why the concept of experientiality has had so many different uses in post-Fludernik narratological discussion.

A trend towards applying experientiality and evidentiality to Greek and Latin texts has emerged in recent years. Raf Van Rooy draws attention to the importance of evidentiality for ancient Greek through a series of case studies from Plato's *Apology* and *Kriton*.[387] From a formal point of view, he gives an overview of possible linguistic devices for marking evidentiality in Ancient Greek, and from a semantic point of view, he examines the ways in which evidentiality values are conveyed. Specific Attic particles, functional oppositions in complementation patterns and 'defective' verbal forms are highlighted as evidentiality markers or 'strategies'. These are capable of expressing different types of evidentiality (namely inferential, presumptive, reportative, quotative, visual or participatory). Van Rooy emphasises evidentiality as a unifying framework for the descriptive analysis of certain Greek phenomena.

In general, as far as the theory of language is concerned, studies are perhaps moving in the opposite direction to the theorisation of language. In the case of ancient languages, given the lack of extensive data on colloquial language, scholars are more interested in borrowing concepts from cognitive linguistics and applying them to enliven their reading of literary texts, where actual language is used for a specific purpose. I mentioned above some projects on papyri that focus precisely on this aspect when scholars want to see what is going on beyond literary language.[388] These studies are indeed very important. However, it is clear that more recently developments in psychology, sociology and discourse analysis, philosophy of language and critical theory have been incorporated into stylistic interpretations based primarily on linguistic movements.[389]

From a narratological perspective, Suzanne Adema operates with the notion of experientiality in relation to Latin texts by discussing passages from Virgil's *Aeneid* to illustrate the types of background that recipients possess. Adema discusses how texts can use this kind of background knowledge.[390] When understanding narra-

---

386 Caracciolo 2012, Caracciolo 2014.
387 Van Rooy 2016.
388 See p. 15 above.
389 Stockwell 2002, 59–60.
390 Adema 2017, Adema 2019, Adema 2022.

tives, readers relate new information to what they already know.[391] The mechanism is a reader's retrieval and use of relevant background knowledge supported by features in the text.[392]

Similarly, Jonas Grethlein looks at experience in the hermeneutic tradition and in the views of the Constance School.[393] Not only the narrating characters, but also the readers have experiences. The experience of reading is shaped by the reader's relationship to the experience of the characters in the story. The reader's experience may overlap or diverge from that of the characters as the story is transformed into a plot. Homeric epics use tragic irony to place their audience above the characters, while novels of consciousness allow the reader to experience the world of the story through the prism of the characters.

Experience thus opens up phenomenological perspectives and is closely related to the current boom in cognitive science, because, among other things, an important aspect of experientiality is embodiment. Marco Caracciolo, for example, has turned to current theories of embodiment to discuss the experientiality of narratives when he emphasises the relevance of the experiential background of the reader involved in the process of reading.[394] They include physical, bodily experiences. They also include perceptions, emotions, and social and cultural conventions. These distinctions promote a fuller understanding of the dynamics of reading by drawing our attention to the importance of the recipient's expectations and emphasising the many levels of the reader's response. In Caracciolo's treatment, however, the concept of experience itself remains ambiguous.[395] Without a specific meaning of its own, experience seems to have become a rather generic term for the reader's reaction in general.

In a stimulating contribution to the dynamisation of the embodied reader model, Karin Kukkonen argues that our bodily engagement with the environment involves anticipatory assumptions about the future that are continually re-evaluated in the light of new evidence, and that the process of reading is no different.[396] The reader's focus is not only on the embodied experience of the story's charac-

---

391 Cf. Sanford and Emmot 2012, Caracciolo 2014, Comer and Taggart 2021.
392 On the structures of epic poetry, see now in detail Reitz and Finkmann 2020.
393 See p. 28–29.
394 Caracciolo 2014.
395 On the vagueness of the term 'experience', see especially Caracciolo and Kukkonen 2021: visual and embodied experience p. 41–43, private experience p. 63–64, proprioceptive experience p. 68, conscious experience p. 70, imaginative and literary experience p. 71, perceptual experience p. 74, affective experience p. 90, spatial p. 97, sensory and somatic experience p. 110, subjective p. 126.
396 Kukkonen 2014 and Grethlein 2023b, 113.

ters, but also on the reader's inferences about the development of the story's plot. More than other models of the embodied reader, Kukkonen is concerned with the temporal dimension of the reading process, while Grethlein argues that the experience of reading is not automatically transferred to the experience of the characters, but rather is predicated on "the sequential form of the narrative".[397]

The same chain of statements and assertions that characterises everyday experience is formed in the reader's consciousness within the plot. In reading, consciousness is subject to the same dynamics of time as our everyday lives, which frames it 'as-if'. The concept of experience is not only about the dynamics of time in the plot and the representation of the mind, but also, with limitations, about the narrative world and its reception by the reader. The legacy of the Constance School as a reader-oriented criticism is thus evident in the cognitive approaches to literary work.

4.2 Experience and 'sensory turn' in the Classics

Another area of cognitive science that is central to ancient studies is concerned with the senses and also cognitive perception in general. The so-called 'sensory turn' that has inspired the humanities in the last decade has enabled scholars to explore a wide range of practices from Greek and Roman antiquity and to investigate the many ways in which smell and taste, sight and sound, individually and together, play a role.[398] For there, music, incense, images and colours, contrasts of light and dark played an important role in creating experiences of all kinds.

While perception refers to the way we receive information from our environment, cognition describes processes such as remembering, learning, problem solving and orientation.[399] It is fascinating to discuss how the senses and sensory perception in the ancient world differed from ours from a cognitive science perspective. The question becomes even more perplexing when one considers that arguably even our perception today is not homogeneous and uniform, but can differ according to gender, age, culture, and the like.

Sight and hearing are the two most important senses with which we can perceive our environment.[400] Questions related to the study of visual perception include how we recognise objects and why we perceive a coherent optical environ-

---

397 Grethlein 2023b, 113.
398 On "sensory change" see Toner 2014b. See also Toner 2014a, Betts 2017, Janik 2020. For studies on the Middle East, see also Neumann and Thomason 2022.
399 Schlicht, Vetter, Thaler, Moss 2013.
400 Hutmacher 2019 with further bibliography. See also p. 81–86 above.

ment even though we can only see small parts of it. Above all, it's exciting to ask whether the world perceived by the ancient Greeks and Romans, and the senses they used to channel that sensory information, might work in a different way to how the modern world perceives and processes it.

In this context, a recent Routledge series, *The Senses in Antiquity*, in six volumes, is very helpful, exploring the connection and interaction between cognition, perception, understanding, feelings, and knowledge in the philosophy, theory, literature, history, culture, and languages of the ancient world.[401] All six volumes form a coherent whole and not just a collection of individual texts, which makes a holistic understanding very productive. This includes the volume of papers on *synaesthesia* in antiquity, edited by Shane Butler and Alex Purves, which is a reassessment of ancient textures, tastes, and flavours, sounds and sight. The introduction situates the senses within the history of aesthetics in order to treat them holistically, beyond the 'visual paradigm', and subsequent essays explore the senses from the classical age to the contemporary reception of classical works.

In contrast, Michael Squire's *Sight and the Ancient Senses* is a thorough guide to the conceptualisation of the ancient 'visual paradigm'.[402] As discussed above in the context of metaphor studies, sight has always held a dominant position among the senses.[403] Depending on the context, it was seen either as a guarantor of truth or as a source of deception. Attitudes to knowledge and ignorance, to remembering and forgetting, to life and death, to the divine and the mortal, are structured by vision and non-vision. From Archaic Greece to the growth of Christianity in Late Antiquity, this volume explores the ways in which the Greeks and Romans understood what they saw, and the wider environmental, intellectual, and political contexts in which ancient theories of vision emerged. Some contributions in this volume deal with ancient theories of vision, while others focus on the eye as a physical entity. Vision and the conceptual framework for the theory of the senses, and finally Greco-Roman visual language are also considered in relation to the other senses.

In parallel, Mark Bradley published the volume *Smell and the Ancient Senses*.[404] Greek and Roman authors describe a whole firework of sublime and an-

---

[401] I discuss these Routledge volumes here as an example, as this is a growing field. On the senses in archaeology, see also Hamilakis 2013.
[402] Squire 2015. On gaze and vision see p. 77–86 above.
[403] See p. 97–105 above.
[404] Bradley 2014. See also Reinarz 2014, Squillace 2020 and Grand-Clément and Ribeyrol 2022. The question is becoming increasingly popular as more and more conferences and workshops are organised on the topic of odour. Cf. e.g. https://www.fu-berlin.de/presse/publikationen/tsp/2021/tsp-april-2021/altaegyptische-duftstoffe/index.html (The Scent of Ancient Egypt, Berlin 2021), https://

imal olfactory sensations and relate them to the social, cultural, or military status of the people and the environment in which they lived. The sense of smell plays a central role: divine incense and burning sacrifices, seductive scents, aromatic kitchen fumes, decaying corpses, pungent and foul-smelling backyards. Different odours can be perceived as either pleasant and sweet or unpleasant and intrusive, but the nose can become accustomed to certain smells, and this is where contemporary sensory research is a great help. The chapter by Neville Morley in particular is a complex examination of the results of the 'sensory turn'.[405] Morley speaks of the smells and odours of the city and calls for a comparison between the smells of historical life and our 'deodorised present'. He points out that while the Romans may have been accustomed to 'unpleasant' smells, for the inhabitants of ancient cities the countryside smelled the worst. This is clearly the case in today's olfactory world. Morley argues that smell of Rome "must be part of a wider study of how Romans received and interpreted sensory information and made use of it in navigating their immediate environment" (p. 112). The cultural and cognitive study of smell relates to ancient medical science and thought, philosophy, religious beliefs, botanical and natural history, satire and comedy cityscapes, food – where tastes, scents, odours, and stenches were abundant and diverse components of the ancient perceptual apparatus.

Alex Purves further continued her research begun in the synaesthesia volume and followed it up with a volume on the sense of touch.[406] The sense of touch is not restricted to a single organ, which distinguishes it from the other senses. It extends to the inside of the body as well as the skin. In antiquity it mediated almost every dimension of human relationships, from the mundane to the sensual, and was also an important interface between the person and the external environment. The extent to which the sense of touch has played a crucial role in the sciences, the visual arts, the humanities, philosophy and medicine, shaping the way we approach subjects ranging from beauty and literature to various forms of religious and ceremonial activity, is the central theme of the book. In enactivist terms, the further question is about the relationship of the body to the object, the environment, and the self. A compelling link with neuroscience and developmental psychology is found in Helen Slaney's chapter on the aesthetic writings of Johann Gottfried Herder and

---

www.hsozkult.de/event/id/event-130221 (The Experience of Smell and Taste in the Greco-Roman World, Dresden 2023), https://www.hsozkult.de/event/id/event-133523 (Olfactory Perspectives on the Large City of the Pre-Modern Era, Regensburg 2023). Last access for all links cited: June 3rd 2024. Cf. also Alvar Nuño, Alvar Ezquerra, and Woolf 2021 and below p. 115–118.
405 Morley 2014.
406 Purves 2017.

classical sculpture.[407] Slaney focuses on the Enlightenment debates about how our minds perceive beauty and whether this ability is innate. Herder argued that tactile memories accumulated since childhood determine our impression of the beauty of a sculpture. Herder's ideas are still relevant to neuroscience today, such as motor theories of perception, supported by Marc Jeannerod's observations of neural activity during 'object-oriented action'. Slaney explores this relationship. We don't realise that it's actually a complex experience made up of our knowledge of how such surfaces feel and our desire to touch them, because the impression is so sudden and seemingly visual. The sensory effect of touch opens up a wide range of interpretative and experiential questions, regardless of whether we locate the sense of touch at the superficial level of the skin, in the flesh or, less tangibly, in the emotions and the mind.

Meanwhile, Kelli Rudolph got to grips with tasting.[408] The functional significance of taste and its value and meaning in the actions, thoughts and words of the Greeks and Romans are reassessed, with the cognitive science question central to how taste in the ancient world differed from ours, and how people then began to understand taste itself in relation to the physical body and other forms of experience. Using literary and material remains from the archaic period to late antiquity, the cultural and intellectual development of attitudes and theories about taste are examined, opening a window on ancient thinking about perception and the body.

The final volume in *The Senses in Antiquity* series, edited by Shane Butler and Sarah Nooter, contributes to the emerging fields of sound and vocal studies by providing the first substantial survey of sound in Ancient Greece and Rome.[409] Sounds and tones play an important role, from the noises of the mortal body to the sounds of the gods, from the home kitchen to the assembly hall, from the chirping of a bird to the music of the heavens. Erika Holter, Susanne Muth and Sebastian Schwesinger present a case study of the *Digital Forum Romanum* in the late Republican period, which uses 3D modelling of the Roman Forum to reconstruct the auditory experience of participants in public assemblies there.[410] A detailed discussion of the acoustic reconstruction is accompanied by an example of the auralisation of Cicero's third speech against Catiline, read in Latin from the perspective of a spectator standing in the Comitia at a distance of 20 metres. The recording is available for free download from the Routledge website (https://s3-eu-west-1.amazonaws.com/

---

407 Slaney 2017.
408 Rudolph 2017.
409 Butler and Nooter 2018. See also Mills 2014. On using sound studies to interpret Greek lyric poetry, see Nooter 2023. See also above p. 80–86.
410 Holter, Muth and Schwesinger 2018.

s3-euw1-ap-pe-ws4-cws-documents.ri-prod/9781138481664/180716_Republik_Pos1_20m_latin.wav, last access June 3rd 2024), and is yet another example of how modern sensory studies can collaborate and interact with ancient material in a mutually enriching way. This volume explores the ways in which sound predetermines our lives in our environment and provides a vital resonant platform for reflection on ecology, experience, the emotional, death and the sacred, oral songs and written texts, the individual self, and its relationship to others. How ancient ideas about sound continue to influence the way we perceive what we hear today can be seen in the various conceptions and uses of hearing and sound production in the contexts of cults, religion, mourning, music, lyric poetry, theatre, and the like.

In general, the Routledge series has provided a holistic overview of Greek and Roman perceptions, opening up a range of new questions and perspectives for study. As the state of research shows, the cognitive perspective on perception and the senses leads to fruitful results when applied to literary studies or to history and archaeology, especially in the analysis of experience in the study of religion.

4.3 'Religious experience' and cognitive science

Of all the fields of ancient history, it is in religious studies, that cognitive approaches have been used most frequently and with fruitful results in recent years. The concept of 'religious experience' is particularly charged with ideological and political significance and has been central to any discussion of the individual's relationship to the powers they worship across all religions.[411] Engaging with 'experience' raises questions about how notions of self, objects and their identities emerge.[412] The questions posed are less about individuals experiencing, and more about entities constituted by experience.

---

[411] The numerous publications of the CAARE network (Cognitive Approaches to Ancient Religious Experience) under the direction of Esther Eidinow and Thomans Harrison as well as the RCC (Religion, Cognition, and Culture, https://rcc.au.dk, last access June 3rd 2024) and the MINDLab (https://neurocampus.au.dk/nca-groups-labs/cfinmindlab, last access June 3rd 2024) in Aarchus in Denmark under the direction of Armin W. Geertz should be mentioned here in particular. Cognitive approaches have already gained acceptance in the study of religion, at least in the last two decades, e.g.: Hick 2006, Sørensen 2007a, Sørensen 2007b, Ustinova 2009, Geertz 2010a, Geertz 2010b, Czachesz 2012, Pachis 2014, Geertz 2016, Geertz 2017, Panagiotidou 2014, Eidinow 2015, Larson 2016, Struck 2016, Panagiotidou and Beck 2017, Grieser and Johnston 2017, Ustinova 2018, Kundtová Klocová and Geertz 2019, Oesterreich 2020, Pachis 2020, Eidinow, Geertz, and North 2022b, Frigerio 2023, Misic and Graham 2024.
[412] Scott 1991.

Through of the concept of experience, it is no coincidence that research on ancient religions has been particularly strongly associated with cognitive analysis for some years. Cognitive approaches have the potential to breathe new life into these fields of study by opening up the theoretical horizon on the physical, emotional and cognitive aspects of ancient religions. The range of new methods takes into account established paradigms applied to the analysis of culture, religious cults and practices, and society. Most importantly, the study of religion today not only applies neurological and physiological patterns to its material, but also establishes a fruitful relationship between ancient religious experiences and modern interpretations of certain experiences on the physiological level. This involves a process of interaction: the current exploration of religious systems as cognitive control systems, new methodologies using Big Data sites, the exploration of the effects of particular experiences, including sensory experiences, the effects of discourse, perceptual illusions and anthropomorphism, the role of the senses and emotions, the interplay of local knowledge and/or understanding with experience, including space and the design of space.

Ultimately, it is the reconstruction of the belief systems, symbols, ideas, customs and practices, social conditions, material and sensory settings and environments in which religiously interpreted experiences take place that reveals their influences. Research on contemporary populations can thus contribute to the understanding of ancient religiously interpreted experiences.

The increasing attention to the way in which the lights, the chants, the smells, and the decoration of the rituals that appealed to the senses of the participants enabled them to touch the gods reveals the sensory universe that the Greeks mobilised in these special moments of activation of supernatural powers. In this field, the research of Adeline Grand-Clément, dealing with the history of colour and sensibility and with the images and representations of the divine in ancient Greece, in the context of the emergence of archaeology and the discovery of polychromy in Greek art, is significant.[413]

The mind, the body and the physical and social environment were inextricably linked in shaping conceptions of the gods in ancient Greek culture. The Greek gods were perceived as anthropomorphic, and this perception may have developed in conjunction with certain cultural forms such as narratives. Anthropomorphism itself is based on experientiality: even the representations of gods in non-human form still conferred human cognitive processes on them. Thus we attribute intel-

---

[413] Grand-Clément 2023. However, much earlier, on the interaction of Aelius Aristides' literary narrative with the material context of the Asklepios sanctuary at Pergamon, and the experience of pilgrimage to this sanctuary, see Petsalis-Diomidis 2010.

lect (intentionality and agency) to them: the only human characteristic that is always projected onto supernatural beings.[414] From a cognitive science perspective, one can examine both narrative as a cultural form and narratives that describe or allude to other cultural forms, including ritual action, and explore how, for example, descriptions of smells might evoke the experience of a divine presence in listeners and in turn influence them.[415] Such an approach allows for cultural groups and individual variations within the constraints of common cultural forms. It illuminates how the ancient Greeks' ideas of the gods were embedded, while allowing for the diversity of a polytheistic culture and, moreover, the personal response of the individual. The approach contributes to the discourse on belief in ancient Greek cultures by suggesting ways in which concepts of the divine might have been shaped, shared, personalised, embodied and embedded within, between and across communities.

Shrines and sanctuaries provide material for analysis. The potential for combining the 'top-down' and 'bottom-up' approaches discussed above with religious experience is particularly important in analysing religious practices and the cognitive dimensions of the experience of those who have participated in them.[416] The ritual affected the state of the body and mind of the participants, a process based on a combination of cognitive and neurophysiological mechanisms found in other initiation and oracle cults. The complex experience of the participant included visual, auditory, tactile, gustatory and kinaesthetic sensations as well as multisensory hallucinations. The rituals of Delphi, Eleusis, the Idaean Cave or Dodone in ancient Greece combined features of a mystical ceremony, such as concealment, contact with the dead, extreme despair, erasure of the past and change of personality, with the interrogation of the oracle by interpreting the hidden wisdom revealed in the sacred cave.[417] Cognitive studies help to explore the physical and mental changes experienced by participants during their stay at the site. The altered state of consciousness experienced was induced by sensory deprivation and included trances and out-of-body experiences, hallucinations, and a sense of direct contact with the supernatural. The main experiential event was accompanied by

---

[414] See Ustinova 2022a with further bibliography.
[415] Alvar Nuño, Alvar Ezquerra, and Woolf 2021. On sensory perception as a central theme in enactive approaches, see above p. 110–114.
[416] See p. 63–64 above and 119–120 below.
[417] See Panagiotidou 2014, Lex 1979. See also Pirenne-Delforge 2018. We are fortunate to have detailed descriptions (Pausanias 9.39, 10–13 and Plutarch *Mor.* 590B-592F) of the ritual and the experience of the participants at the shrine of Trophonius at Lebadeia, providing an opportunity for a comparative case study of the classical record with the findings of contemporary cognitive science research (see Ustinova 2022a).

a series of preparatory acts, each involving a distinct range of cognitive and somatic responses.

Rites that can be described as 'normative sacrifices' are performed in a wide variety of circumstances and with very different purposes, for example to appease and worship a god or goddess, to prepare a meal, to enable prophecy, or to fulfil a responsibility passed on by tradition.[418] The 'normative sacrifice' (to be understood as a sequence of ritual acts: Burning barley groats and animal skins on the altar, killing the victim, examining the entrails, pouring the libations and burning the parts, cooking and eating the flesh remains), according to Hugh Bowden, should be seen as a collection of acts to which the participants bring their individual purposes and which therefore have their own meanings.[419] Cognitive theories explain why 'normative victimisation' has been transmitted in this way, and suggest guidelines for research into the issue.[420]

In particular, sensory associations discussed above and associated with the practice of rituals are the focus of research here.[421] Some of the reservations of ancient historians about the application of cognitive religious studies to the ancient world may be allayed by a deeper awareness of the connection between ritual and memory, and in particular the peculiarities of olfactory memory.

The central act of ancient religious rituals was the burning of substances on the altar, which produced an attractive billowing smoke and with it a series of smells so pleasant and strong that people could believe they were in the presence of the gods. The 'pleasant' smell associated with sacrifice was thus most perceptible near the altar.

As mentioned above in relation to literary sources, smell is closely linked to memory, especially autobiographical or semantic memory. Therefore, it forms one of the central concepts that has recently attracted the attention of science.[422] Smell-triggered memories are much more emotionally charged, activate the neurobiological processes of emotional processing to a greater extent, and people are more likely to be transported to the original time and place of their memories than when the same events are recalled using other modalities.[423] The smell of the victim probably awakens memories in people of their earliest experiences with victims.

---

418 On the "normative victim" see Bremmer 2007.
419 Bowden 2022.
420 McCauley and Lawson 1990, McCauley and Lawson 2002, McCauley and Lawson 2007, Whitehouse 2004, Larson 2016, 195.
421 See above p. 111–114.
422 Rouby et al. 2002, Herz 2016, Olofsson et al. 2020, Keller and Young 2023. See above p. 111–112.
423 Herz 2016.

The role of smell in religious studies is particularly important in activating situated conceptualisations and drawing conclusions from what we can reconstruct, including emotional responses. Smell can influence mood, cognition and behaviour, often evoking memories that are experienced as highly emotional. Smell as a modality may have been particularly effective in making contact with deities. This applies not only to smell as an experience, but also to mere descriptions of smells. The function of olfactory perception is important both in religious rituals and during dramatic performance in theatre for the representation of emotions and for building tension.[424]

The conception of the gods was an elegant process of conceptualisation, both individual and communal, involving sensory, embodied and mental domains, inextricably linked to broader social and cultural contexts, recollections of past memories and situated conceptualisations of earlier ritual experiences. Shared conceptions of gods, it is now *communis opinio*, emerge from shared experiences.[425] This process is called 'situated conceptualisation', which is stored in memory and allows us to draw conclusions about what is likely to happen. In this process, our knowledge constantly grows as we experience new situations.[426]

According to the American psychologist and cognitive scientist Lawrence W. Barsalou, when people experience a situation and process information, sensorimotor processes and brain areas become active on different modalities (visual, auditory, motor, tactile, affective, motivational).[427] Representations do not only occur in the actual experience itself. They are actually, or at least partially, captured during that experience and can then be used again later for conceptual understandings that simulate entities and events in their absence. A concept is a dynamic system, spanning different areas of the brain, designed to represent a particular set of environmental or experiential categories and to guide the way we interact with instances of that set. This process can support representations of entities as well as events that a person has actually experienced, the combination of which also gives rise to new entities.

Furthermore, the question of whether ritual participants in antiquity might have experienced altered states of consciousness and visions of divine apparitions has triggered a long debate about hysteria, belief and the interplay of cult and myth.[428] In the absence of first-hand accounts, historians have struggled to imagine the ecstatic participants of the myth merely from literary descriptions of civic cult

---

[424] Telò 2013, Clements 2014. Cf. Feagin 2018 and Spence 2021.
[425] Luhrmann e.a. 2021.
[426] Barsalou 2008, Barsalou 2009, Barsalou 2016.
[427] Barsalou 2008, cf. also Barsalou e. a. 2003.
[428] See Stein, Costello, and Polinger Foster 2022.

performance, but the apparent gap between ritual performers and mythic models may not be so great. Various miracle workers, Christian martyrs, and maenads (the mythical followers of Dionysus and the most important members of the god's retinue) claimed to have had an experience that was the presence of God.[429]

Recent research has shown, based on biological and physiological data, that this was by no means madness or hysteria, but a natural human response to sensory input and cultural priming: triggered by the high levels of adrenaline, fear, and movement during the ritual.[430] 'Predictive coding', also known as 'predictive processing', is a branch of brain theory which suggests that the brain is in a continuous process of developing and adapting a 'mental model' of the world around it.[431] Such models of one's environment are formed on the basis of information derived from previous expectations and experiences (the 'top-down' input).[432] If sensory information is added at a certain point in time (the 'bottom-up' input), the model formed is compared with these and the model is corrected accordingly. The use of this approach to the cognitive process in the context of lived experience has so far focused on one line of vision: how institutions provide participants in a ritual with certain 'top-down' expectations, but then also make it difficult for participants and limit their ability to verify these with 'bottom-up' sensory information, with the aim of ensuring the widest possible receptivity to the pre-ritual anticipations and post-event explanations that form the basis of a human 'interpretation' of a particular experience. According to the logic of 'predictive processing', such a mind representation is used to generate predictions of sensory input signals, which are then matched to the incoming sensory data.

In addition, cultural knowledge plays a role in how sensory information is processed by the brain. In order to use the environment, the brain must collect and organise information about the environment. Cultural knowledge feeds into the creation of schemas and models and thus also into the way sensory data is interpreted. The cultural knowledge of the participants interacted with the sensory data and activated certain cognitive processes that become visible to us in the form of symbols/images. We know about the visual and auditory confusion caused by shouting, singing, and beating drums or pelvises. In addition, a characteristic posture with the head thrown backwards or forwards appears in vase painting and poetry. This movement seems to be particularly associated with walking, dancing and generally the physical movements during a ritual.

---
429 Clinch 2022, Ustinova 2022b, Lupack 2022, Panagiotidou 2022.
430 Van Leeuwen and van Elk 2018; cf. also Wescoat and Ousterhout 2012.
431 Schjoedt and Andersen 2017, Andersen 2019, Millidge, Seth, and Buckley 2022.
432 Meijs e.a. 2018, Scott 2022.

Another cognitive function that seems to be strongly involved in the experience of felt presence is 'agency detection'.[433] This is the human ability to identify other sentient beings and thus assume that unexpected phenomena are caused by an agent, a sentient being. Thus, we see faces in clouds or in ocean waves, or attribute malevolent properties to a laptop when it suddenly shuts down and unsaved data is lost. This model suggests that when faced with trustworthy sensory data, the brain makes greater use of 'top-down' interpretations of experience and knowledge projections. This results in the tendency to assume the purposeful intervention of a sentient or intelligent agent in certain situations – even if such an agent is not involved at all. To put it another way, the witches, miracle workers, martyrs or maenads were not insane. Our brains merely rely heavily on existing predictive assumptions about the world.

In addition, gender studies have had a strong influence on work in ancient history, and as a result research has been intertwined with cognitive studies, beginning with Joan Scott's seminal article "Gender: A Useful Category of Historical Analysis". This was a large-scale – and successful – attempt to place historical gender studies on a new theoretical foundation.[434] Even then, a distinction was made between biological sex and socially constructed gender. Scott provided her own definition of gender under two aspects: Gender is also a marker of power differentials based on perceptions of sexual difference. The essay was influenced by Jacques Derrida and Michel Foucault as well as by the 'linguistic turn' in history.[435] Scott's research made clear why gender is far more than just another name for 'women's history': Attributions of femininity and masculinity have shaped historical societies in many ways; their analysis can therefore capture power structures in a particularly meaningful way. Especially in the Anglophone and Francophone world, the study of gender in ancient history has experienced a boom since the late 1980s that is both pronounced and fraught with tension.

In recent years, cognitive science has been increasingly actively brought into gender studies.[436] However, a historiography from a cognitive science perspective on sex and gender would require an unprecedented level of interdisciplinary collaboration and interdisciplinary synthesis. Human societies are cultivated neural networks that function on the basis of historically conditioned worldviews and imagined communities. No neurological study can clarify the socio-political coordi-

---

433 Van Leeuwen and van Elk 2018, Andersen 2019. Cf. also Guthrie 1993, Boyer 1994, Barrett 2000, 30–31, Boyer 2001, 51–91, Atran and Norenzayan 2004, Barrett and Lanman 2008.
434 Scott 1986.
435 Foucault 1976–2018, Derrida 2005, Canning 1994.
436 Halpern 2000, Bischof-Köhler 2006, Brannon 2010, Ferstl and Kaiser 2013, Rubin, Atwood and Olson 2019.

nates of ancient Greek and Roman gender politics. Nor can philological or historical analysis alone help to elucidate the neurophysiological extent of religious experience in the ancient world. Therefore, a bold interdisciplinary push for a consistent, biocultural research programme would be necessary in relation to the religious experiences of subordinated and silenced social classes of the past, not only to better decipher the frustratingly fragmentary records, but also to be able to look behind the elitist and male-documentary biases.

This is especially true of the mysteries of Eleusis in Greece or the festivals dedicated to the ancient Roman goddess *Bona Dea*. These were associated with chastity and fertility of women, healing and the protection of the state and the people.[437] Moreover, initiation was a very emotional experience. Today, the most important mythographies are evaluated as violent reminders of gender-specific behavioural norms and as coercive strategies to protect women, supported by religious narratives. Only a cross-disciplinary cognitive historiography on emotions and gender roles in antiquity contributes to overcoming the limitations of research on the religious experiences of ancient women.

Since the male authors had limited knowledge of the rites and attributes of the female mysteries, there is much speculation about their exact sequence. In both Greece and Rome, the male political elite controlled subordinates' access to food, pleasure and rewards, manipulating the nervous systems of the subordinate classes by alternating between ordinary socio-economic stress and extraordinary neurophysiological relief through entertainment, religious rituals and social events that could temporarily alleviate this stress. Such an analysis sheds light on how gender, religion, socio-political discourses on sexual mores and power dynamics were understood and culturally mediated in archaic and classical Greece (e.g. the Mysteries of Eleusis) and in the late Roman Republic (e.g. *Bona Dea*).

4.4 Choruses as vehicles of social, political, and religious life

The institution of the chorus in the ancient world is another significant example of ritual experience to be considered from the perspective of embodied cognition. The forms of production, distribution, communication, and transmission of Greek poetic works in the Archaic and Classical periods, of which choruses were the first interpreters, offer a wide range of material to explore. The choruses sang in ritual contexts, at more secular victory celebrations at competitions, or in the important cultural engine of archaic Greece, the elite male symposium. Such a group present-

---

[437] Foucault 1980, Martin 2018, 113–123.

ed itself and was noticed by its audience; choral performances were often commissioned and financed by tyrants, other prominent figures, or communities. In the social, political, and religious life of classical Greece, choruses were known to play a central role.[438]

The practice of collective social dancing and singing, accompanied by the words and music of the poet, was popular in various parts of Greece in archaic times, but it became absolutely essential to the Athenian conception of ideal education in the city, as Peter Wilson has convincingly argued.[439] Choruses were also a means of "articulating and manifesting exchanges between different cities", as Deborah Steiner has shown in detail.[440] Choruses travelled from where they lived to other cities and re-established their links with them.

Dancing, singing, and playing an instrument were perceived simultaneously and merged into a single whole. The perspective of this perception is particularly thought-provoking when considered from the point of view of neuroscience as a ubiquitous modality. Such research has been carried out in recent years.[441] The cognitive science perspective in this case would mean focusing on their dances and songs and placing a careful analysis of the texts in historical comparisons with other practices of the period.[442]

The Greek audiences themselves were probably very familiar with the dances and songs of the choruses, and thus appreciated the embodied perception of the performance, in other words the extensive use of simulating neurons to experience the spectacle. Dancing, singing, moving in circles – all of these engage the brain's crucial motor networks and are external manifestations of deep thought, a paradigm of embodied cognition.[443] Movement, rhythm, music, poetry are experienced in coexistence and cognitively controlled in a wave of synergy and symmetry, and the spectators, who are intrinsically involved in this process through watching, are conglomerated with the performers in this act of cognition and perception.[444]

---

[438] See especially Pl. *Leg.* 655a-672a, 814e-817a. See Webster 1970, Ley 2007, 114–199, and now recently Steiner 2021. Cf. also Lech 2009, Billings, Budelmann, and Macintosh 2013.
[439] Wilson 2000, which includes an extensive bibliography and lists of the archaeological evidence.
[440] Steiner 2021, 19.
[441] E.g. Ciesielski 2017.
[442] Peponi 2013, Whitmarsh 2013, Budelmann 2019. See also Marseglia 2023.
[443] See e.g. Cruse and Schilling 2010.
[444] For a very useful exploration of the bond between choruses and their audiences, and of *enargeia* as 'visual vividness' in later Hellenistic texts as a bond between authors and readers, see Steiner 2021, 659–669. See above p. 77–86.

A number of experimental studies have shown that belonging to a group, even temporarily, does indeed influence people's thinking, sometimes in such a way that the individual, however, is still able to think individually and to distance himself from the thinking of the other group members. The individual mind is thus contrasted with the group mind or collective mind.[445] Cultural and biological processes are interwoven in this case, and the reception-oriented question is posed as to how the observers, the audience, reacted to the performances. Such an analysis is able to illuminate the choral performances as bodily techniques that go beyond merely facilitating sociality, so that the ritual simultaneously facilitates not being confronted by each other. These techniques change the state of mind of the performers and thereby bring about what can be called a collective ritual experience. Chants can have a corresponding effect on both the performers and the observers.

The physical techniques of dance and song show that such a performance had considerable potential to produce dissociative effects in the performers. Through posture, behaviour and acting, the chorus also forces the audience to think about the political question of the forms and functions of collectivity and the relationship of the individual to the community surrounding and confronting him. The mass as a variable of political mobilisation, the figure of thought of individual self-realisation and the radical questioning of the individual are some of the problems associated with the chorus, raised by the body techniques, costumes and masks and addressed in an enactive and cognitive way. An analysis based on cognitive principles can reconstruct the performances as highly moving. The potential value of recent work on kinesthetic empathy for the study of ancient (nondramatic) choruses has been explored by Sarah Olsen, who suggests that early Greek thought may have constructed "kinesthetic empathy as a product of visual perception combined with kinetic and somatic memory". Furthermore, "this culturally specific model of empathetic identification" could have "an important social resonance", as it could "support an understanding of *choreia* as a vehicle of social continuity and cohesion".[446]

'Experience' is thus another umbrella term that covers a wide range of enquiries in different disciplines that study the ancient world, from the experience of reading and watching to the experience of participating in a ritual, a cult, a political event and the like. It is, in Dewey's way, something that has a personal impact on one's life and affects it. Drawing heavily on biological and psychological re-

---

445 Tomasello 2014, Visvardi 2015, Budelmann 2019.
446 Olsen 2017, 155. On kinesthetic empathy in solo dance in Archaic and classical Greece, see also Olsen 2019 and Olsen 2021. On the concept of kinesthetic empathy across cultural practices as the capacity to experience empathy by watching the movements of another human being, see Reynolds and Reason 2012 and Garner 2018.

search, the actual act of experiencing is then a cultural and aesthetic process, in fact a "bi-product of the continuous and cumulative interaction of an organic self with the world".[447]

---

[447] Dewey 1934, 220.

Chapter 5
Emotions and ancient sources: conversations with David Konstan, Angelos Chaniotis, and Douglas Cairns

Another immediate and natural point of contact between literature and cognitive science is the concept of emotion. Both the creators of all the sources we have from antiquity – literary texts, inscriptions, papyri, coins, works of art – and their addressees were people with cognitions and emotions. There is hardly a written source, including graffiti, that is irrelevant to the study of emotions. The actors and subjects of history are individuals and groups with emotions; therefore, which media and genres we use to study emotions depends on the aims of our enquiry. For the role of emotions in public discourse (as a strategy of persuasion) or for their role in conveying civic values and constructing social and cultural fictions, documentary sources (assembly resolutions, petitions to the authorities, epitaphs, private letters), but also court speeches, are more relevant than, say, comedy. For the ancient perception of emotions, we have to study philosophical treatises; dedications, confessional inscriptions and miracle narratives are fundamental for the study of the emotional background of religion; curses offer important insights into the role of emotions in social interactions. Emotion, then, is an overarching field that provides a necessary framework for exploring all the discussed above areas of cognitive classics – material agency, space, imagination and experientiality.

It is likely that research on emotions and affects in cognitive poetics will become even more prominent in the future, as there have been a number of recent cognitive poetic calls for more attention to be paid to this particular phenomenon.[448] Major centres and journals have been established for the interdisciplinary study of emotions and affective sciences.[449] The growing concern with emotions

---

[448] Stockwell 2002, 171–173.
[449] See e.g. the journals *Emotion* (https://www.apa.org/pubs/journals/emo), *Motivation and Emotion* (https://www.springer.com/journal/11031/, last access June 3rd 2024), *Cognition and Emotion* (https://www.tandfonline.com/journals/pcem20, last access June 3rd 2024), *Emotion Review* (https://journals.sagepub.com/description/EMR, last access June 3rd 2024), *Emotions: History, Culture, Society* (EHCS, https://societyhistoryemotions.com/journal/, last access June 3rd 2024). On emotion research and affective sciences cf. Schiewer 2014, 12–77 with further bibliography. For the most influential theories on emotions and the most important debates of the last decades in philosophy, psychology and biology, see Campeggiani 2023.

https://doi.org/10.1515/9783111577371-008

in the humanities is one facet of these trends, and at the heart of this development is the impetus given to the study of emotions in history by the work of, for example, William Reddy (the key concept of 'emotional regime') and Barbara Rosenwein (the key concept of 'emotional communities').[450]

In addition, Magda Arnold was one of the first in modern research to consider emotions as something that can be analytically dissected and understood: as a cognitive phenomenon. She introduced the concept of appraisal, which is the origin of emotional experience.[451] This concept was further developed by Richard Lazarus in psychology, who saw appreciation as the cognitive evaluation of the significance of our environmental relationships, and by Robert Solomon in philosophy, who emphasised the subjective nature of the value judgements that make up emotions.[452]

According to Keith Oatley, who is known as a leading exponent of a link between the study of emotions and the practice of writing and appreciating literature, emotions are mental states with coherent psychological functions. They contain two components: the functional aspect, which marks the readiness to act or a point at which the readiness to act changes, and a phenomenological colouring in the form of a felt experience, often a physical reaction or expression.[453]

Contemporary emotion research also focuses on the affective quality and nature of literary works. An overarching feature of this strand of research, however, is its emphasis on the emotional responses of recipients: it combines the interests and questions of modern emotion studies with those of classical poetics, aesthetics and rhetoric. Emotions are seen as an essential element of audience engagement with writing, acting and storytelling, and the ways in which writing, acting and storytelling can facilitate this engagement.[454]

There is neither a common understanding of emotions nor an accepted account of what constitutes an emotion across the various academic disciplines that study these issues and their manifestations. However, there is *the Component Process Model*, a multidimensional and multi-factorial framework developed by Klaus Scherer's Geneva School, which includes a number of cognitive and biolog-

---

[450] Cf. Plamper 2010 and the German version "Wie schreibt man die Geschichte der Gefühle?" in https://werkstattgeschichte.de/wp-content/uploads/2017/02/WG54_039-069_PLAMPER_GESCHICHTE.pdf, last access June 3rd 2024.
[451] Arnold 1960, 171, and Campeggiani 2023, 83–85.
[452] Lazarus 1991, 121, 144; Solomon 1993a, 19, 127. See Campeggiani 2023, 85–93.
[453] Oatley 2004, Oatley and Jenkins 1996. On 'experience' see p. 106–110. above.
[454] Mar, Oatley, Djikic, and Mullin (2011).

ical pathways.[455] Such models can be adapted to take account of cross-cultural and historical variations, and some projects explore labels, categories and the different ways in which language can be used to influence emotions.[456]

Jesse Prinz's embodied appraisal model is another notable example. He recognises that affective experiences are multi-component processes, but first tries to identify the one constituent that makes up emotion, and finds it (as William James and Carl Lange had done before him in the 19th century) in the perception of bodily changes.[457] Later, Prinz develops an enactivist theory of emotional content and claims that emotions "bring new properties into existence".[458] In a similar vein, Lisa Barrett and James Russell study how the brain creates emotional experiences, viewing emotions as constructed events rather than fixed entities. They examine the neurobiological, cognitive, perceptual, and social processes that lead to experiences such as sadness, anger, and fear.[459]

Many other researchers focus on the physical experience of the individual, whether this is expressed through facial expressions or neurophysiological changes. But the underlying difficulty is that the events and features that we classify as emotions, and that other societies have classified using other, at least partially equivalent concepts, involve much more than these approaches attempt to capture as features of language, thought and culture.

Literary genres offer different views of characters' motivations and extensive evidence of the circumstances in which their emotional states are triggered, which can help us to interpret explicitly attributed emotions and implicit accounts of their behaviour. They rely on the construction of narratives of distinctive affect settings as contexts for portraying and appealing to emotions.

The multiple ways in which affect is staged and narrated in literature then reflect in quite concrete ways the paradigmatic settings of affect in the broader cultural arena, or in specific 'emotional communities' within the given culture.

Medievalist Barbara Rosenwein introduced the term 'emotional communities', explaining that it refers to groups that share the same norms and values regarding

---

455 Scherer 2009. The model is built around appraisal mechanisms; thus it can be considered as a continuation of Arnold's appraisal theory. See Campeggiani 2023, 88–89.
456 See e.g. Christina Soriano's project on language and culture in the Swiss Center for Affective Sciences (*CISA*) in Geneva: https://www.unige.ch/cisa/research/current-specific-research-projects/language-and-culture/, last access June 3rd 2024.
457 Prinz 2004, Prinz 2007. Cf. James 1884 and Lange 1885. See also Cairns and Nelis 2017b, 12–13, and Campeggiani 2023, 65–75.
458 Shargel and Prinz 2017, 110.
459 Barrett and Russell 2015.

emotional behaviour and even feelings themselves.[460] In the cultures we have studied, where there are successful literary descriptions of emotion, we have strong evidence for the experience of affect. In appealing to the feelings of 'external' spectators and modern recipients, the actors portrayed in literary artefacts interact with other actors and with the intended recipients. This is one of the reasons why classical philologists have rightly made extensive and detailed use of literary sources in their historical analyses of emotions: The emotional dimension of a text is often a reason for the recipient's attraction to a particular work. Literary imagined empathy, or the kind of vicarious emotions that arise when reading literature, feel just as real as physiologically generated emotions.[461]

The role of cognitive science in this context is obvious. By drawing on the paradigmatic emotional attitudes of the specific context in which they are produced, literary texts contribute to the creation, circulation, and dissemination of the affective codes embedded in a literary text. The particular recipients for whom the affective codes serve as a model, may find their affective palette expanded by the impact of literary texts. Literary works not only anchor and incorporate the affective codes of their respective communities and societies, but also become affective codes themselves. They can enter, reorient, and expand the affective registers and capacities of their recipients.

Viewing the processes of emotion as culturally and chronologically embedded and considering their place in framing the ways in which people, communities and states experienced and acted, seems to be an interpretive key that sheds light on areas of the ancient world that would otherwise remain hidden. The ways in which emotions are conceived and experienced in a variety of historical or culturally diverse contexts, from classical times to the present day, the implications of these emotions for processes of human behaviour and change, and the impact of past affective legacies on contemporary political, economic and civic action are all crucial to our reading of ancient texts, and a crucial point at which ancient sources can be particularly helpful to contemporary cognitive scientists.

As far as ancient sources are concerned, it was perhaps David Konstan, Angelos Chaniotis and Douglas Cairns who laid the foundations and set the focus for the study of emotions.[462] This chapter is built around my conversations with these three scholars. I asked them the same questions – basically the questions that form the *fil rouge* of this book – about whether they believe that cognitive science's

---

460 Rosenwein 2006, Rosenwein 2020, 3. See also above p. 126 f. 450.
461 For a more detailed overview, see Cairns and Nelis 2017b.
462 Another seminal book – a kind of Roman counterpart to Cairns' study of Greek *aidōs* – should be mentioned here: Robert Kaster's analysis of five Latin emotion terms: *verecundia, pudor, paenitentia, invidia,* and *fastidium* (Kaster 2005).

dialogue with the classics is possible or even productive, whether the 'cognitive turn' in the classics is a fad or whether there is something more substantial going on here, and the reasons why emotions are so fundamental to the study of ancient sources. Their answers to these questions form the main body of this chapter.

There is widespread agreement that the core of human emotion – love, fear, anger, envy, shame – has remained unchanged since the dawn of civilisation. David Konstan, however, postulated that basic human emotions – love, fear, anger, envy, shame – differed from our own in some key ways in antiquity, and that recognising these differences is essential to our appreciation of ancient literary and cultural life.[463]

Konstan challenged the traditional view that the Greek terms for emotions were essentially the same as those used today. Alongside the parallels, there are also striking differences. For example, when we speak of Greek 'anger', 'love' or 'envy', we often overlook the fact that the Greeks did not use these terms themselves. Instead, they used words from their mother tongue, such as ὀργή, φιλία and φθόνος, which are not easily translated into our modern vocabulary of emotions. Konstan argued that representations of emotion in classical antiquity corresponded to a world in which there was fierce competition for recognition and in which the behaviour, motivation and actions of others were triggers of emotion rather than random or natural events. Konstan interpreted several works of ancient literature, ranging from epic and drama to history and oratory, using Greek concepts of emotion. He also showed how the Greek view of emotion reflects something of our own beliefs, either about the nature of certain feelings or about the class of feelings themselves.

From a slightly different perspective, Angelos Chaniotis outlined and implemented a programme to expand the material available for the study of ancient sentiments, moving from a conventional and almost exclusive concern with literary and philosophical documents to a richer range of non-literary and sub-literary sources, and a much stronger focus on material culture: "The social and cultural construction of emotions: the Greek paradigm" (2009–2013).[464] This research has led to a deeper assessment of the social and cultural determinants of emotional expression in written sources (papyri, inscriptions, literary texts) and physical remains from the Greek and Greek-speaking world (ci. 800 BCE-600 CE). In a variety

---

463 Konstan 1997, Konstan 2003a, Konstan 2003b, Konstan 2006a, Konstan 2006b, Konstan 2017, Konstan and Rutter 2003.
464 Chaniotis 2011, Chaniotis 2012a, Chaniotis 2012b, Chaniotis 2012c, Chaniotis 2012d, Chaniotis 2013a, Chaniotis 2013b, Chaniotis 2013c, Chaniotis 2013d, Chaniotis 2013e, Chaniotis 2015, Chaniotis 2016, Chaniotis 2017, Chaniotis and Ducrey 2013, Chaniotis, Kaltsas, and Mylonopoulos 2017.

of contexts (religion, litigation, politics, art, private life) and genres (miracle stories, dedications, curses, petitions, letters of condolence, court speeches, architecture, images), the evocation of fear, anger, jealousy, sadness or hope has been studied.

As for the last name on this list, the importance of Douglas Cairns' decades of work in the field of ancient emotions cannot be overstated.[465] His work is concerned with the role of emotions in the way the Greek and Roman world lived and thought, from the earliest Greek literature and history to the Byzantine period. His work examines the affective life of the Greeks and Romans from a variety of perspectives – philosophy, science, medicine, literature, music, theatre, religion, domestic life, politics, art history and history. It covers a wide range of texts in both ancient languages and in all possible contexts.

From this point on, and for the remainder of this chapter, I will be giving the floor to these three scholars. There are several reasons why I have chosen this format. Two are crucial. First, their work on emotions in antiquity, and thus their connection with the explosion of cognitive approaches to the classical sources, is vast and cannot be easily reduced to a brief synopsis. Rather than paraphrase the monographs and numerous publications that have appeared over the last thirty years, I have decided to talk to them live and to build our conversation on the corpus of studies that the three of them have undertaken in depth. The second reason – in the spirit of contemporary cognitive experiments! – is an attempt to be innovative: I asked them more or less the same questions and received, as expected, different and varied answers. Responses were spontaneous and stimulating. From these interwoven conversations a new way of exploring, reflecting on or looking at emotions in classical studies emerged.

The fact that I have chosen these three scholars does not in any way imply that emotions have been studied exclusively by them. New publications are increasingly appearing that deal with emotions such as anger, fear, pity, joy, love, and grief in a variety of ancient texts and genres.[466] The latest findings in affective narratology are used to examine the ways in which ancient narratives evoke emotions in their readers. However, at the time when Konstan, Chaniotis and Cairns started analysing emotions in Greece and Rome, this field was unnoticed, and it seems that their studies in particular are closely linked to the developing and growing dialogue between classicists and cognitive scientists.

---

[465] Cairns 1993, Cairns 2003a, Cairns 2003b, Cairns 2008, Cairns 2009, Cairns 2011a, Cairns 2011b, Cairns 2013, Cairns 2014, Cairns 2015, Cairns 2016a, Cairns 2016b, Cairns 2016c, Cairns 2017a, Cairns 2017b, Cairns 2019, Cairns and Fulkerson 2015, Cairns and Nelis 2017a, Cairns, Hinterberger, Pizzone, and Zaccarini 2022, Cairns and Virág 2024.
[466] E.g. Pachis 2019, De Bakker, van den Berg and Klooster 2022.

5.1 David Konstan

David Konstan. Interview via zoom, 6th February 2023

What does the word "cognitive" mean in the context of classics?
'Cognitive' is understood to mean so many different things these days, what exactly do I mean by 'cognitive'? We used the word 'cognitive' in those days basically to mean 'mental'. It involved thinking. Some people more recently wanted to make the meaning more particular, not as general as to mean absolutely anything that involves thinking.

I can give you an example that motivated me at the time, – I use it in several places, – if you're standing on a street corner, or on the street, and somebody pushes you violently, you might feel angry. But if you then discover that the person saved your life, by pushing you out of the way of a car, you wouldn't feel angry now! You would, however, still feel excited, and you will still feel tense, because the tension doesn't go away at once. But you won't be angry, you will be grateful or the like.

So the fact of somebody pushing you and the tension that you feel, by itself doesn't constitute anger. Anger requires some appreciation, some evaluation of the situation. And in this sense, anger is cognitive, and the Stoics went so far as to make it entirely cognitive. It is not entirely clear, but my own view of the Stoics is that the so called 'pre-emotion', the προπάθεια, is the instinctive response that anybody has to something, as somebody pushes you, and your whole body reacts in a certain way that stays even when you know you know the motive. And so you may be grateful, or you may be angry, but either way, you are in an excited state. And that excited state persists. And that's not strictly intellectual.

Similarly, with heights, you might take a person and put them over a precipice, and they would feel queasy. But that is independent of their evaluation of the situation. So I think something similar would be the case with anger: the sage, when pushed, would feel a reaction, but wouldn't make a judgement about it. And even if he did, he would make a judgment, for example, that, – well, it doesn't matter if somebody pushes me because I don't care about insults. I only care about my virtue.

So the Stoics haven't omitted the corporeal dimension completely. But they have really emphasized the intellectual side, the mental side, the evaluation and judgment, the assessment. That is where we all got started with that kind of distinction, which to me, I have to say, was very enlightening.

In general, the Greeks do not think of emotions as rational or irrational (*logos* vs. *pathos*,), they think of causes, in part because they are forensic in their behaviour (at least, the Athenians were) and there is so much emotional argument in the courtroom or in the Assembly. They realised that emotions are responsive to the way you appraise things and are not just instinctive reactions. So, when the Stoics (and even Aristotle) make this clear distinction between primitive pre-emotions, *propatheiai*, and real, – they are responding to something that a Greek would understand easily.

The conception was lost for centuries, wherein people regarded the emotions as irrational. That was my introduction to the cognitive side. Recently, I've been working on Aristotle's *De anima*, to incorporate something of the physical dimension of emotion. People have accused me in my work of ignoring the fact that the emotions are embodied. And they're right. I did ignore that. Of course, when you're trying to develop an idea, you push too much to one side, and that's natural. But it is as clear as can be that emotions are embodied.

But what does that mean? And what does that entail? It means for me, that if you didn't have a body, you would not feel an emotion. So God (if he is incorporeal) cannot feel an emotion. Strictly speaking, God would not have emotions, because emotions are embodied perceptions. God's perceptions have to be different in nature. There is a similar dilemma when Aristotle says we only learn from experience. God obviously doesn't learn from experience. So you need to have emotions in body.

But does that mean that the emotions can be defined looking only at their physical manifestation? Or is that not enough? If I look at the intellectual side, I know what anger is: I've been insulted, and I want revenge. I know what shame is: I have been exposed as doing something I disapprove of. Now, I can also tell you, anger is movement, hot blood around the heart. Anger is accompanied by that. But if I say hot blood around the hot heart, is that enough to distinguishing anger from other emotions? My answer is no. It is not, that is, the physical correlate of mental events is not sufficient to define the emotion. The physical explains the emotion physically but can't tell you which emotion is. In this, I'm going exactly the opposite of David Charles's recent book, where he argues just the contrary. He uses that, if I find the neurons and synapses where everything goes on with anger, that's enough to tell me you're angry.

So anger has two dimensions. I can look at it physically, or I can look at it intellectually, and they correspond to each other. Aristotle does think emotions have to be embodied. But he doesn't think that looking only at their embodiment is enough to tell you what the emotion is. However, looking only at the intellectual is enough. So I think there's a real difference there in the way Aristotle treats these two aspects. This is what I'm coming to think. Nevertheless, the emotions do have to be embodied. So I'm going to be differing here for many people who want to see the correspondence on both sides as equally valid.

But there are further dimensions to emotions. Take, for instance, the famous example of a mathematician solving a problem on the blackboard. Suppose that he says: if I didn't have this chalk and blackboard, I couldn't solve the problem. Are we saying that the process of thinking is going on in the hand and the blackboard, as well as in the mind? In other words, that cognition is not just in the brain, but everywhere, dispersed, disseminated. The question becomes still more interesting when you think that human beings, other human beings, may be involved. When Aristotle says that a friend is one soul in two bodies, which today we would express rather as one mind and two bodies, is he anticipating distributed cognition?

Indeed, when you look at the conditions that Aristotle imposes on friendship, for instance that friends want to live together all the time, the conditions come very close to what modern students of distributed cognition say about the conditions under which another person might be part and parcel of one's own thinking. I didn't start with these ideas, but now they seem intensely relevant.

And yet, thinking now about the cognitive dimension, I probably am still inclined to look more at the intellectual side and think of cognition that way. As I mentioned, I've been looking at the body in relation to the mind and emotions, even if, as David Charles rightly argues, there are two dimensions to the emotions, cognitive and physical, they do not give the same information. There must be a physical basis, but we must not be misled by a tendency in neuroscience today to reduce emotions to functions of the brain. I doubt that this is what Aristotle meant, and I think he may have the better view.

Taking for a moment a longer view, as is well known, William James argued that the emotions are entirely corporeal: fear is nothing more than the response of running away. A strong reaction to this view set in with appraisal theory, which reintroduced the intellectual or cognitive dimension very strongly. But appraisal theory suffers, I think, from a certain vagueness, because it invites us to make appraisals of so many different things. On one account, there are five dimensions to appraisal theory: one appraises the stimulus, the effects, one's own reaction, a wide range of information, not just the motives of the person who elicits the response, as in Aristotle.

A further aspect of appraisal theory that worries me, and which is common today, is to maintain that the emotions are infinite in number. They are unlimited. We maybe talk about anger. But between anger and the nearest emotion, say rage or irritation or fury, there's an entire spectrum, and not just that, there's no point on the spectrum that's fixed. So when we talk about emotions, we're linguistically fixing points on the spectrum as though they had natural function, whereas in fact, every point along the line counts equally as a distinct emotion, and has to be treated in its own right.

One of the places in antiquity where a similar view is expressed is in the essay, *On the sublime*, ascribed to a certain Longinus; here, he affirms at one point, rather casually, it must be said, that the *pathē* are limitless. Yes, in one sense they are. But if you push that to the point in which we no longer can speak of any single emotion, then it's becoming just a blur. If very case is absolutely unique, then there arises a kind of nominalism, each item unique and of equal significance. There are some psychologists who are inclined to go in that direction.

In my own view, the naming of separate emotions is valid. There are nuclei, which mark out the boundaries where one emotion changes. It's like saying that we shouldn't talk about blue, red or green, because the spectrum is continuous spectrum. But it's very useful to talk about blue, red and green, because that's how our eyes are constructed. And I would say it's very useful to talk about anger, shame and pity, because that's how our psyches are constructed. That's why we pick those emotions in particular, and this is not arbitrary. It's true that just which ones are selected varies from one culture to another, but every culture locates certain emotions as salient, and picks out, as it were, the relevant points on the spectrum. To put it in Hegelian terms, it is where quantity turns into quality. So too, our colour vocabulary is culturally determined. But it doesn't mean that you can have a society where there are no such determinations. Every culture will map them in one way or another.

Methodological quibbles: Why are classicists sceptical about the need for cognitive research in Classics?
People who apply cognitive approaches on Classics often meet from 'traditional Classicists' a question: how can you be sure? How can you measure emotions with your modern means, and think that they are applicable to a society that flourished two or three thousand years ago? Here again, I would not take a nominalist position on the emotions and assume that, every time we see an emotion label, it is necessarily a distinct emotion. It may be subtly different from our conception, and

we need to be alert to that. In that respect, our labels are not just imprecise. They are also misleading.

I would say every culture constructs its focal points. So it makes a difference, for instance, that Greeks in antiquity thought of colours more in connection to their light saturation, a brighter black or white versus what we call the matte colour. In this regard, they may identify things as sharing the same colour, depending on reflectivity or albedo, where we wouldn't see the resemblance because we are brought up to think more in terms of the linear spectrum. Phrases like "the wine-dark sea" are a case in point.

But that is not to say that there is a society where there are no colour terms. Every society will have colour terms, and they will condition the way they view things. And every society will have emotion terms, and that will condition the way they feel things. And that's what we want to study. Of course, they are also vague. We get angry sometimes for one reason and other times for another. Is the anger the same when you are angry with your children because they act up, and when you get angry with a colleague who has insulted you? They are not exactly the same feeling: we can understand that. But this is not to say that every single instance of anger is different.

Let us return, then, to cognitive science. Cognitive science, as we have noted, is often treated as though it were a subfield of brain science. Which is to say, the the emphasis is on neural connections. As I have observed, this is entirely productive, but at the same time has its limitations. An example: neuroscientists sometimes affirm that theirs is an intimate connection between fear or other emotions, and what goes on in brain, or, to be more inclusive, the glands and other body features. But I am not wholly convinced that the way they express it is right. I would go rather for the way the Stoics looked at it. They offered, as we have observed, the most narrowly cognitive interpretation of the emotions we know in antiquity, insisting that they were simply the result of judgments, usually, a pair of judgments. For instance, this particular stimulus can do me harm, and I am right to fear it. And yet, to repeat the earlier point, if the emotion were just these judgments, why is it so hard to change somebody's mind when they are emotionally excited, as opposed to when they make a different kind of mistake? Why is so hard to calm angry people down? Very often, when people are angry, they say, No, I didn't misunderstand, I am right to feel this way. No matter how much evidence you give them, they will find reasons for their fear or anger. Whereas if they say, it's cold outside, and you say, oh, no, I just went outside, it's actually warmed up a lot, they are far more likely to believe you. That's the question I have asked about the Stoics. It's just a judgment. Why is it so hard to change a qualitative value judgment? Why is this judgement different from all other judgments?

Now, the Stoic Seneca does have an answer, of sorts. He says that once a passion gets out of control – and remember this, is a kind of judgment – it occupies the whole of one's mental space, what the Stoics referred to as the *hegēmenikon* or "controlling function." And so there is no room for countervailing judgments, unless perhaps another passion of equal intensity should supervene. But why is this not the case also for any firmly held belief or judgment? I return to the idea that, for the Stoics too, there is the physical side to the emotions, blood boiling around the heart and the like (they were Aristotelian in this regard). But again, while this lends emotions their powerful character, it does not suffice to define an emotion on its own. Or at least, that is what I have suggested in the most recent incarnation of my views.

The emotions, excite things in our bodies. We would say they trigger adrenaline, they get your hormones working, raise your blood pressure, cause the heart to beat more quickly. But if you add all those things together, they are still necessary accompaniments of emotion, but in and of themselves, they don't tell you what the emotion is. I would go so far as to say that you can get angry without there being a very strong physiological dimension, at all. And it's still anger. Just as one can feel pity or even fear without obvious correlative corporeal effects. Perhaps, however, this is a sort of a enduring or stable anger, anger that has settled into a disposition. As Achilles say in the *Iliad*, his gorge rises when he remembers how Agamemnon treated him. At other times, when he is playing the lyre and singing of the glories of old heroes, presumably he is still angry but without the accompanying physical symptoms.

Very broadly, I believe that the intellectual and emotional world of Homer and that of Aristotle are pretty much the same. There has been no substantial psychological change, contrary to the view advanced by Bruno Snell, which posited a discovery of the self in the post-Homeric world. If there was a change in emotional subjectivity, perhaps we might locate it in the rise of Christianity, with its emphasis on hope of salvation vs. the extreme despair of hell. I heard a very interesting talk not long ago by Lawrence Kim, in which he argued that the application of the word 'archaic' to seventh and sixth century literature in Greece is an 18th century invention. There seems to be no ancient precedent for it. No ancient writer uses the word *palaios* or any comparable term to distinguish the universe of Homer from that of Aristotle.

Aristotle was absolutely right, then, to use Homer as an illustration for his theoretical analysis of anger. It fits perfectly. Of course, there is the matter of genre. Literature is different from philosophy, but the kinds of feelings described are roughly the same. True, in the Iliad, we are dealing with people at war, and war does make people think differently. It can, for example, induce a kind of fatalism that is not simply a sign of a primitive mentality, but common in modern battle contexts, as when soldiers under fire console themselves with the idea that "that bullet doesn't have my name on it." But the Greeks never stopped fighting. They were at war throughout the fifth century, as much as they were in the twelveth century. They were always at war. And when you're at war, your sentiments are intensified. You're out there, and the odds are high that you're going to get killed. Of course, this is fantasy, but it does help people to survive under extreme conditions of danger. And so I see Homer very much that way. Achilles is, perhaps, a bit on the pathological side. He ought really to have given in when the embassy from Agamemnon came to appease him. And there is some indication that, in an earlier form of the *Iliad*, he did just that. For Athena says he will. In Book One, she tells him that the Achaeans will come and you will be rewarded. Only at the end of Book Eight do we hear for the first time in the poem, at a second assembly of the gods, that Achilles will not go back to battle just yet, but only after the death of his dearest friend, Patroclus. As Albert Lord said long ago, this is a deliberately new development in the story.

But then something new happens, as Achilles seeks to avenge himself on Hector, who was chiefly responsible for slaying Patroclus. Is this still anger? It is not, strictly speaking, Aristotelian anger. Achilles is deeply hurt and perhaps even feels a kind of guilt, and he certainly wants desperately to kill Hector, but he has not been insulted, which is the condition that Aristotle specifies for anger in his discussion in the *Rhetoric*. As he puts it, anger is a desire for revenge in response to a slight. Indeed, there is a scholium, that is, an ancient comment on the text recorded in the margins of the manuscript, which says that there are two emotions or *pathē* at war in Achilles. One is anger, and the other is grief. And the ancient commentator avers that grief, *lypē*, is stronger and drives out the anger. I think that's exactly the right interpretation of this portion of the *Iliad*. And I think that Aristotle would likely agree.

Is a 'cognitive turn' something en vogue or is it something more profound, which might have an influence on different levels of interpretation?
I don't think this is just a trend or a fad. I believe that it will endure, because it is correct in respect to the emotions, which are, as I have been arguing, deeply cognitive. To be sure, there is still work to be done, because we are so steeped in the idea that the emotions are somehow irrational. It will take time for this to change. The great classicist Kenneth Dover said about his autobiography that he was responsible for what he did, but not for his emotions, that is, what he felt – provided he did not act on them. But the cognitive view of the emotions implies that we may also be responsible for how we feel. Emotions, as we have seen, are judgments, and depend on evaluations, assessments, appraisals if you like, that are cognitive and are, within limits, subject to our control, if we exercise sufficient introspection and

self-discipline. If we take account of the way the ancients considered the emotions, we can see why they practiced what Martha Nussbaum called a therapy of desire, or of the pathē more generally. We have ways to evaluate our character, and our dispositions. And so, when I look at cognitive aspects of emotions, not now from a physiological and neurological point of view, but from a standpoint that suggests that our passions respond to our evaluations or judgments of things, and that we can and should be responsible for those evaluations, I conclude not only that the cognitive approach to emotions will endure, but that it is morally urgent. But that is not to deny that it will face challenge that built into our natures, as these have been culturally constructed.

So cognitive science is relevant because it represents a revolution in the way we understand ourselves, our complex selves. Let me conclude with one more example of its relevance. Imagine you are reading an epigram, that is, a short poem, perhaps with a twist or punchline at the end. In doing so, you implicitly reconstruct the context, imagine where the person who is speaking is located, whether they're sitting at feast, drinking, or perhaps even dead, as in a funerary epigram. You also reconstruct the sentiments in play: what is the speaker feeling, what is the reader expected to feel? You judge, not just from emotive words, but from the acknowledged stimuli to emotions, which may not be identical for us and for the ancient Greeks or Romans. So you make an effort to acquire the cultural knowledge needed to understand what emotions may have been aroused, and under what circumstances. This again is an aspect of cognitive science, closely linked, in this instance, to literary criticism. And no less important, ethically and socially, for that.

5.2 Angelos Chaniotis

Angelos Chaniotis. Interview via zoom, 15th June 2023

How did you come to study emotions and how did your interest in this area first begin?
My interest in emotions actually started very early and it was indirect. It is related to a series of projects in Heidelberg that I either co-directed or participated in. One of them was dedicated to rituals. And of course, rituals have an emotional dimension. The project's title was *Ritual dynamics*; what we studied is not rituals as a stable, non-changing form of behaviour and performance, but how rituals are "lived", that is, experienced in real life. And of course, when you talk about experience in rituals, whether these are religious rituals or not, you are involving emotions, because for instance, religious rituals are connected with the fear of God, with the expression of gratitude or with hope. For this reason, some of my earliest work on emotions is related to religion.

The second project which is indirectly related to emotions was a project on persuasion strategies. We published a small volume in Heidelberg that approached case studies of persuasion strategies in various disciplines, from musicology to ancient history and from literary studies to Chinese studies.[467] When I was dealing with persuasion strategies, I was very much interested among other things, in forms of behaviour – for instance, in the theatrical behaviour of statesmen; this is also the subject of a book that I wrote in Greek (*Theatricality and public life in the Hellenistic world*, 2009). So when, in 2008, I was asked by an administrator in Oxford, responsible for external funding, whether I would be interested in applying for a major grant with the European Research Council, and if I had a subject that would interest me, I spontaneously responded: "emotions". I did this without having previously studied in detail the theoretical works that had been written up to that time. I knew, of course, the book of William Harris on *Restraining Anger* (2004). Harris had given a lecture in Heidelberg, long before the book was published, while he was still working on it. So, I was familiar with the fact that there is an interest in emotions in Ancient History.

I was also familiar with cognitive aspects in Classical Archaeology and Prehistorical Archaeology. Cognitive archaeology was a thriving field, beginning in the 90s and booming in the early part of this century. But for me, the study of emotions was just the natural continuation of my research on rituals, persuasion strategies, and theatrical behaviour. This was my motivation. Of course, when I applied for a major grant with the European Research Council, I realized that something that seemed to me a necessity in Classical Studies had already had a relatively long tradition in other fields, especially in Modern and Early Modern History, less so at

---

[467] A. Chaniotis, A. Kropp, and C. Steinhoff (eds.), *Überzeugungsstrategien* (*Heidelberger Jahrbücher* 52), Heidelberg: Springer 2008.

that time in Medieval Studies. It was in connection with that grant application that I really started reading the theoretical literature on emotions in history.

For me, the impetus for the study of emotions was basically given by texts, by inscriptions. Inscriptions are not "my theory", but they did trigger my interest in emotions, leading me to the study of theoretical works. As regards theory, my position has always been that theory is important when it helps us understand something that we wouldn't have understood without theory. I am not someone who starts his work by choosing a theoretical framework; instead, I try to produce the theoretical framework suitable for my subject. I do not always succeed in this enterprise, and sometimes it's just a minor contribution. I think that my minor contribution to the study of emotions in history is the concept not of 'emotional communities' (in the plural), as defined by Barbara Rosenwein, but 'emotional community' (in the singular), that is, the *ad hoc* creation of shared emotions in certain situations. I study emotional community basically through the epigraphic material and other documentary sources.

The second important thing in my work, is my effort to try to understand – not always successfully – the research of the neurosciences on how the brain works. When I was discussing my project with a psychologist in Berlin – it was around 2010, when scientists were talking about the *amygdala* and its importance for emotions –, he told me that in 10 years things may change. So, what neuroscientists discuss in one day is not necessarily written in stone; it may be revised. And this was a warning for me not to take every idea proposed by the neuroscientists for granted, but to use the information provided by scientific and psychological discussions as an inspiration and trigger for questions and thoughts appropriate for historical studies. This is what I have gained from neuroscientific literature, whether this is the work of Raymond Dolan or of Joseph LeDoux; both of them have influenced the way that I see how emotions work. This doesn't necessarily mean that I adopt their theories without limitations, or even that I understand all the details of their theoretical work. But it has been a very important influence on my work.

For me, cognitive studies and the study of emotions are intrinsically connected with the study of texts, because the study of texts is the window for our understanding of the ancient world. We do not have a time machine (yet) that would allow us to walk in the streets of Classical Athens and ask the Athenians what they think about the Peloponnesian War or the plague in 430 BCE. What we have are texts, and texts are filtered. This is why, for me, the study of verbal communication is so important: for instance, the use of metaphors, repetition, the use of what I call 'acoustic signals', that is, words that in particular situations and in particular historical periods trigger specific emotions. The selection of vocabulary in verbal communication is the most important aspect in the interpretation of historical sources, and it is impossible to study this, without a cognitive approach. We cannot directly talk to people; we cannot conduct experiments; we cannot conduct interviews; all this is important for cognitive studies. But what we can do is this: when we have a critical mass of texts, we can compare them and see how linguistic expression may give us clues perhaps not about what people felt, but about the factors that influenced the way people speak about their emotions.

This is the main difference between cognitive science and the work of an ancient historian. I do not believe that as a historian I am in a position to really understand what people had felt; but what I can study are the parameters that influence the way emotions are controlled, intensified, expressed, manipulated, described, and so on. And this is, I think, an important difference between the work of cognitive science and the work of a historian.

Is a 'cognitive turn' something en vogue or is it something more profound, which might have an influence on different levels of interpretation?
I think that in Ancient Studies, in any form that they take – whether this is philology, history, archaeology, linguistics, and so on – the 'cognitive turn' is not a temporary trend, but something that will have a sustainable influence on the way we conduct our research.

What I have discovered in my work and also try to communicate to others is the fact that historians – whether they are historians of political history, social history or religion, or even historians of art, literature, or philosophy –, cannot approach their sources without trying to take into consideration how emotions have shaped them. This is why I think that that the interest in emotions and cognition is not a temporary 'turn', but a path that will be followed; it will be a methodological requirement for the future of Ancient Studies, with lasting influence.

We need to put aside all the reservations that people have had, for many years, to approach something that cannot be studied through interviews or discussions with real, living human beings, but can only be approached through the study of texts and material evidence. For me, the cognitive approach to ancient history is a very important methodological matter. I don't think that in historical studies this methodological approach has had yet reached the diffusion and the importance that it deserves. Historical studies are still very hesitant in using cognitive approaches for the understanding of phenomena, and this, especially true in the study of political history, but to a large extent, also on the study of social, legal, or economic history.

Let me give you just one example. Let's take, for instance, Diocletian's price edict, which is one of the longest inscriptions of antiquity, and which determines the highest price of products (301 CE). When we look at developments in the stock exchange market in our time, we read in the news that these developments are determined by fear, hope, anxiety, and so on, that is, by emotions. And yet, we do not attempt to understand the economic developments in antiquity by taking into consideration such elementary things as emotions. And this despite the fact that many developments in the ancient economy were intrinsically connected with emotions. I don't mean to say that to understand the role of emotions in ancient economic developments is an easy task; it is not. But if historians were only to do the easy things, then ancient history would be a terribly boring discipline, incapable of producing any results that make us think.

So, it is my conviction that in every aspect of historical studies emotions need to be one of the components that form the basis for the analysis of both sources and historical phenomena. Therefore, the 'cognitive turn' is one of the 'turns' with a lasting influence in classical studies such as, for instance, the 'linguistic turn', or the turn towards studies of gender and sexuality. The interest in gender studies first started as a trend in the 1970s, became very popular in the 1980s, and nowadays, it is no longer a trend or a 'turn', but a more or less self-evident component of the study of antiquity. You cannot ascertain aspects of ancient history and classical studies without taking into consideration gender and sexuality; gender has now become an integral part of the way we look at the antiquity.

I think that cognition and emotion are something similar. We can see that whole areas of relevant research have been underdeveloped for many years. For instance, the study of the senses, such as the sound. Taste is surely less easy to study. But, for instance, sound in religion and politics, i.e. the role of acclamations and loud cries in gatherings or in the assembly, is both a well attested phenomenon in documentary and literary sources and an important component of political life. These are important issues, a by-product, so to say, of the cognitive turn. The interest in the history of the senses is an additional reason for me to think that the cognitive turn has come to stay and to allow us to discover unexplored areas that still need research.

Can ancient sources be somehow of use for cognitivists and for cognitive research?
Usually, we regard Ancient Studies as an importer, and not an exporter of theory. Classicists are expected to "import", e.g., theoretical models from literary theory, from anthropology, from sociology, from economic theory, from cognitive science and so on. The question is, what do we give back? And how do we give it? I am not very happy with the way that the discussion between the neurosciences, in general, and the humanities have been conducted in the past. There have been efforts for a dialogue, for instance, through the organization of conferences. I attended such a conference in New York, in 2012. For me, it was a rather disappointing experience, because it was a conference of parallel monologues; that is, scholars

who represented the humanities essentially talked to other scholars who represented the humanities. Every now and then there was some question from neuroscientists to Classicists and vice versa. What the representatives of neurosciences presented was mainly a discourse with other neuroscientists who study emotions, basically disagreeing on a generally acceptable definition of emotions.

I don't have a recipe for a better dialogue between Classics and the neurosciences – and admittedly, there have been successful collaborations, e. g., concerning traumatic experiences in war. What I have tried to do, whenever I was asked by neuroscientists to make a contribution, was to offer the perspective of a historian. I did it, for instance, in an article that I wrote for *Current Opinion of Behavioural Sciences*.[468] I offered my response as an Ancient Historian to the perception of emotions as survival circuits or survival mechanisms, which is an influential theory about how we define emotions. And I think that I was able to comment on the findings of this theory from the perspective of a historian through examples that I had collected in my study of ancient sources. Actually, I was impressed by the similarity of their findings and mine. I mean that if we look at how societies operate, emotions are a sort of a survival mechanism both of a community and of an individual. For instance, if you do not feel indignation, you will be the victim of injustice. If you do not know fear, you will expose yourself to dangers. If you do not show love and affection, you endanger the continuation of the species – I mean, the love of parents for their children and so on. If you do not feel disgust, you will expose yourself to pathogens. I could go on listing emotions and explaining how they contribute to the survival both of individuals and of societies. The Spartan society would not have survived from the Archaic to the Hellenistic period without the emotion of fear, because it was exposed to the threat of revolts of the dependent population.

So this is, I think, a way we can have a dialogue. One does not need to completely understand the methods and procedures that neuroscientists apply in order to formulate a hypothesis. What one needs to understand is the questions that drive their research and see whether the same questions can be asked in connection with the materials that we have as ancient historians, philologists and so on, and to try to provide some answers.

Another example, that I often mention in my publications, is how my work was influenced by brain imaging. It was just a sentence that I had read in a paper published by Raymond Dolan in *Science*,[469] in which he discussed the inter-

---

[468] A. Chaniotis, The Social Construction of Emotion: A View from Ancient Greece, *Current Opinion in Behavioral Sciences* 24, 2018, 56–61.
[469] R. J. Dolan, "Emotion, Cognition, and Behavior", *Science* 298, 2002, 1191–1194.

dependence that exists between attention, emotion, memory, and decision making, or belief. And this is precisely what I see in my sources, especially in inscriptions, but also in other types of material evidence. An inscription attracts your attention, especially if it is decorated with an image; then you read the text, which commemorates something – the reason for which an epitaph, a dedication, or a decree was written. This triggers the memory of certain events – for instance, divine punishment –, let's say the fact that thunder had killed a sinner and so on. Remembrance arouses emotions: the emotion of fear for divine wrath or, if you read, for instance, a healing miracle, the emotion of hope. "If God has healed that person, why shouldn't he heal me?" Finally, this contributes to something that one may describe, depending on the situation, as faith, belief, attitude, ideology, values, approach to life, or decision making.

A brief remark of Raymond Dolan that was based on what he has been researching with brain imaging, allowed me to clearly see a phenomenon that otherwise I might not have noticed. What he actually said is that it cannot be understood yet, how emotion contributes to belief.[470] I think that my material can provide the answer to this particular specific question of how the interplay of attention, memory, and emotion contribute to belief and faith. I wouldn't have studied this material if I hadn't read this remark by Dolan. So, I think that possibilities for a cooperation between cognitive scientists and representatives of the humanities exist, when they address the same questions from their perspective and with the material that they best understand. I wouldn't expect a neuroscientist to understand my sources, and a neuroscientist cannot expect from me to understand the methods that they apply. But asking the same questions can create a common ground for both approaches.

---

[470] "Emotion exerts a powerful influence on reason and, in ways neither understood nor systematically researched, contributes to the fixation of belief".

5.3 Douglas Cairns

Douglas Cairns. Interview via zoom, 13th February 2023

I got the impression that you were surprised that I invited you to take part in a study on cognitive classics, since you think that you have been dealing with emotions for so many years. Would you like to comment on this?

I have over the years found out a bit more about cognitive approaches to classical texts and especially a bit more about 4E cognition in general. I guess I was semi-consciously aware of some of these issues, and had come to some kind of position on some of them without much of a theoretical basis, but my work was originally on emotion, and I have continued to work on emotion. That's by no means the sum total of human cognition, and it's by no means the sum total of areas in which cognitive approaches have been valuable so far. There are lots of people who do what I would see as much more readily accessible and identifiable forms of cognitive humanities, in areas such as narratology, the uses of memory or aesthetics, for example, whereas I stay pretty much firmly within what I know best, which is emotions.

But if you do work in emotions, and you are aware of cognitive approaches to emotions, or indeed to other phenomena, you begin to see how all of the various strands of especially 4E cognitive theory begin to be helpful. You begin to see with certain limitations and restrictions how they tend to blend into each other – certainly embeddedness and embodiedness interact very closely with each other. From there, you can make a fairly short step towards enactive approaches. The one that maybe stands out as different is extended cognition, or at least some versions of extended cognition, that some people have found more difficult to apply to emotions. Many aspects of cognitive approaches shade into each other when you begin to think about emotions, and you find yourself using all these approaches

– and in fact not really clearly distinguishing between any of them or any of the possible domains in which they might be significant.

What does the word 'cognitive' mean in the context of classics?
There are differing accounts of what cognition means and of what counts as 'cognitive'. There are very narrow accounts and there are broader and much more inclusive accounts. And part of it depends on which background you're coming from, which approaches and methods you favour, and how well those approaches and methods work for you. So I take an inclusive approach. I would say I'm a 'second generation' cognitivist. So I'm not one of these people who thinks of it all in terms of a computing model of the mind, an input-output processing model of the mind.

And I've certainly moved on from the very narrow definition of cognitivism, as it first existed in emotion studies – and still exists to some extent in emotion studies – where people say emotions are cognitive and mean by that that they involve judgments. 'Cognitive' is much more than that. I'm thinking of the very narrow, so-called cognitivist approach to emotion that actually predates modern cognitivism, the kind of thing you get in Martha Nussbaum and Robert Solomon, and others, where they just mean that emotions are judgments, that they involve evaluations of states of affairs. But that's a very narrow approach to what 'cognitive' might mean, what cognitivism might be.

I think we need to go back to the Latin. *Cognoscere* means getting information about the world, in order to acquire knowledge of the world. It's about getting to know things. So it's really about what the enactivists call sense-making. Obviously, everything we do, in that sense, if we're aware of it and we're using it to make sense of our environment – and even if we're using it to make sense of that part of our environment that's constructed by ancient writings and artefacts and the evidence that survives from the ancient world – all of that is cognitive. And all of the things that we study that survive from the ancient world, they are cognitive too – they're all ways in which the ancients have left traces of how they made sense of the world. So it's all about that very broad type of cognition, I think. And therefore any branch of classics can be cognitive, and any of the activities and spheres of activity that you might study in the ancient world – like narrative, like drama, like technology, like medicine, like the use of language – that's all about cognition as well. Once you get into it, I think there's no getting away from it. There's no escaping it. It is absolutely everything, everywhere.

Back to what the enactivists call 'sense-making': Would you now call 'enactive' and 'cognitive' synonyms?
For enactivists the way that organisms live is crucial – it's a very biological approach; it's an ecological approach to cognition. And in fact extended mind theo-

rists like Andy Clark accuse enactivists of bio-chauvinism because they don't make enough of artefacts and technology, in his view. But for the enactivists themselves, the way that the organism reacts to, interacts with, and makes use of the feedback from its actions and the environment in order to organize itself, that's cognition, and that's what enactivism is all about. So for *them*, all cognition is enactive; but I don't think that's necessarily the case for the exponents of the other branches of 4E cognition.

For example, if you follow the extended view, cognition is defined by what happens in the brain, and the condition for cognition in other parts of the organism and the environment, including external physical objects (and so on), is that those things should enable processes to go ahead that might otherwise happen in the brain. So it has a very internalist, mentalist definition of what cognition is – it's just that, under certain circumstances, it finds those processes elsewhere.

Is a 'cognitive turn' something en vogue or is it something more profound, which might have an influence on our reading?
No, I think it is more than that. Obviously, there are interpretative methodological trends. There are lots of approaches that compete with cognitive approaches. There are lots of traditional approaches that carry on much as though nothing had ever happened in any other theoretical discipline or sub-discipline at all. And I guess that's always going to be the way it is. So, I mean, I guess it would be too optimistic to imagine that the cognitive approaches are ever going to carry the board to the extent that everyone recognizes that they're not just desirable, but essential.

But equally, I think we're only at the beginning. If this goes the way I think it should go, then everyone will have to realize – whether they use cognitive approaches or what they would define as cognitive approaches themselves or not – that these approaches are making a difference, and they need to know what difference they're making. So I think it's not just a fad. But at the same time, you could say that these are probably stylistic and personality differences between individuals. So some people approach, let's say, Classical Studies, or whatever discipline, humanities discipline, it is that they're involved in, like golf. So you've got a bag, and you've got lots of clubs in it, and you use lots of different clubs for different kinds of shots. Or maybe it's even more like playing different sports on different days, rather than having different clubs for different shots. There are people who are eclectic in their use of methods and theories.

From my point of view, it's not one theory among many. So I use it because I've not just found the utility of it, as the years have gone by, but because I've begun to see, I think, how it connects up. And because I think I was always interested in what classics had to offer me as an individual and us as moderns, as denizens of contemporary societies. So right from the very beginning, when I first started learning Latin and Greek in secondary school, it was what it did for me that I was interested in; it was what I was then able to do, because I'd studied Latin and Greek, that really excited me. For example, I understood so much more about language; I understood so much more about the elevated discourse of a variety of different disciplines, from practical politics to more theoretical subjects. And so you're bootstrapping yourself there into new ways of thinking on the basis of the disciplines you're studying and the methods you're using to study them, and you're learning something about yourself.

When I got into my PhD and started doing stuff about honour and shame, the thing that really excited me about it was that it didn't have to be about the Greeks. One of the exciting things about it was that people were applying to the Greeks generalizations that had been drawn from other societies – so there was a strong comparative element. And I think, in fact, there always is a strong comparative element, even if we don't engage fundamentally in explicit comparativism. So even if we don't say here are the Greeks and here are the Japanese, and here are the Finns, and here are the Touareg, and all the rest of it; even if we just say 'here are the Greeks', we're never just saying 'here are the Greeks'. We're always saying: here are the Greeks and here are we. None of us is an ancient Greek; none of us is an ancient Roman. There's got to be a comparative element involved when we study these ancient societies, or when we study any other society – either we are doing it unconsciously, not activating our own cultural background and assumptions, or, better, we do it consciously and do activate our cultural background and assumptions and we interrogate them too, and we use the comparison, the comparative perspective that we get from the other culture, to interrogate our own culture, and vice versa. So we activate what conditions our thinking, and we use that to interrogate ancient Greek thinking. And I think that's a kind of cognitive approach in its own right.

I came relatively late to the work of Kahneman and Tversky, through Kahneman's book *Thinking, Fast and Slow*. But when you look at that, you see what a difference comparison makes. People make better decisions when they compare *this* with *that*, rather than when they just go for *this*. That's the fast version of it – oh, that sounds good! I'll do that! But if you say, what about this in comparison with that? If you put two things in explicit relation to each other, you begin to see what's characteristic of each one in the light of the other. So that's the kind of process of cognition I think we go through, or we should go through when we think about ancient societies.

And then you begin to think, how does this mode of approaching information and processing information in the hope of acquiring some kind of knowledge about the world, whether ancient or modern, how does that square with the way that *they* [sc. the ancient Greeks and Romans] did it? How did they process their information about the environments that they moved in and the worlds they lived in? And how did they represent that in their artefacts, material culture, and writing? So, for these reasons, I think we are deeply embedded or we should be deeply embedded in a cognitive approach. And therefore, it's not something that you can just leave in the bag, like one of the golf clubs – it's the golf club that you've always got to choose. It's an all-purpose golf club for everything.

Methodological quibbles: to what extent can we use modern cognitive categories for ancient societies?
I have heard people questioning that. These are people who think, paradoxically, that you can obtain a completely emic perspective on the ancient world: that the only thing you can do, or the only thing you should do, is think of the material in ancient terms. We can't do that. Even when we are working with emic categories, and we're trying to understand what those categories are and how they operate, and how the ancients used them to make sense of their worlds, you're never anyone else, you're always yourself. You can never wholly inhabit the perspective of another individual, not in everyday interaction in the here and now in the modern world, and you certainly can't do it with regard to people who lived in societies very different and distant in time and space.

So, we can't inhabit their perspectives; we can only activate our perspectives on their perspectives. And there's always got to be that element of duality and dialogue from a certain distance – there's always a distance between us and them. So, we can't say, cast out theory, and just approach these texts and artefacts in some kind of unmediated way. That is a very naive way of thinking of it. It's also a theory in its own right: there's no one who comes to anything, any form of study, without some kind of theory. It's just that some of the theories are better than others, and some of them are more explicit than others too. So, it's important to get them out there. If there are theories that are – at least on the face of it, until you begin to interrogate them – holding their own, proving to be robust, standing up against criticism, proving to be useful and enlightening when applied to other contexts, then there's every chance that they will be useful when we apply them to ancient contexts as well.

We are not saying that everything is universal; we're not saying that you can reduce the mentalities of different societies to common terms which are translatable and explicable in the terms of another culture. But I think we are assuming that there's something that imposes some kind of constraint, maybe with a very wide norm of reaction in which a variety of different reflexes are possible, but still, nonetheless, imposing some kind of constraint on what can be said, and what can be thought, in terms of the way that we are located in the world as physical organisms, and the way that our brains make sense of the world and the way that our brains are moulded by culture, and create culture, in interaction with our bodies, with other people, and with the environment.

So I'm not saying the circumstances between cultures are inevitably closely comparable, but at some kind of level, and in some kind of degree, there are fairly basic constraints that make us all representatives of the same broad type, the same species that has approached the world in at least basically, rudimentarily similar terms.

For me, the proof of the pudding is in the eating. Has any of this worked? I would say it has. Take, for example, all the good work that's been done on the topic of *enargeia* in ancient texts. That's a significant emic term. It's a term that the ancients use to talk about a particular quality that texts and visual artefacts may have. How do we understand it? Well, the headline way of understanding it [sc. in ancient sources] tends to be in terms of pictorialism and representationalism. You get all of this stuff about putting things before the eyes and so on, both in Greek and in Latin. And then you look at the examples that are cited as good examples of this phenomenon, and you look at what is being done there, and it seems that, in fact, it's not about painting mental pictures at all – it's about placing human beings in situations in which they react to circumstances in their environment, in ways that are fundamentally accessible to us as human beings who might react in similar ways in circumstances of that sort. And so it tends not to be a static picture of lots of details, painted in very sort of flat terms, painted in static terms, but something that is full of action, and full of features of the environment, natural or social, with which the individuals in the narrative interact, in ways in which, in principle, we could also interact. So it's full of affordances for action.

The best example I can think of is one that clearly is a textbook case of *enargeia*, and the operation of *phantasia*, and all that. And that's the description of the cannibal feast of Mary in Flavius Josephus' *Jewish War*, Book 6. Mary, having been reduced to starvation by the guards during the siege of Jerusalem, cooks and eats her own son as a way of getting revenge on the guards. They smell the cooking; they would like to have some of the meat; but they come and find that she's killed her son and cooked him and eaten him. They are completely horrified. She is completely triumphant. They tell people, and so they (the primary internal audience) tell a story to a secondary internal audience. And that internal audience, the narrator says, put this scene before their eyes as if they were the ones that had done it. So a key term of what *enargeia* is is activated; it's made clear that we're talking about *enargeia* now. And yet that's not about them being Mary; it's not about them imagining what Mary feels like, because Mary is triumphant. She's gone mad, because of the dire straits that she's been forced to exist in. So, in some sense, they put themselves in that position, as if they were confronted with doing a deed of this kind. And yet, they're still themselves; they're still seeing it from their own perspective. It's not from Mary's perspective at all. It's not in any way empathy or (German) *Empathie*. But it is *Einfühlung*: it's the old [Romantic] notion of *Einfühlung* – they feel themselves into that scene as though they were there. So the sense in which this is *sub oculis subiectio* (or πρὸ ὀμμάτων τίθεσθαι) isn't just that you visualize it like a picture; rather, it's as if you go there, you get into it, you get involved as though you were actually taking part. And that's because of the way that the narrative is constructed not in terms of visuality, but in terms of action and affordances for action, things that you might be able to manipulate, things that you might do, things to which you might respond.

So that little cue about the reaction of the secondary internal audience is a cue for us, the external audience, that we should be responding in a certain way. You can think of that in cognitive terms, in terms of the way that there are prompts and cues, both in the world and in texts, that predispose you to respond in certain ways, that prime you to respond in a particular way. Just as the internal audience of the guards' tale were drawn in, by the description of what Mary had done, and they put themselves there as though they were confronted with doing that thing as well, so are we. So we've got one primary internal audience focusing on this deed, and one secondary one, and these focus our attention as external audience, even as our own attention remains focused on the deed itself. We've got various forms of what Noël Carroll calls criterial pre-focusing taking place. And then we're beginning to understand how a text like this is constructed, and how it achieves its effects. And I think, basically, we're seeing that it does achieve those effects by exploiting the active potential of our cognitive apparatus.

So here, modern cognitive approaches help us understand ancient texts, but they also help us understand ancient theory. We could take the ancient descriptions of *enargeia* at face value – we could say it's all about 'visualizations' or about painting mental pictures, the kind that Plato talks about in the *Philebus*, for example. And yet when you look at what they actually do, it's not about painting mental pictures at all. It's all about depicting characters in action, in scene, in ways that we can relate to. And so it's precisely what's going on in the circumstances that first gave rise to the older German notion of *Einfühlung*, the idea that you put a figure in the landscape, so that the external viewer of the painting of the landscape has something to latch on to, something that puts them there, as if they could move through this space as well.

Metaphor (as Aristotle observes) also makes things vivid – it makes things *enarges*. And part of that is that it gives you these more primary things, these more concrete and physical and interactive things, to latch on to. So in particular, in my field, when it is about emotion, the great thing about emotion metaphor, I think, is that we can get close to what ancient subjects experienced, because they tell us, and they tell us in metaphor, and the metaphors that they use to tell us about these experiences are above all designed to tell us what they felt like. They're above all phenomenological. They're experiential. So clearly, they're not private, internal, subjective experiences, but they still represent first-person subjective experience, insofar as it's understood intersubjectively in language, intersubjectively in a shared culture. In a recent piece in the *London Review of Books*, for example, Terry Eagleton points out that because we're linguistic creatures, it's not true that we have no access to the inner lives and mental states of other people. Because other people can tell us. And they can do other interesting things with language that give us some kind of access to their thought processes, their feelings, and so on, including not what it actually felt like, but what it's supposed to feel like to be in a particular affective state. That is a way in which our access to each other as people living in the here and now is no different from our access to the ancient Greeks.

More fundamentally, other-understanding can be a matter of perception. Again, the phenomenological tradition tells us that we can directly perceive other people's states of mind, at least sometimes. Sometimes people don't hide their thoughts and feelings. Sometimes they're immediate – as Wittgenstein says, just try to imagine that that person is not in pain. It is impossible if they're actually showing you spontaneous signs of, say, physical pain. You can see people's emotions in their faces and their bodies. And that's, of course, a big premise of what we might call pre-cognitive modern emotion research too – we do see emotions in the body and in the face. But you don't always: some people are very good at concealing them. Some people will tell you the opposite of what they're actually feeling. Some people tell you all kinds of lies. And so when perception gives out, what we rely on is narrative. One of the great things about the cognitive approaches is that they've been so useful for narrative, for narratology. And that's useful because – well, I don't want to say that what other people study is narrative, but certainly what I study, in terms of emotion, is narrative. I'm attracted by the idea that self-understanding is narrative in form. So the metaphor of the self is just a long-term story that we tell ourselves about persistence, through time, in a narrative shape. And equally our understanding of others is typically narrative in form as well. It is about the context in which their actions have taken place, the antecedent causes of those actions, how those causes may have influenced them, how they process them, what they felt in the light of these circumstances, and what they do as a result. It is a sequential event-structure type of narrative. And of course, those things then get into actual narratives – literary narratives, Homeric narratives, and historiographical narratives. So these things are narratival in mode to start with, and they lend themselves to representation and to reconstitution in narratives.

And the thing is, we have loads of narratives of the ancient world. So we can go back to Homer and get rich information about how people behave in context, in the light of certain events in their lives, such as the loss of a companion or an insult. We can see them using their own vocabulary to process these experiences. We can see them using their own metaphors to process them as well. We can see them talking about anger as something that's sweeter than honey and rises like smoke in your breast, and so on. And we get a sense of what it's supposed to feel like for someone in that situation to experience that emotion. These are metaphors of a recurrent and familiar type that continues to exist.

Can ancient sources be somehow of use for cognitivists and for cognitive research?
In some cases, the rich data of the classical world give us a lot to work on. There are single sources like Homer that are incredibly rich in themselves. You could spend your whole life just going back to Homer for whatever it was you were interested in, in cognitive terms or in other terms. I'm interested in emotion, and I still go back to Homer all the time and still find more every time I do so. When I started my PhD, and I got interested in trying to figure out what *aidōs* was, one of the things that struck me – and of course one of the things that people find difficult about the concept – is that the stock translations of *aideomai* are "I feel shame" and "I respect". So how are "I feel shame" and "I respect" related? Well, they're related in ways that are independent of the conceptualization of the Greek notion of *aidōs*, because they are facts of social interaction as it inevitably manifests itself. If we're dealing with interaction, rather than just action, then it's going to involve these two-way negotiations of how I'm responding to the other person's self-representation and how I'm representing myself for their response. I'm constantly monitoring how they're presenting themselves and how I'm dealing with it, and how that impinges on my self-representation and how they're dealing with it. We're constantly looking back and forward – at ourselves, how am I doing, and at the other, how are they doing?

And again, people have noticed this, people like Erving Goffman in particular – long before the so-called cognitive turn. And they're right – these are genuine features of social interaction. And they are also features of social interaction that bring home to us how to this metaphor of the self, this narrative of the self, isn't a narrative that we write all by ourselves. Other people write part of it too, and we do the same for them. What you are isn't just what you would like to be (for example, when you're sitting in the bathtub); at some stage, you've got to get out of the bathtub, into the world, and then what you are isn't entirely up to you – you paint some of the picture, but other people colour in the rest of it. They have a role too in constituting your identity, your social roles, your place in society, and – fundamentally – what you are. And to a large extent, our existence is as difficult as it is because we are not in charge of these things, but – to some extent at least – at the mercy of other people's constructions, and the best we can do is to influence them, to the best of our ability.

I started thinking about these things before I came across any cognitive psychology or even social psychology to any great extent. But when you do know the social psychology and the cognitive psychology, it just takes on a completely different significance. And then, for example, I have noticed recently, in Book 2 of Aristotle's *Rhetoric*, where he's talking about the emotions, how, first of all, he presents them in narrative terms. He breaks up the elements of the narrative – those before whom you feel this emotion, the things about which you feel this emotion, the targets of this emotion. He talks about the elements of a narrative separately, but they come together to form a scenario, so that the emotion, whatever it is (let's say anger), turns out to be a short story, about eliciting conditions, how you feel when you experience it, and then what you do as a result of it.

And then some of these, in fact, are themselves sub-emotions. So, part of the emotion of anger is the desire for retaliation, and part of that involves *elpis*, the expectation or hope of retaliation one day. And some of that involves feeling pleasure *now*, because you're thinking, if I get my revenge, that will be great, and you feel actually pleased in the moment, and not just in the future when you achieve the actual revenge. So, there's a little scenario, but some of it is not just about inert features of the world, but about what other people have thought of you, and how what they think of you matches what you think of yourself, often in the light of what you think of others. A lot of the emotions in *Rhetoric* 2 are about what we think they think about us, given what we think about them. It's enormously embedded, and it all involves whatever you want to call it – other understanding, social cognition or, as some people call it, theory of mind – whatever. But the point is, you can't approach these issues without using the best theories and approaches to those phenomena, those cognitive phenomena, in your own society and in your own scientific context. We need to draw on the other scientific disciplines in order to make sense of these things now, and in principle the data that we have from the ancient world lend themselves to being understood in those terms, using the same tools and techniques.

You mentioned the question of materiality. This is an interesting issue, I think. Just as there's an 'affective turn' that has very little to do with the kind of thing I'm interested in and very little to do with more scientific emotion studies, equally there is a 'material turn' that has very little to do with cognitivism, I think. There is the whole 'thing theory' approach, in which you're using what are sometimes called post-humanist approaches to these things. The idea is that it involves an unduly anthropocentric perspective to see things and objects as things that we manipulate and use to extend our own cognitive processes. So, this is an approach that de-centres the human and then wants to argue that things in themselves have agency. And well, I just don't buy that. One of the fundamental cognitive distinctions that human beings make – and I think any other mammal like ourselves is also going to have to make – is a distinction between agents and objects. We just *do* categorically distinguish between agents and objects. Objects can be endowed with agency, but only by other agents. My prime example here would be the well-known Heider and Simmel animation, where you have the three geometric shapes, and if you just show them on a plane surface, without moving, they're just geometric shapes. If you were to show them ricocheting off each other, they would still be geometric shapes and would be treated as objects. But if you make the big square look like a house with a door that opens and make the big triangle guard the door and then try to come between the small triangle and the circle (and so on), then they all begin to – as we would say – interact with each other and we begin to interpret them as agents, because they have been manipulated to behave in those ways by human agents. In the experiment, they are credited with agency by the experimental subjects (ourselves) because they are behaving *as if* they were agents. So, we can do that – by ontological metaphor, for example, by personification, we can turn things into agents; but they're not agents as such. It takes a human mind to do that.

So, you can take things or objects and you can build them into systems at the heart of which is a human being. Clothes, for instance, are a really good example when it comes to the expression of emotions. So that raises the question, can we say that extended cognition exists also in the case of emotions? I think in some ways that might be the wrong question. It involves a presupposition that there will be something out there in the world, in an object or in the environment, that replicates the kind of thing that might go on in the brain. But that may be to start from the wrong premise, because emotions just are so extended anyway – they involve so many features that aren't in the head or in the body that to treat them in that way, and to look for things out there in the world that mirror what's going on internally in the organism might be the wrong approach.

But emotions certainly are extended using features of the world. There are things like clothes, or things like your furniture, or paintings on your wall, or the décor of your room, where what you're doing is cognitive niche construction – you are setting things up in your environment, creating an environment in order to feel a certain way. And you do that when you pour yourself a glass of wine as well. These are all props for emotional experience, where we're creating an environment to have an affective experience of a certain sort. And equally, if we think of emotions as conditioned by some kind of evaluation or appraisal of an object, an intentional object in the world, then that appraisal could come from us, or it could come from someone else. It could be someone else who supplies the crucial trigger that makes you feel the emotion rather than something that you come up with, entirely spontaneously, by yourself. So another person may be the appraiser. And of course, you would have then to appraise their appraisal, but still, that's then a form of participatory, interactive sensemaking that's going on.

Conclusion: Off to new shores?

How can cognitive insights inform our understanding of ancient texts and of the broader of ancient world? It has long been debated whether the last millennia have been too short an evolutionary period for human cognition to have changed significantly.[471] In other words, can today's knowledge of the human mind be applied not only to the study of different world cultures, but also to the understanding of history as a whole.

The topics and issues outlined here by no means claim to cover the entire range of cognitive approaches to the interpretation of ancient sources. But it is time to take stock of much that has been done so far and to get an idea of the extent to which the cognitive sciences can be helpful to and benefit from collaboration with the classics. This collaboration is important not only because it applies contemporary theories to ancient sources, or because it combines literary, linguistic and historical-archaeological methods with the sciences of cognition and emotion, but also because it makes use of ancient thought to challenge modern presuppositions. Classical scholars can provide important insights for cognitive science research by discussing when, where and how different processes might have varied and changed. It seems that the perspective of cognitive science contributes to a better interdisciplinary understanding of the ancient world as a whole, to mutual communication between these disciplines and sub-disciplines, and to bridging the inevitable gaps and rifts between them.

Studies in cognitive science have transformed the understanding of human thought, and their importance for historical research can no longer be overlooked. Cognitive classics could thus be defined as the study of how people in the past used their thinking skills to understand and orient themselves and the world around them, and conversely, how the environment influenced their thinking. Cognitive classics thus represent a synthesis and symbiosis between the techniques and methods of the study of history and the concepts of cognitive science in order to explain and understand human behaviour, thought and communication throughout history. Rather than anachronistically applying modern thinking to ancient material, the most fruitful results are achieved when cognitive science is used as a means of highlighting some intriguing facets of the ancient sources. The relationship between history, literature and cognition is seen as the interaction of the mind with the environments of time and place. Thus, the historical record can be used to explore specific capacities of cognition in interacting with the world, such

---

[471] On the debates, see above p. 29–30.

as the capacities of language, thought, memory, space, and matter.[472] The study of Greek and Roman texts in terms of memory, imagination and emotion brings together classical and cognitive studies. Cognitive classics can provide a richer insight into how – and not just what – humans have thought, and how the brain has interacted with its environment.

The non-verbal evidence of ancient peoples' thoughts, feelings, reactions, behaviours, habits, and practices is not something to which we have unlimited access. We should not assume that what is natural or obvious to us was also so the Greeks or the Romans, and this means that many types of behaviour are culturally specific, although may also be true that some aspects of body language are universal and cross-cultural.[473] Sometimes there is evidence to suggest that a certain gesture, ritual, or practice is common in different cultures or forms of society. This does not mean that these gestures, rituals, or practices correspond to what we know from ancient texts or archaeological material, even if they seem very familiar. Evidence from material and textual sources, but also from descriptive and thus imaginative sources, is needed to avoid biased assumptions and to establish a link with ancient thought and perception.

As cognitive theory contributes to ongoing research into cultural evolution, history provides important data on how our distant ancestors gradually improved their cognitive skills and techniques thousands of years ago.[474] For example, studies in anthropology and psychology have shown that people around the world form associations with natural objects – including other people, plants, animals, and artefacts – from a very young age. Since a culture is made up of different concepts and ideologies, we should ask how these concepts have been transmitted between people over time. A kind of epidemiological view of culture is helpful.[475] Just as the physical body is prone to disease, the human mind is prone to belief. From this perspective, some approaches will be more effective than others in reaching out to society and capturing people's attention.

One of the achievements of cognitive approaches is to ask new questions about much discussed topics or to return to questions that were asked in the past but

---

[472] On 'cognitive history' cf. Atran 1990, Harré 2002, Lawson 2004, Heintz 2004, Frith 2007, Heintz 2011, Dunér 2011, Martin and Sørensen 2011, Xygalatas 2014, Dasgupta 2016, Sutton and Keene 2017. See also *Journal of Cognitive Historiography* https://journal.equinoxpub.com/JCH, last access June 3rd 2024.

[473] See Cairns and Nelis 2017b, 14.

[474] See above p. 33–39, 86–97, 131–138 (David Konstan), 139–144 (Angelos Chaniotis), 146–156 (Douglas Cairns). See also Dunér and Ahlberger 2019 and especially Dunér 2019.

[475] See Trostle 2005, 21–41 (chapter "The Origins of an Integrated Approach in Anthropology and Epidemiology").

then abandoned as unanswerable. Hypotheses that are universal rather than specific to particular societies are generated by such an access to ancient material.[476] There is a growing tendency to consider ancient material objects not only as evidence for the representation of a particular practice or experience, but also in their broader original setting, as objects that functioned in particular geographical and physical environments.[477] Statues, for example, are not only a vehicle for the expression of feelings, but can also be an expression of devotion and a trigger for certain reactions. Epigraphic texts, dedications, the geographical and architectural location and arrangement of archaeological sites in general help to create a common ground and space for experience and performance, a place for the cognitive realisation on which all experience depends. A wide variety of ancient contexts and sources allow literary, epigraphic, visual, and archaeological evidence to be studied from the perspective of human experience and integrated into our experience, taking into account the complexity, multimodality and multicausality of human life. This raises new questions and develops new insights into the physical, emotional and cognitive aspects of the study of antiquity.[478]

The 'second generation' of cognitive scientists argue that the 'cognitive' is to a greater extent than previously thought 'enactive': a reaction to the cognitivism of thirty years ago, initiated then by the concept of the 'embodied mind'. This reaction has been advocated by Shaun Gallagher, Dan Zahavi, Alva Noë and Daniel Hutto, among others.[479] It emphasised the embodied nature of the mind and the fluid connections between the brain and its immediate environment. Drawing on the phenomenological work of Edmund Husserl, Martin Heidegger and especially Maurice Merleau-Ponty, enactivists use the four *E*'s discussed above to describe the mind: *embodied, embedded, enactive* and *extended*.[480]

Conceived as a stocktaking in different fields of ancient studies, this book aims to pose a question which branches of cognitive research are particularly favoured or have proved particularly fruitful when applied to ancient material, and which branches of the classics are particularly involved in such interaction. Both diachronic and synchronic engagement with different genres and media in philology,

---

[476] On the question and related debates about the applicability of 'universal' human presuppositions to particular societies, especially to societies distant in time such as those of antiquity, see above p. 29–30, 142–144 (Angelos Chaniotis), 149–153 (Douglas Cairns).
[477] See above chapter 1. Cf. also Chaniotis 2014, Chaniotis 2016, Chaniotis 2017.
[478] On the role of cognitive metaphor in the perception of what ancient people thought and felt, see Dunér 2014 and Cairns 2019, 23–24; see also Carroll 2023 and p. 97–105. above.
[479] Varela, Thompson, und Rosch 1991, Gallagher 2000, Gallagher und Zahavi 2008, Noë 2004, Noë 2009, Hutto 2000, Hutto 2008, Hutto and Myin 2012, Zahavi 2014. See above p. 5–10, p. 16 f. 52.
[480] Anderson, Wheeler and Sprevak 2019, 6–8. See above p. 8–10 and p. 145–147.

history and archaeology would appear to contribute to better interaction and exchange between these fields and to the elaboration and presentation of new and unexpected results.

'Cognitive' fields themselves (such as material agency, perception, memory, artificial intelligence) penetrate every ancient sub-discipline and show themselves relevant in linguistics, literary criticism, theatre research, history, and archaeology. And the boundaries between the sub-disciplines are blurred. 'Cognitive' approaches and concepts, terms such as 'experience', 'embodiment' or 'distributed cognition' open up new views and perspectives in archaeology, history and philology.

The aim of this book has been to reveal the current developments associated with the so-called 'cognitive turn' in classical studies in recent decades from the perspective of material agency, spatial perception, imagination and visuality, experience and emotions.

We experience ourselves and the world through constant cognitive acts. David Konstan explains in detail that although emotions such as colours were perceived very differently in ancient Greece than in modern societies today, there are nevertheless rudimentary bases that we can draw on to imagine what wonder, expectation, love or hate felt like.[481] The cognitive sciences provide the classics with insights into the workings of the brain that can be used to make more informed and nuanced reflections on the thoughts of poets, writers, viewers, listeners, actors or readers. Authors construct cognitive patterns for their audience. If the audience has been inspired to actively participate in then the narrative will be perceived as engaging and enjoyable.

Returning to the crucial question of what the cognitive approaches actually bring, what they change in our perception of classical texts or more generally of ancient materials, the simple answer would be that they perhaps change the perspective a little, away from meaning as a goal towards the nature and functions of meaning itself. In other words, we are not only dealing with the quality of a text's meaning and thus with a new reading of the text, but above all with thinking about how meaning comes about, which per se also creates meaning.[482] In a long-standing debate between hermeneutics and cognitive poetics, it is argued that hermeneutics interprets forms and seeks to understand what they mean, while cognitive poetics also asks how meanings are created.[483]

It is true that cognitive science, by revealing how the thinking mind grasps literary texts, can illuminate certain facets of the imaginative world that need to be

---

[481] See p. 131–138 above.
[482] Brône and Vandaele 2009b. See also Budelmann 2023, 13–16.
[483] See Carroll 2023, 64 with bibliography.

clarified. However, reading and interpreting texts is closely linked to the question of how they come about, what constitutes the essence of reading and what is actually meant by reading. This brings us back to Hans-Georg Gadamer and hermeneutics on a new level and from a new perspective.[484] For Gadamer, hermeneutics is an interpretation contained in an act of understanding, with the act of reading serving as a model for interpretation and translation, which is always an interpretation.[485] More generally, Gadamer's hermeneutics is rooted in the act of experience (German *Erfahrung*), which is inseparable from language as it formulates our world. It is the encounter with a meaning (in art, in the words we speak, in our actions in life) that is at first foreign or strange and that through the process of interpretation comes to understanding. What is understood is always something individual: the text we read, the play we watch, what someone tries to communicate to us in a conversation, what the respective image means as a material image.[486] In this sense the act of interpreting is a completion of meaning that takes place in the experience of language.[487] So I would not speak of a demarcation from hermeneutics, but rather of an additional sense-making and thus an extension of hermeneutics through cognitive approaches.

Cooperation between Classics and cognitive science is therefore important not only when it comes to adapting modern theories to ancient material, or when our theoretical approaches to literature, linguistics and historical archaeology enter into dialogue with the sciences of cognition and emotion. The cooperation is also important in using the richness of ancient thought to challenge modern presuppositions and assumptions. Classicists, ancient historians and archaeologists can provide important insights into contemporary cognitive science debates by discussing on what occasion, where, why and how different processes might have manifested themselves. On the other hand, cognitive scientists can elucidate how similar these processes may or may not be to today's scientific laboratory accounts. Interdisciplinary exchange can improve our understanding of common and changing cognitive patterns in the past, present, and future.

---

[484] See Gadamer 1959 and Gadamer 1990, 352–368. See also p. 28–29 above. See also a useful analysis of this issue in Fricke and Müller 2010.
[485] See Gadamer 1992, 387–392, cf. also Gadamer 1984 ("Hören-Sehen-Lesen") und Gadamer 1989 ("Lesen ist wie Übersetzen").
[486] Gadamer's argument predates the concept of contemporary immersive theatre (such as Felix Barrett's *Punchdrunk* or Thomas Oberender's *Immersion* programme series at the Berliner Festspiele) in which no two spectators will have the same experience.
[487] I owe this understanding of Gadamer to the colloquia on hermeneutics in Freiburg that I have attended for many years, and especially to James Risser for long and detailed discussions of this specific question.

Cognitive perspectives lead classicists, linguists, historians and archaeologists to ask new epistemological questions about their own fields and bring them together to think about the ancient world. Cross-disciplinary competence and interdisciplinarity are necessary or unavoidable when working on cognitive approaches in classics, as the methods, tools, resources, and approaches of all these disciplines overlap and prove to be mutually useful. Analogous questions, comparable tools, parallel approaches in textual analysis, in ritual experience or in the study of archaeological sites and material objects help to understand antiquity and the ancient world, albeit from different perspectives, as a living organism, holistically.

Bibliography

Aase 1994: Aase, T. H. (1994), Symbolic Space: Representations of Space in Geography and Anthropology, *Geografiska Annaler. Series B, Human Geography*, 76/1: 51–58

Adams und Jansson 2012: Adams, P.C. and Jansson, A. (2012), Communication Geography. A Bridge between Disciplines, *Communication Theory* 22: 299–318

Adema 2017: Adema, S.M. (2017). *Speech and thought in Latin war narratives. Words of Warriors.* Leiden, Boston: Brill.

Adema 2019: Adema, S.M. (2019). *Tenses in Vergil. Narrative Style and Structure.* Leiden, Boston: Brill.

Adema 2022: Adema S.M. (2022), Unhappy Dido, Queen of Carthage. In: Bakker M.P. de, Berg B. van den & Klooster J. (Eds.) *Emotions and Narrative in Ancient Literature and Beyond.* Leiden: Brill. 554–568.

Agarwal 2018: Agarwal, P. (2018) Place, D. R. Montello (ed.), *Handbook of behavioural and cognitive geography*, Edward Elgar Cheltenham, UK, Northampton, MA, USA, 291–306

Aikhenvald 2004: Aikhenvald, A. (2004). *Evidentiality.* Oxford University Press, Oxford.

Alaimo and Hekman 2008: Alaimo, S., S. Hekman (2008), *Material Feminisms*, Indiana University Press.

Alexiadou 2013: Alexiadou, A. (2013), Kognitive Linguistik, A. Stephan und S. Walter (hrsg.), *Handbuch Kognitionswissenschaft*, Metzler Stuttgart, Weimar, 63–66.

Allan 2008: Allan, K. (2008). *Metaphor and Metonymy. A Diachronic Approach.* Malden, MA.

Allan 2020: Allan, R. (2020). Narrative Immersion. Some Linguistic and Narratological Aspects. In J. Grethlein, L. Huitink and A. Tagliabue, eds., *Experience, Narrative, and Criticism in Ancient Greece. Under the Spell of Stories*, Oxford, 15–35.

Allan and Bijs 2007: Allan, R. and M. Bijs (2007, eds.), *The Language of Literature. Linguistic Approaches to Classical texts*, Leiden: Brill.

Allison 1983: Allison, R. H. (1983), Amphibian Ambiguities: Aristophanes and His Frogs, *Greece & Rome* 30/1: 8–20

Alvar Nuño, Alvar Ezquerra, and Woolf 2021: Alvar Nuño, A., Alvar Ezquerra, J., and G. Woolf, eds. (2021), *SENSORIVM: The Senses in Roman Polytheism.* Leiden, The Netherlands: Brill.

Andersen 2019: Andersen, Marc. (2019). Predictive coding in agency detection. *Religion, Brain & Behavior* 9(1), 65–104.

Anderson 2015: Anderson, M. (2015). *The Renaissance Extended Mind.* Palgrave-Macmillan.

Anderson, Cairns and Sprevak 2019: Anderson, M., D. Cairns, and M. Sprevak, eds. (2019), *Distributed Cognition in Antiquity*, Edinburgh Univ. Press.

Anderson, Wheeler and Sprevak 2019: Anderson, M., M. Wheeler, and M. Sprevak (2019), Distributed cognition and the Humanities, Anderson, M., D. Cairns, and M. Sprevak, (eds.), *Distributed Cognition in Antiquity*, Edinburgh Univ. Press, 1–17.

Angelopoulou 2024: Angelopoulou, A. (2024), The Dynamics of Physical, Aesthetic and Cultural Taste in Aristophanes, in: Z. Case, M. Ellis, A. M. Reinke (eds.), *Sensing Greek Drama*, Cambridge Philological Society, 50–66.

Antović and Cánovas 2016: Antovic, M. and Cánovas, C. P., eds. (2016). *Oral Poetics and Cognitive Science*, Berlin, Boston: De Gruyter.

Aoki 1999: Aoki, Y. (1999), Trends in the study of the psychological evaluation of landscape. *Landscape Research* (24), 85–94.

Apostel 2020: Apostel, L. (2020), Rezension von Henley, T. B., Rossano, M. J. & Kardas, E. P. (eds) (2020). Handbook of Cognitive Archaeology: Psychology in Prehistory, New York: Routledge, *Archäologische Informationen* 43: 431–434.

Apperly 2010: Apperly, I.A. (2010). *Mindreaders: the cognitive basis of theory of mind*, Hove: Psychology Press / Taylor & Francis Group.

Armstrong 2013: Armstrong, P. B. (2013), *How Literature Plays with the Brain: The Neuroscience of Reading and Art.* Baltimore: Johns Hopkins UP.

Armstrong 2020: Armstrong, P. B. (2020), *Stories and the Brain. The Neuroscience of Narrative.* Baltimore: Johns Hopkins UP.

Arnold 1960: Arnold, M. B. (1960), *Emotion and Personality*, New York: Columbia University Press.

Arnott 1996: Arnott, W. G. (1996). *Alexis: the fragments. A commentary.* Cambridge, CUP.

Arvanitakis 2015: Arvanitakis, K. I. (2015), *Psychoanalytic Scholia on the Homeric Epics.* Leiden, Niederlande: Brill.

Assmann 1992: Assmann, J. (1992), *Das kulturelle Gedächtnis. Schrift, Erinnerung und politische Identität in frühen Hochkulturen*, C. H. Beck, München.

Assmann 2006a: Assmann, A. (2006). *Erinnerungsräume. Formen und Wandlungen des kulturellen Gedächtnisses.* 3. Aufl. Beck: München.

Assmann 2006b: Assmann, J. (2006), *Thomas Mann und Ägypten. Mythos und Monotheismus in den Josephsromanen.* Beck: München.

Assmann and Assmann 1994: Assmann, A., J. Assmann (1994), Das Gestern im Heute: Medien und soziales Gedächtnis, K. Merten, S. J. Schmidt, S. Weischenberger (Hrsg.), *Die Wirklichkeit der Medien. Eine Einführung in Kommunikationswissenschaften.* Westdeutscher Verlag, Opladen, 114–140.

Atran 1990: Atran, S. (1990). *Cognitive foundations of natural history: Towards an anthropology of science.* Cambridge University Press; Editions de la Maison des Sciences de l'Homme.

Atran and Norenzayan 2004: Atran S, Norenzayan A. (2004), Religion's evolutionary landscape: counterintuition, commitment, compassion, communion. *Behav Brain Sci.* 27(6):713–30; discussion 730–770.

Bacon 1994/1995: Bacon, H. H. (1994/1995). The Chorus in Greek Life and Drama, *Arion*, Third Series, 3/1: 6–24

Bakker 1997: Bakker, E. (1997). *Poetry in speech: orality and Homeric discourse.* Ithaca.

Bakker 2005: Bakker, E. (2005). *Pointing at the past: from formula to performance in Homeric poetics.* Cambridge, MA.

Bakker and Kahane 1997: Bakker, E. and A. Kahane, eds. (1997). *Written voices, spoken signs: tradition, performance, and the epic text.* Cambridge, MA.

Bakker and Wakker 2009: Bakker, S. and G. Wakker, eds. (2009). *Discourse cohesion in ancient Greek.* Leiden – Boston.

Bär and Domouzi 2024: Bär, S. and A. Domouzi (eds.) (2024), *Artificial Intelligence in Greek and Roman Epic*, Bloomsbury Publishing.

Barad 2001: Barad, K. (2001), Re(con)figuring Space, Time, and Matter, M. DeKoven (Hrsg.): *Feminist Locations: Global and Local, Theory and Practice.* Rutgers University Press, New Brunswick, 75–109.

Barad 2007: Barad, K. (2007), *Meeting the Universe Halfway: Quantum Physics and the Entanglement of Matter and Meaning.* Durham, North Carolina: Duke University Press.

Barcelona and Valenzuela 2011: Barcelona, A., J. Valenzuela (2011), An overview of cognitive linguistics, Brdar, M., Žic Fuchs, M., Gries, S. Th., (eds.), *Cognitive Linguistics: convergence and expansion*, Amsterdam/Philadelphia: John Benjamins Publishing Company, 17–44

Barham and Everett 2021: Barham, L., Everett, D. (2021), Semiotics and the Origin of Language in the Lower Palaeolithic. *J Archaeol Method Theory* 28, 535–579

Barrett 2000: Barrett J. L. (2000), Exploring the natural foundations of religion. *Trends Cogn Sci.* 4(1):29–34.

Barrett and Lanman 2008: Barrett, J L. and J. A. Lanman (2008), The science of religious beliefs, *Religion* 38:2, 109–124

Barrett and Russell 2015: Barrett L. F., Russell J. A. (2015). An introduction to psychological construction. In: Barrett L. F., Russell J. A. (Eds.), *The psychological construction of emotion* (pp. 1–17). Guilford Press.

Barrios-Lech 2016: P. Barrios-Lech (2016), *Linguistic Interaction in Roman Comedy*, Cambridge CUP.

Barsalou 2008: Barsalou, L. W. (2008), Grounded Cognition, *Annual Review of Psychology* 59:1, 617–645

Barsalou 2009: Barsalou L. W. (2009), Simulation, situated conceptualization, and prediction. *Philos Trans R Soc Lond B Biol Sci.* 364(1521):1281–9.

Barsalou 2016: Barsalou, L. W. (2016). Situated conceptualization: Theory and applications. Y. Coello & M. H. Fischer (Eds.), *Foundations of embodied cognition: Perceptual and emotional embodiment*, 11–37. Routledge/Taylor & Francis Group.

Barsalou e.a. 2003: Barsalou L. W., Kyle Simmons W., Barbey A. K., Wilson C. D. (2003), Grounding conceptual knowledge in modality-specific systems. *Trends Cogn Sci.* 7(2):84–91.

Bartolomeo 2002: Bartolomeo, P. (2002), 'The Relationship Between Visual Perception and Visual Mental Imagery: A Reappraisal of the Neuropsychological Evidence', *Cortex* 38: 357–378.

Bartsch and Elsner 2007: Bartsch, S., and Elsner, J. (2007). Introduction: Eight Ways of Looking at an Ekphrasis. *Classical Philology* 102(1), i–vi.

Bennett 2001: Bennett, J. (2001), *The Enchantment of Modern Life: Attachments, Crossings, and Ethics*. Princeton University Press.

Bennett 2010: Bennett, J. (2010), *Vibrant Matter: A Political Ecology of Things*. Duke University Press.

Bennett and Joyce 2010: Bennett, T., P. Joyce eds. (2010), *Material Powers. Cultural Studies, History and the Material Turn*, Routledge.

Bentein 2015a: Bentein, K. (2015), Particle-usage in documentary papyri (I – IV AD): an integrated, sociolinguistically-informed approach, (2015) *Greek, Roman, and Byzantine Studies* 55: 721–753

Bentein 2015b: Bentein, K. (2015), The Greek documentary papyri as a linguistically heterogeneous corpus: the case of the katochoi of the Sarapeion-archive, (2015) *Classical World* 108(4): 461–484

Bentein 2016: Bentein, K. (2016), *Verbal Periphrasis in Ancient Greek: have- and be- constructions*, Oxford classical monographs, OUP Oxford.

Bentein 2020: Bentein, K. (2020), Deictic shifting in Greek contractual writing (I-IV AD). *Philologus* 164(1): 83–106

Bentein, Janse, and Soltic 2017: K. Bentein, M. Janse, Jorie Soltic, eds. (2017), *Variation and change in Ancient Greek tense, aspect and modality* (2017), Leiden: Brill.

Bergen 2015: Bergen, B. (2015). "1. Embodiment". *Handbook of Cognitive Linguistics*, E. Dabrowska and D. Divjak, Berlin, München, Boston: De Gruyter Mouton, 2015:10–30.

Bergen 2019: Bergen, B. (2019), "Chapter 1: Embodiment". *Cognitive Linguistics – Foundations of Language*, E. Dabrowska and D. Divjak, Berlin, Boston: De Gruyter Mouton, 2019: 11–35.

Bernini and Caracciolo 2013: Bernini, M. and Caracciolo, M. (2013), *Letteratura e scienze cognitive*. Carocci editore, Rome.

Berti 2019: Berti, M. (2019), *Digital Classical Philology: Ancient Greek and Latin in the Digital Revolution*, Berlin, Boston: De Gruyter Saur.

Betts 2017: Betts, E., ed. (2017), *Senses of the Empire: Multisensory Approaches to Roman Culture*, Routledge.

Billings, Budelmann, and Macintosh 2013: Billings, J., F. Budelmann, and F. Macintosh, eds. (2013), *Choruses, Ancient and Modern*, Oxford: OUP.

Bianchi, Brill, and Holmes 2019: Bianchi, E., S. Brill, and B. Holmes, eds. (2019), *Antiquities Beyond Humanism*, Oxford: OUP.

Binford 1962: Binford, L. R. (1962), Archaeology as Anthropology, *American Antiquity* 28/2:217–225

Binford 1972: Binford, L. R. (1972), *An Archaeological Perspective*. Seminar Press, New York and London.

Binford 1989: Binford, L. R. (1989), *Debating Archaeology*, New York; Academic Press.

Binford and Binford 1968: Binford, S.R., L.R. Binford, eds. (1968), *New perspectives in archaeology*, Chicago (IL): Aldine.

Bischof-Köhler 2006: Bischof-Köhler, D. (2006). *Von Natur aus anders. Die Psychologie der Geschlechtsunterschiede* (3. Aufl.). Stuttgart: Kohlhammer.

Bjork and Bjork 1996: Bjork, E. L., R. A. Bjork, eds. (1996), *Memory. Handbook of Perception and Cognition*, Academic Press.

Blackmore and Troscianko 2018: Blackmore, S. and E. Troscianko (2018), *Consciousness: an introduction*. Routledge.

Blair 2007: Blair, R. (2007), *The Actor, Image, and Action. Acting and Cognitive Neuroscience*, Routledge.

Blair 2009: Blair, R. (2009). Cognitive Neuroscience and Acting: Imagination, Conceptual Blending, and Empathy, *The Drama Review* 53: 92–103.

Blair 2020: Blair, R. (2020). Acting and Science, K. E. Shepherd-Barr, ed., *The Cambridge Companion to Theatre and Science*, Cambridge CUP, 162–175

Blair and Cook 2016a: Blair, R. and A. Cook, eds., (2016), *Theatre, Performance and Cognition: Languages, Bodies and Ecologies*. London: Bloomsbury Methuen Drama.

Blair and Cook 2016b: Introduction, in: Blair, R. and A. Cook, eds., (2016), *Theatre, Performance and Cognition: Languages, Bodies and Ecologies*. London: Bloomsbury Methuen Drama, 1–15.

Blundell e.a. 2013: Blundell, S. / D. Cairns / N. Rabinowitz (eds.) (2013), Vision and Viewing in Ancient Greece, *Helios* 40, 1–2, special issue.

Boden 1990: Boden, M. A. (1990), *Artificial Intelligence. Handbook of Perception and Cognition*, Academic Press.

Boegehold 1999: A. L. Boegehold (1999), *When a gesture was expected: a selection of examples from archaic and classical Greek literature*. Princeton: Princeton University Press.

Boivin 2008: Boivin, N. (2008), *Material Cultures, Material Minds. The Impact of Things on Human Thought, Society, and Evolution*, CUP Cambridge.

Bol 2005: Bol, P. C. (2005), *Frühgriechische Bilder und die Entstehung der Klassik: Perspektive, Kognition und Wirklichkeit*, Utz Verlag GmbH.

Bond, Craps, Vermeulen 2016: Bond, L., S. Craps, P. Vermeulen, eds., (2016), *Memory unbound: Tracing the Dynamics of Memory Studies*, New York: Berghahn.

Bonifazi 2001: Bonifazi, A. (2001). *Mescolare un cratere di canti. Pragmatica della poesia epinicia in Pindaro*. Alessandria: Edizioni dell'Orso.

Bonifazi 2008: Bonifazi, A. (2008). Memory and Visualization in Homeric Discourse Markers. E. A. Mackay (ed.), *Orality, Literacy, Memory in the Ancient Greek and Roman World*, 35–64. Leiden and Boston: Brill.
Bonifazi 2009: Bonifazi, A. (2009). The pragmatic meanings of some discourse markers in Homer. E. Rieken & P. Widmer (eds.), *Pragmatische Kategorien: Form, Funktion und Diachronie. Akten der Arbeitstagung der Indogermanischen Gesellschaft von 24. bis 26. September 2007 in Marburg*, 29–36. Wiesbaden: Reichert.
Bonifazi 2012: Bonifazi, A. (2012). *Homer's Versicolored Fabric: The Evocative Power of Ancient Greek Epic Word-Making*. Hellenic Studies Series, Washington D.C. and Cambridge, MA: Harvard University Press.
Bonifazi 2018: Bonifazi, A. (2018). Embedded focalization and free indirect speech in Homer as viewpoint blending. J. Ready and C. Tsagalis (eds.), *Homer in Performance: Rhapsodes, Narrators, and Characters*, 230–254. Austin: University of Texas Press.
Bonifazi 2019: Bonifazi, A. (2019). *Autos* and the Center-Periphery Image Schema. W.M. Short and E. Mocciaro (eds.), *The Embodied Basis of Constructions in Greek and Latin*, 126–148. Berlin: De Gruyter.
Bonifazi 2021: Bonifazi, A. (2021), Particle Use in Herodotus and Thucydides. Part IV (pp. 565–879) in A. Bonifazi, A. Drummen and M. de Kreij, *Particles in Ancient Greek Discourse: Exploring Particle Use across Genres*. Hellenic Studies Series 74. Washington, DC: Center for Hellenic Studies. https://chs.harvard.edu/book/bonifazi-drummen-de-kreij-eds-particles-in-ancient-greek-discourse/ , last access June 3rd 2024.
Bortolussi and Dixon 2015: Bortolussi, M. and Dixon, P. (2015). 'Transport: Challenges to the Metaphor', in L. Zunshine, (ed.), *The Oxford Handbook of Cognitive Literary Studies*, 525–40. New York.
Bottemanne, Longuet, and Gauld 2021: Bottemanne, H., Longuet, Y., Gauld, C. (2021). *The predictive mind: introduction to Bayesian brain theory*. L'Encéphale 48(4):436–444
Bowden 2022: Bowden, H. (2022), A cognitive approach to Ancient Greek animal sacrifice, E. Eidinow, A. Geertz and J. North (eds), *Cognitive Approaches to Ancient Religious Experience*. Cambridge University Press, Cambridge, 19–43.
Boyd 2009: Boyd, B. (2009), *On the Origin of Stories: Evolution, Cognition, and Fiction*, Harvard University Press, Belknap Press.
Boyer 1994: Boyer, P. (1994). Cognitive constraints on cultural representations: Natural ontologies and religious ideas, L. A. Hirschfeld and S. A. Gelman (eds.), *Mapping the mind: Domain specificity in cognition and culture* (391–411). Cambridge: Cambridge University Press.
Boyer 2001: Boyer, P. (2001). *Religion Explained: The Evolutionary Origins of Religious Thought*. New York: Basic Books.
Bradley 2014: Bradley, M., ed. (2014), *Smell and the Ancient Senses*, Routledge.
Braidotti 2002: Braidotti, R. (2002), *Metamorphoses: Towards a Materialist Theory of Becoming*, Blackwell.
Brannon 2010: Brannon, L. (2010). *Gender. Psychological perspectives* (6th ed.). Boston, MA: Pearson.
Brdar, Žic Fuchs, and Gries 2011: Brdar, M., Žic Fuchs, M., Gries, S. Th., eds. (2011) *Cognitive Linguistics: convergence and expansion*, Amsterdam/Philadelphia: John Benjamins Publishing Company.
Bremmer 2007: Bremmer, J. N. (2007). Greek Normative Animal Sacrifice, D. Ogden (Ed.), *A Companion to Greek Religion* (132–144). Blackwell Publishing.

Brône and Vandaele 2009a: Brône, G. and Vandaele, J. (2009), *Cognitive Poetics: Goals, Gains and Gaps*, Berlin, New York: De Gruyter Mouton.
Brône and Vandaele 2009b: Brône, G. and Vandaele, J. (2009), "Cognitive poetics. A critical introduction". In: *Cognitive Poetics: Goals, Gains and Gaps*, ed. by G. Brône and J. Vandaele, Berlin, New York: De Gruyter Mouton, 1–32.
Brook 1968: Brook, P. (1968), *The empty space: a book about the theatre.* New York: Scribner.
Brown 2001: Brown, B. (2001). Thing Theory. *Critical Inquiry*, 28(1), 1–22.
Bruner 2023: Bruner, E. ed. (2023), *Cognitive Archaeology, Body Cognition, and the Evolution of Visuospatial Perception*, Elsevier Academic Press.
Bruner et al. 2018: Bruner, E., Fedato, A., Silva-Gago, M., Alonso-Alcalde, R., Terradillos-Bernal, M., Fernández-Durantes, M. Á., & Martín-Guerra, E. (2018). Cognitive archeology, body cognition, and hand-tool interaction, G. S. Forrester, W. D. Hopkins, K. Hudry, & A. Lindell (Eds.), *Cerebral lateralization and cognition: Evolutionary and developmental investigations of behavioral biases* (pp. 325–345). Elsevier Academic Press.
Budelmann 2019: Budelmann, F. (2017). Group Minds in Classical Athens? Chorus and Dēmos as Case Studies of Collective Cognition, M. Anderson, D. Cairns, M. Sprevak (Eds.), *Distributed Cognition in Classical Antiquity* (pp. 194–212). Edinburgh University Press.
Budelmann 2023: Budelmann, F. (2023), Introduction, in: F. Budelmann and I. Sluiter (eds.), *Minds on stage: Greek tragedy and cognition*, Oxford OUP, 1–21.
Budelmann and Easterling 2010: Budelmann, F. and Easterling, P. E. (2010), 'Reading Minds in Greek Tragedy' *Greece & Rome* 57(2): 289–303
Budelmann and Power 2015: Budelmann, F. & Power, T. (2015). Another Look at Female Choruses in Classical Athens. *Classical Antiquity* 34 (2):252–295.
Bundrick 2005: Bundrick S. D. (2005). *Music and Image in Classical Athens.* New York NY: Cambridge University Press.
Burke and Troscianko 2017: Burke, M., and E. T. Troscianko, eds. (2017). *Cognitive Literary Science: Dialogues between Literature and Cognition.* Oxford University Press.
Butler and Nooter 2018: Butler, S., S. Nooter, eds. (2018), *Sound and the Ancient Senses*, Routledge.
Butler and Purves 2014: Butler, S., A. Purves, eds. (2014), *Synaesthesia and the Ancient Senses*, Routledge.
Buzan and Buzan 1993: Buzan, T. and Buzan, B. (1993), *The Mind Map Book: How to Use the Radiant Thinking to Maximize Your Brain's Untapped Potential.* Penguin Book Ltd., London.
Cairns 1993: Cairns, D. L. (1993), *Aidōs: The Psychology and Ethics of Honour and Shame in Ancient Greek Literature.* Oxford: Clarendon Press.
Cairns 2003a: Cairns, D. L. (2003), Myths and Metaphors of Mind and Mortality. *Hermathena* 175: 41–75.
Cairns 2003b: Cairns, D. (2003). Ethics, ethology, terminology: Iliadic anger and the cross-cultural study of emotion. In S. Braund & G. Most (Eds.), *Ancient Anger: Perspectives from Homer to Galen* (Yale Classical Studies 32, 11–49). Cambridge: Cambridge University Press.
Cairns 2008: Cairns, D. L. (2008), Look both ways: studying emotion in ancient Greek, *Critical Quarterly* 50/4: 43–62
Cairns 2009: Cairns, D. L. (2009), Weeping and Veiling: Grief, Display and Concealment in Ancient Greek Culture. T. Fögen (ed.), *Tears in the Graeco-Roman World*, Berlin 37–57
Cairns 2011a: Cairns, D. L. (2011), 'Honour and shame: Modern Controversies and Ancient Values', *Critical Quarterly*, 531: 23–41

Cairns 2011b: Cairns, D. L. (2011), 'Looks of Love and Loathing: Cultural Models of Vision and Emotion in Ancient Greece', *Mètis* 9: 37–50

Cairns 2013: Cairns, D. L. (2013), A Short History of Shudders, A. Chaniotis, P. Ducrey (eds.), *Unveiling Emotions II. Emotions in Greece and Rome: Texts, Images, Material Culture*, Stuttgart, 85–107.

Cairns 2014: Cairns, D. L. (2014). Ψυχή, θυμός, and Metaphor in Homer and Plato. *Études platoniciennes* 11: 1–37.

Cairns 2015: Cairns, D. L. (2015). "The Horror and the Pity: *Phrikē* as a Tragic Emotion," *Psychoanalytic Inquiry* 34, 75–94.

Cairns 2016a: Cairns, D. L. (2016), Mind, Body, and Metaphor in Ancient Greek Concepts of Emotion, *L'Atelier du Centre de recherches historiques [En ligne]*, 16. URL: http://journals.openedition.org/acrh/7416, last access June 3rd 2024.

Cairns 2016b: Cairns, D. L. (2016), Metaphors for hope in archaic and classical Greek poetry. R. Caston and R. Kaster (eds.) *Hope, joy, and affection in the classical world*, 13–44. Oxford: Oxford University Press.

Cairns 2016c: Cairns, D. L. (2016), Clothed in shamelessness, shrouded in grief: The role of "garment" metaphors in Ancient Greek concepts of emotion, G. Fanfani, M. Harlow, M. L. Nosch, eds., *Spinning Fates and Song of the Loom: The Use of Textiles, Clothing and Cloth Production as Metaphor, Symbol and Narrative Device in Greek and Latin Literature*, Oxford, Oxbow Books, 25–41

Cairns 2017a: Cairns, D. L. (2017), Mind, metaphor, and emotion in Euripides (*Hippolytus*) and Seneca (*Phaedra*), MAIA: Rivista di Letterature Classiche 69/2: 247–267

Cairns 2017b: Cairns, D. L. (2017), The Tripartite Soul as Metaphor, R. G. Edmonds III and P. Destrée, eds., *Plato and the Power of Images*, 219–238, Leiden Brill.

Cairns 2018: Cairns, D. (2018/2019). ΘΥΜΌΣ in Homer: Philological, oral-poetic, and cognitive approaches, *Quaestiones Oralitatis* 4:13–30

Cairns 2019: Cairns, D. (2019). Distributed Cognition and the Classics, M. Anderson, D. Cairns, and M. Sprevak, eds., *Distributed Cognition in Antiquity*, Edinburgh Univ. Press, 18–36.

Cairns and Fulkerson 2015: Cairns, D. L., L. Fulkerson, eds. (2015), *Emotions between Greece and Rome*, BICS Supplement 125, London.

Cairns and Nelis 2017a: Cairns, D. L., D. P. Nelis, eds. (2017), *Emotions in the Classical World: Methods, Approaches, and Directions*, Stuttgart: Steiner.

Cairns and Nelis 2017b: Cairns, D. L., D. P. Nelis (2017), Introduction, Cairns, D. L., D. P. Nelis, eds. (2017), *Emotions in the Classical World: Methods, Approaches, and Directions*, Stuttgart: Steiner, 7–30

Cairns, Hinterberger, Pizzone, and Zaccarini 2022: D. Cairns, M. Hinterberger, A. Pizzone, and M. Zaccarini, eds. (2022), *Emotions through Time. From Antiquity to Byzantium*. Mohr Siebeck Tübingen.

Cairns and Virág 2024: Cairns, D. and Virág, C. (eds.) (2024), *In the Mind, in the Body, in the World: Emotions in Early China and Ancient Greece*, New York: OUP.

Calabrese and Ballerio 2014: S. Calabrese and S. Ballerio, eds. (2014), *Linguaggio, letteratura e scienze neuro-cognitive*, Ledizioni Collana.

Campbell 1984: Campbell, D. A. 1984. The Frogs in the Frogs, *The Journal of Hellenic Studies*, Vol. 104, 163–165

Campeggiani 2023: Campeggiani, P. (2023), *Theories of Emotion: Expressing, Feeling, Acting*. Bloomsbury Academic.

Canevaro 2019: Canevaro, L. (2019), Materiality and Classics: (Re) Turning to the Material. *The Journal of Hellenic Studies*, 139, 222–232.

Canevaro 2023: Canevaro, L. (2023), *Theocritus and things: material agency in the Idylls*. Edinburgh Univ. Press.

Canino et al. 2022: Canino S., Raimo S., Boccia M., Di Vita A., Palermo L. (2022), On the Embodiment of Social Cognition Skills: The Inner and Outer Body Processing Differently Contributes to the Affective and Cognitive Theory of Mind. *Brain Sciences*, 12(11):1423.

Canning 1994: Canning, K. (1994), Feminist History after the Linguistic Turn: Historicizing Discourse and Experience, *Signs* 19/2: 368–404

Cánovas 2011: Cánovas, C. P. (2011). The genesis of the arrows of love: diachronic conceptual integration in Greek mythology. *American Journal of Philology* 132(4): 553–579.

Cánovas 2014: Cánovas, C. P. (2014), Cognitive patterns in Greek poetic metaphors of emotion: A diachronic approach, J. E. Díaz Vera (ed.), *Metaphor and Metonymy through Time and Cultures: Perspectives on the Sociohistorical Linguistics of Figurative Language*, 295–318, Mouton de Gruyter.

Cánovas 2016: Cánovas, C. P. (2016), Rethinking image schemas. *Journal of Literary Semantics*, 45(2): 117–139;

Cánovas and Antović 2016a: Cánovas, C. P. and Antović, M. (2016), "Introduction: Oral Poetics and Cognitive Science". M. Antovic and C. P. Cánovas (eds.), *Oral Poetics and Cognitive Science*, Berlin, Boston: De Gruyter, 1–11.

Cánovas and Antović 2016b: Cánovas, C. P. and Antović, M. (2016), "Construction grammar and oral formulaic theory". M. Antovic and C. P. Cánovas (eds.), *Oral Poetics and Cognitive Science*, Berlin, Boston: De Gruyter, 79–98.

Caracciolo 2012: Caracciolo, M. (2012), Notes for a(nother) Theory of Experientiality. *Journal of Literary Theory* 6/1: 177–194.

Caracciolo 2014: Caracciolo, M. (2014), *The Experientiality of Narrative: An Enactivist Approach*, Berlin, Boston: De Gruyter.

Caracciolo and Kukkonen 2021: Caracciolo, M. and K. Kukkonen (2021), *With bodies: narrative theory and embodied cognition*. The Ohio state univ. press, Columbus.

Cardeña 2022: Cardeña, E. (2022), Not Only Ecstasy: Pouring New Concepts into Old Vessels, D. Stein, S. K. Costello, K. Polinger Foster (eds.), *The Routledge Companion to Ecstatic Experience in the Ancient World*, Routledge, 26–40

Carlson 1990: Carlson, M. (1990). *Theatre semiotics*. Bloomington: Indiana University Press.

Carroll 2023: Carroll, M. (2023), Space for deliberation: image schemas, metaphorical reasoning, and the dilemma of Pelasgus, in: F. Budelmann, I. Sluiter (eds.), *Minds on Stage. Greek Tragedy and Cognition*, Oxford, 60–78

Casey 1997: Casey, E. S. (1997), *The Fate of Place: A Philosophical History*, University of California Press.

Casey 2009: Casey, E. S., ed. (2009). *Getting Back into Place*, Second Edition: *Toward a Renewed Understanding of the Place-World*. Indiana University Press.

Cassin 2014: Cassin, B., Ed. (2014). *Dictionary of Untranslatables: A philosophical lexicon*. Transl. by S. Rendall, C. Hubert, J. Mehlman, N. Stein & M. Syrotinski. Princeton: Princeton University Press.

Caston and Weineck 2016: Caston, V. and Weineck, S.-M., eds. (2016), *Our Ancient Wars: Rethinking War through the Classics*, Ann Arbor: Univ. of Michigan Press.

Cave 2016a: Cave, T. (2016), *Thinking with Literature: Towards a Cognitive Criticism*, OUP Oxford.

Cave 2016b: Cave, T. (2016), " Penser la littérature : vers une approche cognitive ", F. Lavocat (éd.), *Interprétation littéraire et sciences cognitives*, Paris, Hermann Editeurs, 15–32

Cecchet, Degelmann, Patzelt 2019: L. Cecchet, Ch. Degelmann, M. Patzelt eds., (2019),*The Ancient War's Impact on the Home Front*, Cambridge Scholars Publishing.
Chafe 1994: Chafe, W. L. (1994), *Discourse, consciousness, and time: The flow and displacement of conscious experience in speaking and writing*. University of Chicago Press
Chaniotis 2011: Chaniotis, A. (2011), Emotional Community through Ritual. Initiates, Citizens, and Pilgrims as Emotional Communities in the Greek World, A. Chaniotis (ed.), *Ritual Dynamics in the Ancient Mediterranean: Agency, Emotion, Gender, Representation*, Stuttgart: Steiner Verlag, 264–290.
Chaniotis 2012a: Chaniotis, A. ed. (2012), *Unveiling Emotions: Sources and Methods for the Study of Emotions in the Greek World*, Stuttgart: Steiner Verlag
Chaniotis 2012b: Chaniotis, A. (2012), Unveiling Emotions in the Greek World. Introduction, A. Chaniotis (ed.), *Unveiling Emotions: Sources and Methods for the Study of Emotions in the Greek World*, Stuttgart: Steiner Verlag, 11–36
Chaniotis 2012c: Chaniotis, A. (2012), Moving Stones: The Study of Emotions in Greek Inscriptions, A. Chaniotis (ed.), *Unveiling Emotions: Sources and Methods for the Study of Emotions in the Greek World*, Stuttgart: Steiner Verlag, 91–129
Chaniotis 2012d: Chaniotis, A. (2012), The Ritualised Commemoration of War in the Hellenistic City: Memory, Identity, Emotion, in P. Low, G. Oliver, and P. Rhodes (eds.), *Cultures of Commemoration: War Memorials, Ancient and Modern*, Oxford: Oxford University Press, 41–62
Chaniotis 2013a: Chaniotis, A. (2013), Empathy, Emotional Display, Theatricality, and Illusion in Hellenistic Historiography, in A. Chaniotis and P. Ducrey (eds.), *Unveiling Emotions II. Emotions in Greece and Rome: Texts, Images, Material Culture*, Stuttgart: Steiner, 53–84.
Chaniotis 2013b: Chaniotis, A. (2013), Under Siege: Challenges, Experiences, and Emotions, in B. Campbell and L. Tritle (eds.), *The Oxford Handbook of Warfare in the Classical World*, Oxford: Oxford University Press, 438–456.
Chaniotis 2013c: Chaniotis, A. (2013), Paradoxon, Enargeia, Empathy: Hellenistic Decrees and Hellenistic Oratory, in C. Kremmydas and K. Tempest (eds.), *Hellenistic Oratory: Continuity and Change*, Oxford: Oxford University Press, 201–216
Chaniotis 2013d: Chaniotis, A. (2013), Staging and Feeling the Presence of God: Emotion and Theatricality in Religious Celebrations in the Roman East, in L. Bricault and C. Bonnet (eds.), *Panthée: Religious Transformations in the Roman Empire*, Leiden: Brill, 169–189
Chaniotis 2013e: Chaniotis, A. (2013), Emotional Language in Hellenistic Decrees and Hellenistic Histories, in M. Mari and J. Thornton (eds.), *Parole in movimento. Linguaggio politico e lessico storiografico nel mondo ellenistico*, Pisa: Fabrizio Serra Editore, 339–352
Chaniotis 2014: Chaniotis, A. (2014), "Mnemopoetik: Die epigraphische Konstruktion von Erinnerung in den griechischen Poleis". O. Dally, T. Hölscher, S. Muth und R. Schneider (hrsg.), *Medien der Geschichte – Antikes Griechenland und Rom*, Boston: De Gruyter, 132–169.
Chaniotis 2015: Chaniotis, A. (2015), Affective Diplomacy: Emotional Scripts between Greek Communities and Roman Authorities during the Republic, in D. Cairns and L. Fulkerson (eds.), *Emotions between Greece and Rome*, London, 87–103.
Chaniotis 2016: Chaniotis, A. (2016), Displaying Emotional Community: The Epigraphic Evidence, in E. Sanders and M. Johncock (eds.), *Emotion and Persuasion in Classical Antiquity*, Stuttgart: Steiner Verlag, Stuttgart, 93–111.
Chaniotis 2017: Chaniotis, A. (2017), The Life of Statues: Emotion and Agency, in D. Cairns and D. P. Nelis (eds.), *Emotions in the Classical World: Methods, Approaches and Directions*, Stuttgart: Steiner Verlag, 143–158.

Chaniotis and Ducrey 2013: Chaniotis, A. and P. Ducrey, eds. (2017), *Unveiling Emotions II. Emotions in Greece and Rome: Texts, Images, Material Culture*, Stuttgart: Steiner.

Chaniotis, Kaltsas, and Mylonopoulos 2017: Chaniotis, A., N. Kaltsas, and I. Mylonopoulos, eds. (2017), *A World of Emotions: Greece, 700 BC-200 AD*, New York: Onassis Foundation USA.

Chaston 2010: Chaston, C. (2010), *Tragic Props and Cognitive Function: Aspects of the Function of Images in Thinking*, Mnemosyne, 317, Brill.

Chesi and Spiegel 2020: Chesi, G. M. and F. Spiegel (2020, edd.), *Classical Literature and Posthumanism*. London and New York: Bloomsbury Academic.

Chomsky 1959: Chomsky, N. (1959), A Review of B. F. Skinner's *Verbal Behavior*. Language 35/1: 26–58

Christensen 2022: Christensen, J. (2022), *The Many-Minded Man: The "Odyssey", Psychology, and the Therapy of Epic*, Ithaca, NY: Cornell University Press.

Chronopoulos, Maier, Novokhatko 2020: Chronopoulos, S., F. K. Maier, and A. Novokhatko, eds. (2020), *Digitale Altertumswissenschaften: Thesen und Debatten zu Methoden und Anwendungen*, Heidelberg: Propylaeum (Digital Classics Books, Band 4).

Chronopoulos, Maier, Novokhatko 2022: Chronopoulos, S., F. K. Maier, and A. Novokhatko, eds. (2022), *Classics@20: Digital Text Analysis of Greek and Latin sources; Methods, Tools, Perspectives*, CHS Harvard, https://classics-at.chs.harvard.edu/volume/classics20-digital-text-analysis-of-greek-and-latin-sources/, last access June 3rd 2024.

Chuanji Gao et al. 2022: Chuanji Gao, J. J. Green, Xuan Yang, Sewon Oh, Jongwan Kim, S. V. Shinkareva (2022), Audiovisual integration in the human brain: a coordinate-based meta-analysis, *Cerebral Cortex* 2022, bhac443

Ciesielski 2017: Ciesielski, T. (2017), Ancient *choreia* in neurocognitive context, *Studia UBB dramatica* LXII, 2, 115–130

Clark 1996: Clark, H. (1996). *Using Language*. 'Using' Linguistic Books, Cambridge: Cambridge University Press.

Clark 2003: Clark, A. (2003), *Natural-Born Cyborgs: Minds, Technologies, and the Future of Human Intelligence*, New York OUP.

Clark 2008: Clark, A. (2008), *Supersizing the Mind: Embodiment, Action, and Cognitive Extension*, New York OUP.

Clark 2009: Clark, A. (2009), Spreading the joy? Why the machinery of consciousness is (probably) still in the head, *Mind* 118 (472):963–993

Clark 2015: Clark, A. (2015), *Surfing Uncertainty: Prediction, Action, and the Embodied Mind*, New York OUP.

Clark 2019: Clark, T. (2019). *The Value of Ecocriticism*, Cambridge: Cambridge University Press.

Clark and Brennan 1991: Clark, H. H., S. E. Brennan (1991), Grounding in Communication, In: L. B. Resnick, J. M. Levine, S. D. Teasley (eds.): *Perspectives on Socially Shared Cognition*, Amer Psychological Assn. 27–149.

Clark and Chalmers 1998: Clark, A., Chalmers, D. (1998). The Extended Mind. *Analysis*, 58(1), 7–19.

Clay 2011: Clay, J. S. (2011), *Homer's Trojan Theater: Space, Vision, and Memory in the Iliad*. Cambridge/New York: Cambridge University Press.

Clements 2014: Clements, A. (2015). "Divine Scents and Presence." M. Bradley, (ed.), *Smell and the Ancient Senses*, Routledge, 46–59.

Clinch 2022: Clinch, A. (2022), Ecstasy and Initiation in the Eleusinian Mysteries, D. Stein, S. K. Costello, K. Polinger Foster (eds.), *The Routledge Companion to Ecstatic Experience in the Ancient World*, Routledge, 314–331

Cline 2024: Cline, E. H. (2024), *After 1177 B.C.: The Survival of Civilizations*, Princeton Univers. Press.
Cohen 2015: Cohen, J. J. (2015), *Stone: An Ecology of the Inhuman*, University of Minnesota Press.
Cole 2005: Cole, S. G. (2005), *Landscapes, Gender, and Ritual Space: The Ancient Greek Experience*, University of California Press.
Collin 2010: Collin, F. 2010. L'art de la parole imagée chez Fronton: philosophie et pensée littéraire, *L'art du discours dans l'antiquité: de l'orateur au poète*, dir. de P. Voisin et M. de Béchillon. Paris: L'Harmattan, coll. "Kubaba", 213–234.
Colombetti 2014: Colombetti, G. (2014), *The feeling body: Affective science meets the enactive mind*, MIT Press.
Colombetti and Roberts 2015: Colombetti, G. Roberts, T. (2015). Extending the extended mind: the case for extended affectivity. *Philosophical Studies* 172 (5):1243–1263.
Colston 2008: Colston, H. L. (2008), "A new look at common ground: memory, egocentrism, and joint meaning", in I. Kecskes and J. Mey (eds.), *Intention, Common Ground and the Egocentric Speaker-Hearer*, Berlin, De Gruyter, 151–188.
Comentale 2017: Comentale, N. 2017. *Ermippo. Introduzione, traduzione e commento*. Heidelberg, Verlag Antike.
Comer and Taggart 2021: C. Comer, A. Taggart (2021), *Brain, Mind, and the Narrative Imagination*, Bloomsbury Academic.
Conroy Dalton, Krukar and Hölscher 2018: Dalton, R. C., Krukar, J., and Hölscher, C. (2018). Architectural cognition and behavior, D. R. Montello (Ed.), *Handbook of behavioral and cognitive geography* (337–356). Edward Elgar Publishing.
Coole and Frost 2010: Coole, D. and Frost, S., eds. (2010), *New Materialisms: Ontology, Agency, and Politics*, New York, USA: Duke University Press.
Costello 2022: Costello, S. K. (2022), Contextualizing the Study of Ecstatic Experience in Ancient Old World Societies, D. Stein, S. K. Costello, K. Polinger Foster (eds.), *The Routledge Companion to Ecstatic Experience in the Ancient World*, Routledge, 15–25
Cox and Colledge 1969: Cox, K. R. and Colledge, R. G. (Eds.) (1969). *Behavioural Problems in Geography: A Symposium*, London, Routledge.
Cresswell 2015: Cresswell, T. (2015), *Place: An Introduction*, 2nd Edition, Wiley-Blackwell.
Croft and Cruse 2004: Croft, W., and Cruse, D. A. (2004), *Cognitive Linguistics*. Cambridge: Cambridge University Press.
Crownshaw 2016: Crownshaw, R. (2016), Cultural Memory Studies in the Epoch of the Anthropocene. L. Bond, S. Craps and P. Vermeulen, (eds.) *Memory Unbound: Tracing the Dynamics of Memory Studies*. Oxford: Berghahn, 242–257
Cruse and Schilling 2010: Cruse H., Schilling, M. (2010), Getting cognitive, In: Bläsing B., Puttke M., Schack T. (Eds.), *The Neurocognition of Dance: Mind, Movement and Motor Skills*, London: Psychology Press: 53–74.
Csapo (2014): Csapo, E. (2014), "The Iconography of Comedy", in: M. Revermann (ed.), *The Cambridge Companion to Greek Comedy*, Cambridge: CUP, 95–127.
Czachesz 2012: Czachesz, I. (2012), *Changing Minds: Religion and Cognition Through the Ages*, Peeters, Leuven-Paris.
D'Angour 2020: D'Angour, A. (2020). The musical Frogs in *Frogs*, A. Fries and D. Kanellakis (eds.), *Ancient Greek Comedy: genre – texts – reception*, De Gruyter, 187–197
Dąbrowska and Divjak 2015: Dąbrowska, Ewa and Divjak, D., eds. (2015). *Handbook of Cognitive Linguistics*, Berlin, München, Boston: De Gruyter Mouton.

Dąbrowska and Divjak 2019: Dąbrowska, Ewa and Divjak, D., eds. (2019). *Cognitive Linguistics – Foundations of Language*, Berlin, Boston: De Gruyter Mouton.
Damásio 1994: Damásio, A. (1994), *Descartes' error: emotion, reason, and the human brain*, Avon books, New York
Dancygier 2017: Dancygier, B. (Ed.). (2017). *The Cambridge Handbook of Cognitive Linguistics*. Cambridge: Cambridge University Press.
Dancygier and Sweetser 2014: Dancygier, B., & Sweetser, E. (2014). *Figurative language*. Cambridge University Press.
Danesi 1995: Danesi, M. (1995). The iconicity of metaphor, M. E. Landsberg (Ed.), *Syntactic iconicity and linguistic freezes: The human dimension* (265–283). Berlin/Boston: De Gruyter.
Dasen 2022: Dasen, P. R. (2022), Culture and Cognitive Development, *Journal of Cross-Cultural Psychology* 53, 7–8: 789–816
Dasgupta 2016: Dasgupta, S. (2016), From the Sciences of the Artificial to Cognitive History, R. Frantz, L. Marsh (eds.), *Minds, Models and Milieux: Commemorating the Centennial of the Birth of Herbert Simon*, Palgrave Macmillan, 60–70
De Bakker, van den Berg and Klooster 2022: Bakker M.P. de, Berg B. van den & Klooster J., Eds. (2022), *Emotions and Narrative in Ancient Literature and Beyond*. Leiden: Brill.
De Bakker and de Jong 2022: Bakker, M. P. de, and I. J. F. de Jong (2022, eds.), *Speech in Ancient Greek Literature*. Studies in Ancient Greek Narrative; Vol. 5, Mnemosyne. Supplements; Leiden: Brill.
De Jong 2012: de Jong, I. J. F. (2012), *Space in Ancient Greek Literature*. Leiden; Boston: Brill.
DeLanda 1991: De Landa, M. (1991), *War in the Age of Intelligent Machines*, Zone Books.
DeLanda 2021: De Landa, M. (2021), *Materialist Phenomenology, A Philosophy of Perception*, Bloomsbury.
Denizot and Spevak 2017: Denizot, C. and O. Spevak, eds., (2017). *Pragmatic Approaches to Latin and Ancient Greek*, Amsterdam/Philadelphia: John Benjamins Publishing Company,
Denschlag 2017: Denschlag, F. (2017), *Vergangenheitsverhältnisse: Ein Korrektiv zum Paradigma des "kollektiven Gedächtnisses" mittels Walter Benjamins Erfahrungstheorie*, Bielefeld: transcript Verlag.
Derrida 1974: Derrida, J. (1974), White Mythology: Metaphor in the Text of Philosophy, transl. by F. C. T. Moore, *New Literary History* 6/1, On Metaphor, 5–74 (Orig. in French La mythologie blanche: La métaphore dans le texte philosophique, *Poetique* 5 (1971) 1–52).
Derrida 2005: Derrida, J. (2005), James Adner, Kate Doyle, Glenn Hendler, Women in the Beehive: A Seminar with Jacques Derrida. *differences* 16 (3): 139–157.
Devellennes and Dillet 2018: Devellennes, C., & Dillet, B. (2018). Questioning New Materialisms: An Introduction. *Theory, Culture & Society*, 35(7–8), 5–20.
Devereaux 2016: Devereaux, J. (2016). Embodied historiography: models for reasoning in Tacitus's *Annales*, in: W. M. Short (ed.), *Embodiment in Latin Semantics*. Amsterdam: Benjamins, 237–268
Devereaux 2019: Devereaux, J. (2019), The body-as-metaphor in Latin literature, P. Meineck, W. M. Short, J. Devereaux, eds., *The Routledge Handbook of Classics and Cognitive Theory*, Routledge, 169–188
Dewey 1934: Dewey, J. (1934), *Art as experience*, New York: Minton Balch.
Di Biase-Dyson 2016: Di Biase-Dyson, C. (2016), Spatial metaphors as rhetorical figures. Case studies from Wisdom texts of the Egyptian New Kingdom, Horn, F. and C. Breytenbach, eds., *Spatial Metaphors. Ancient Texts and Transformations*, Berlin, Edition Topoi, 45–68

Di Paolo 2018: Di Paolo, E. (2018). "The enactive conception of life," *The Oxford Handbook of 4E Cognition*. L. de Bruin, A. Newen and S. Gallagher, eds. (Oxford: Oxford University Press). 71–94.

Di Paolo, Cuffari, De Jaegher 2018: Di Paolo, E. A., Cuffari, E. C., and De Jaegher, H. (2018). *Linguistic Bodies: The Continuity Between Life and Language*. Cambridge, MA: MIT Press.

Di Paolo, Rohde, and De Jaegher 2010: Di Paolo, E.A., Rohde, M., Jaegher, H.D. (2010). Horizons for the Enactive Mind: Values, Social Interaction, and Play, J. Stewart, O. Gapenne, and E. A. Di Paolo (eds), *Enaction: Toward a New Paradigm for Cognitive Science*, MIT Press, 33–87

Dirven and Verspoor 1998: Driven, R., & Verspoor, M. (1999). *Cognitive Exploration of Language and Linguistics*. Amsterdam/Philadelphia: John Benjamins Publishing Company.

Donald 1991: Donald, M. (1991). *Origins of the Modern Mind: Three stages in the evolution of culture and cognition*. Cambridge, MA: Harvard University Press.

Dove 2014: G. Dove (2014), Thinking in Words: Language as an Embodied Medium of Thought, *Topics in Cognitive Science* 6/3 Special Issue: *Action and Language Integration: From Humans to Cognitive Robots*, by A. Cangelosi and A. M. Borghi, 371–389

Dovey 2010: Dovey, K. (2010). *Becoming Places: Urbanism/Architecture/Identity/Power*. London; New York: Routledge.

Duncan 2023: Duncan, A. C. (2023), Seeing together: joint attention in Attic tragedy, in: F. Budelmann, I. Sluiter (eds.), *Minds on Stage. Greek Tragedy and Cognition*, Oxford, 173–195

Dunér 2011: Dunér, D. (2011), Astrocognition: Prolegomena to a future cognitive history of exploration, U. Landfester, N.-L. Remuss, K.-U. Schrogl, J.-C. Worms (eds.), *Humans in Outer Space—Interdisciplinary Perspectives*, Wien Springer, 117–140

Dunér 2014: Dunér, D. (2014), Conceptual Metaphors of Science Prolegomena to a Cognitive History of Science, *Journal of Foreign Language Teaching and Applied Linguistics* 2/2, 49–57

Dunér 2019: Dunér, D. (2019), "Human Mind in Space and Time: Prolegomena to a Cognitive History". D. Dunér and C. Ahlberger (eds.), *Cognitive History: Mind, Space, and Time*, Berlin, Boston: De Gruyter Oldenbourg, 3–32.

Dunér and Ahlberger 2019: Dunér, D. and Ahlberger, C. (2019), *Cognitive History: Mind, Space, and Time*, Berlin, Boston: De Gruyter Oldenbourg.

Dünne and Günzel 2006: Dünne, J. und S. Günzel, hrsg. (2006), *Raumtheorie: Grundlagentexte aus Philosophie und Kulturwissenschaften*, Frankfurt am Main: Suhrkamp Verlag.

Easterlin 2012: Easterlin, N. (2012), *A Biocultural Approach to Literary Theory and Interpretation*, Johns Hopkins University Press.

Eco et al. 1994: Eco, U., Niklas, U. & Edeline, F. (1994). Metaphor, T. A. Sebeok (Ed.), *Encyclopedic Dictionary of Semiotics*, vol. 1 (2nd edition, 534–549). Berlin/New York: Mouton de Gruyter.

Eden 1988: Eden, C. (1988), Cognitive mapping, *European Journal of Operational Research*, 36/1: 1–13

Eidinow 2015: Eidinow, E. (2015). Ancient Greek Religion: 'Embedded'... and Embodied, C. Taylor, & K. Vlassopoulos (Eds.), *Communities and Networks in the Ancient Greek World*, Oxford University Press, 54–79

Eidinow, Geertz, Deeley, and North 2022a: E. Eidinow, A. Geertz, Q. Deeley, J. North (2022), Introduction, E. Eidinow, A. Geertz, and J. North, Eds., (2022), *Cognitive Approaches to Ancient Religious Experience*, Cambridge: Cambridge University Press, 1–16.

Eidinow, Geertz, and North 2022b: E. Eidinow, A. Geertz, & J. North, Eds., (2022), *Cognitive Approaches to Ancient Religious Experience*, Cambridge: Cambridge University Press.

El Refaie 2017: El Refaie, E. (2017). Analysing metaphors in multimodal texts, E. Semino and Z. Demjén, eds., *The Routledge Handbook of Metaphor and Language*, London and New York, 148–162

Epstein, Patai, Julian, Spiers 2017: Epstein R. A., Patai E. Z., Julian J. B., Spiers H. J. (2017), The cognitive map in humans: spatial navigation and beyond. *Nat Neurosci.* 20(11):1504–1513.

Erll 2008: Erll, A. (2008), Kollektives Gedächtnis und Erinnerungskulturen. Nünning, A., Nünning, V. (Hrsg.), *Einführung in die Kulturwissenschaften*. Stuttgart: Metzler, 156–185

Erll 2011a: Erll, A. (2011), *Kollektives Gedächtnis und Erinnerungskulturen. Eine Einführung*, Springer.

Erll 2011b: Erll, A. (2011), Travelling Memory, *Parallax*, 17:4, 4–18.

Erll and Nünning 2008: Erll, A. Nünning, A. Hrsg. (2008), *Cultural Memory Studies. An International and Interdisciplinary Handbook*, Berlin De Gruyter.

Escobar 2001: Escobar, A. 2001. Culture sits in places: reflections on globalism and subaltern strategies of localization, *Political Geography*, 20/2, 139–174.

Evans 2007: Evans, V. (2007). *A glossary of cognitive linguistics*. Edinburgh: Edinburgh Univ. Press Ltd.

Evans and Green 2006: V. Evans, M. Green (2006), *Cognitive Linguistics: An Introduction*, Routledge.

Evans, Bergen, and Zinken 2007: V. Evans, B. Bergen, and J. Zinken, eds. (2007), *The Cognitive Linguistics Reader*, Equinox Publishing Limited.

Fagan 2011: Fagan, G. G. (2011), *The Lure of the Arena: Social Psychology and the Crowd at the Roman Games*, CUP Cambridge.

Falletti, Sofia, and Jacono 2016: C. Falletti, G. Sofia, and V. Jacono, eds. (2016), *Theatre and Cognitive Neuroscience*, London: Bloomsbury.

Fauconnier 1997: Fauconnier, G. 1997. *Mappings in Thought and Language*. Cambridge.

Fauconnier and Turner 2002: Fauconnier, G., Turner, M. (2002). *The way we think: Conceptual blending and the minds hidden complexities*. New York: Basic Books.

Feagin 2018: Feagin, S. L. (2018), Olfaction and Space in the Theatre, *The British Journal of Aesthetics*, 58/2: 131–146

Fedriani 2011: Fedriani, Chiara. 2011. Experiential Metaphors in Latin: feelings were containers, movements and things possessed. *Transactions of the Philological Society* 109 (3): 307–326.

Fedriani 2014: Fedriani, C. (2014). *Experiential Constructions in Latin*. Leiden: Brill.

Fedriani 2016: Fedriani, C. (2016). Ontological and orientational metaphors in Latin: evidence from the semantics of feelings and emotions. W. M. Short (ed.), *Embodiment in Latin Semantics*. Amsterdam: Benjamins, 115–140.

Fedriani 2017: Fedriani, C. (2017). *Quapropter, quaeso?* 'Why, for pity's sake?'. Questions and the pragmatic functions of *quaeso, obsecro,* and *amabo* in Plautus, O. Spevak & C. Denizot (eds.), *Pragmatic Approaches to Latin and Ancient Greek*, 83–109. Amsterdam/Philadelphia: John Benjamins Publishing Company.

Fedriani 2019: Fedriani, C. (2019). A pragmatic reversal: Italian *per favore* 'please' and its variants between politeness and impoliteness. *Journal of Pragmatics* 142: 233–244.

Fedriani 2020: Fedriani, C. (2020). Conventionality, deliberateness, and creativity in metaphors: toward a typology of figurative expressions in Latin semantics. *CLUB Working Papers in Linguistics* 4: 33–48.

Fedriani et al. 2021: Fedriani, C., A. Buccheri, I. De Felice, and W. M. Short (2021). "Semantic analysis and frequency effects of conceptual metaphors of emotions in Latin. From a corpus-based approach to a dictionary of Latin metaphors" *Journal of Latin Linguistics*, 20/2: 163–189.

Fedriani and Unceta Gómez 2021: Fedriani, C., L. Unceta Gómez (2021), The metaphorical conceptualization of politeness in Latin. Embodiment and social relations of distance and solidarity. *Studi italiani di linguistica teorica e applicata* 50 (3): 521–542

Feng and O'Halloran 2013: Feng, W. and K. O'Halloran. (2013). The Visual Representation of Metaphor: A Systemic Functional Approach. *Annual Review of Cognitive Linguistics* 11/2: 320–335

Ferstl and Kaiser 2013: Ferstl, E. C. and Kaiser, A. (2013). Sprache und Geschlecht: Wie quantitative Methoden aus der Experimental- und Neuropsychologie einen Beitrag zur Geschlechterforschung leisten können. *Gender* 5(3), 9–25.

Finley 1955: Finley, J. H. 1955. *Pindar and Aeschylus*. Cambridge, Mass.

Finnegan 1988: Finnegan, R. (1988), *Literacy and Orality: Studies in the Technology of Communication*. Oxford: Basil Blackwell.

Fludernik 1996: Fludernik, M. (1996), *Towards a 'Natural' Narratology*, Routledge.

Fludernik 2003: Fludernik, M. (2003), Chronology, Time, Tense and Experientiality in Narrative, *Language and Literature* 12.2: 117–34.

Fludernik 2010: Fludernik, M. (2010), "Experience, Experientiality and Historical Narrative: A View from Narratology", T. Breyer and D. Creutz, eds., *Erfahrung und Geschichte: Historische Sinnbildung im Pränarrativen*. Narratologia 23. Berlin: De Gruyter, 40–72.

Fludernik 2011: Fludernik, M. ed., (2011), *Beyond Cognitive Metaphor Theory: Perspectives on Literary Metaphor*. London: Routledge.

Folkers 2013: Folkers, A. (2013): Was ist neu am neuen Materialismus? Von der Praxis zum Ereignis, T. Goll, D. Keil, T. Telios (Hrsg.) *Critical Matter: Diskussionen eines neuen Materialismus*, Münster: edition assemblage, 16–33.

Forceville 2009: Forceville, C. J. (2009), The role of non-verbal sound and music in multimodal metaphor, C. J. Forceville and E. Urios-Aparisi (eds.), *Multimodal metaphor*, Berlin – New York: Mouton De Gruyter, 383–400

Foucault 1980: Foucault, M. (1980), *Power/Knowledge: Selected Interviews and Other Writings, 1972–79*, ed. C. Gordon, New York: Pantheon.

Foucault 1976–2018: Foucault, M. (1976–2018), *The History of Sexuality (*Or. in French *Histoire de la sexualité)*: Vol. 1: *The Will to Knowledge [An Introduction]*. London: Allen Lane 1978 (Or. in French *La volonté de savoir.* Gallimard, Paris 1976), Vol. 2: *The Use of Pleasure,* London: Penguin Books 1985 (Or. in French *L'usage des plaisirs.* Gallimard, Paris 1984), Vol. 3: *The Care of the Self,* London: Penguin Books 1986 (Or. in French *Le souci de soi.* Gallimard, Paris 1984), Vol. 4: *Confessions of the Flesh,* London: Penguin Books 2021 (Or. in French *Les aveux de la chair.* Gallimard, Paris 2018).

Fowler 1977: Fowler, R. (1977), *Linguistics and the novel*, London: Methuen and Co.

Frankish and Ramsey 2014: Frankish, K. Ramsey, W. M., eds. (2014). *The Cambridge Handbook of Artificial Intelligence*. Cambridge University Press.

Freeman 2007: Freeman, M. (2007). Cognitive Linguistic Approaches to Literary Studies: State of the Art in Cognitive Poetics, D. Geeraerts and H. Cuyckens (eds.), *The Oxford Handbook of Cognitive Linguistics*, Oxford, 1175–1202

Fricke and Müller 2010: Fricke, H., and R. Müller (2010). "Cognitive Poetics Meets Hermeneutics" *Mythos-Magazin* 1–9, https://www.mythos-magazin.de/erklaerendehermeneutik/hf-rm_cognitive poetics.pdf, last access October 2nd 2024.

Frigerio 2023: Frigerio, G. (2023), *A Cognitive Analysis of the Main Apolline Divinatory Practices: Decoding Divination*, London: Routledge.

Frith 2007: Frith, C. (2007), *Making Up the Mind: How the Brain Creates our Mental World*, Blackwell Publishing.
Frontisi-Ducroux 1995: Frontisi-Ducroux, F. (1995), *Du Masque au Visage. Aspects de l'identité en Grèce ancienne*. Paris: Flammarion.
Fuchs 2020: Fuchs, T. (2020), *Verteidigung des Menschen. Grundfragen einer verkörperten Anthropologie*. Suhrkamp Berlin.
Gadamer 1959: Gadamer, H.-G. (1959): "Vom Zirkel des Verstehens". In: Neske, G. (Hrsg.). *Martin Heidegger zum siebzigsten Geburtstag. Festschrift*. Pfullingen: Neske, 24–34.
Gadamer 1984: Gadamer, H.-G. (1984), Hören – Sehen- Lesen, in: Gadamer, H.-G., *Gesammelte Werke*, Band 8: *Ästhetik und Poetik*, Tübingen: Mohr Siebeck 1993, 271–278
Gadamer 1989: Gadamer, H.-G. (1989), Lesen ist wie Übersetzen, in: Gadamer, H.-G., *Gesammelte Werke*, Band 8: *Ästhetik und Poetik*, Tübingen: Mohr Siebeck 1993, 279–285
Gadamer 1990: Gadamer, H.-G. (1990/1960), *Wahrheit und Methode. Grundzüge einer philosophischen Hermeneutik*, Tübingen: Mohr Siebeck.
Gadamer 1992: Gadamer, H.-G. (1992), Wort und Bild – ‚so wahr, so seiend', in: Gadamer, H.-G., *Gesammelte Werke*, Band 8: *Ästhetik und Poetik*, Tübingen: Mohr Siebeck 1993, 373–399
Gallagher 2000: Gallagher, S. (2000), Philosophical conceptions of the self: implications for cognitive science. *Trends Cogn Sci*. 4(1):14–21.
Gallagher 2005: Gallagher, S. (2005), *How the Body Shapes the Mind*, Oxford, Oxford University Press.
Gallagher 2017: Gallagher, S. (2017). *Enactivist interventions: Rethinking the mind*. Oxford: Oxford University Press.
Gallagher and Zahavi 2008: Gallagher, S., D. Zahavi (2008), *The Phenomenological Mind: An Introduction to Philosophy of Mind and Cognitive Science*, Routledge.
Gander and Kinsella 2012: Gander, F. and J. Kinsella (2012), *Redstart: An Ecological Poetics*, University of Iowa Press.
García Jurado 2000: García Jurado, F. (2000), Las "metáforas de la vida cotidiana" ("metaphors we live by") en latín y su proyección etimológica en castellano, *Cien años de investigación semántica. De Michel Breal a la actualidad: actas del Congreso Internacional de Semántica* / coord. por M. Martínez Hernández, D. del Pino García Padrón, D. Corbella Díaz, C. J. Corrales Zumbado, F. J. Cortés Rodríguez, J. S. Gómez Soliño, M. L. Izquierdo Guzmán, J. M. Oliver Frade, B. Pico Graña, L. M. Pino Campos, F. del Mar Plaza Picón, G. Santana Henríquez, Vol. 2, 1571–1584
Garland 1987: Garland, R. (1987), *The Piraeus from the fifth to the first century B.C.* London: Duckworth.
Garner 2018: Garner, S. B. (2018), *Kinesthetic Spectatorship in the Theatre: Phenomenology, Cognition, Movement*, Palgrave Macmillan.
Garratt 2016: Garratt, P. (2016), *The Cognitive Humanities: Embodied Mind in Literature and Culture*, Palgrave Macmillan.
Gauvain et al. 2011: Gauvain, M., H. Beebe, and S. Zhao (2011), Applying the Cultural Approach to Cognitive Development, *Journal of cognition and development* 12(2):121–133
Gauvain and Munroe 2012: Gauvain, M., Munroe, R. L. (2012). Cultural change, human activity, and cognitive development. *Human Development*, 55(4), 205–228
Gavins and Steen 2003: Gavins, J., Steen, G. (Eds.). (2003). *Cognitive Poetics in Practice*. Routledge.
Geeraerts 2006: Geeraerts, D. (ed.) (2006), *Cognitive linguistics: basic readings*. Berlin: Mouton De Gruyter.

Geeraerts 2022: Geeraerts, D. (2022), Cognitive linguistics, in: J. Verschueren, J.-O. Östman, and J. Blommaert (eds.), *Handbook of Pragmatics: Manual*, Second edition, Amsterdam/Philadephia: John Benjamins, 178–184.

Geeraerts and Cuyckens 2007a: D. Geeraerts and H. Cuyckens (eds.) (2007), *The Oxford handbook of Cognitive Linguistics*. Oxford: Oxford University Press.

Geeraerts and Cuyckens 2007b: D. Geeraerts and H. Cuyckens (2007), Introducing cognitive linguistics, D. Geeraerts and H. Cuyckens (eds.), *The Oxford handbook of Cognitive Linguistics*. Oxford: Oxford University Press, 3–21

Geertz 2010a: Geertz, A. W. (2010), Brain, Body and Culture: A Biocultural Theory of Religion, *Method & Theory in the Study of Religion* 22(4): 304–321

Geertz 2010b: Geertz, A. W. (2010), Too much mind and not enough brain, body and culture: On what needs to be done in the cognitive science of religion, *Historia religionum: an international Journal* 2: 21–37

Geertz 2016: Geertz, A. W. (2016), Conceptions of religion in the cognitive science of religion, Antes, P., Geertz, A. W., Rothstein, M. (eds.), *Contemporary Views on Comparative Religion. In Celebration of Tim Jensen's 65th Birthday*, Sheffield and Bristol, CT, 127–139.

Geertz 2017: Geertz, A. W. (2017), Religious Bodies, Minds and Places: A Cognitive Science of Religion Perspective, L. Carnevale (ed.), *Spazi e luoghi sacri: espressioni ed esperienze di vissuto religioso*, Bari, 35–52

Gerolemou 2019: Gerolemou, M. (2019), Staging artificial intelligence, P. Meineck, W. M. Short, J. Devereaux, eds., *The Routledge Handbook of Classics and Cognitive Theory*, Routledge, 345–355

Gerolemou 2022: Gerolemou, M. (2022), *Technical Automation in Classical Antiquity*, Bloomsbury Publishing.

Gerolemou and Kazantzidis 2023: Gerolemou M., Kazantzidis G., eds. (2023), *Body and Machine in Classical Antiquity*. Cambridge: Cambridge University Press.

Gerrig 1993: Gerrig, R.J. (1993) *Experiencing Narrative Worlds. On the Psychological Activities of Reading*. New Haven, CT.

Ghezzi and Molinelli 2014: C. Ghezzi, P. Molinelli, eds. (2014), *Discourse and Pragmatic Markers from Latin to the Romance Languages*. Oxford: Oxford University Press.

Gibbs 1994: Gibbs, R. W. (1994), *The Poetics of Mind-Figurative Thought, Language, and Understanding*. Cambridge: Cambridge University Press.

Gibbs 1996: Gibbs, R. W. (1996), Why many concepts are metaphorical. *Cognition* 61, 309–319.

Gibbs 2005: Gibbs, R. W. (2005), *Embodiment and Cognitive Science*. New York, NY: Cambridge University Press.

Gibbs 2006: Gibbs, R. W. (2006), Metaphor Interpretation as Embodied Simulation, *Mind and Language* 21/3: 434–458

Gibbs 2017: Gibbs, R. W. (2017), *Metaphor wars: Conceptual metaphors in human life*, Cambridge Univ. Press, Cambridge.

Gibbs and Stehen 1999: Gibbs, R. W. Steen, G. (Eds.), (1999). *Metaphor in Cognitive Linguistics*. Amsterdam/Philadelphia: John Benjamins Publishing Company.

Gibson 1979: Gibson, J. (1979), *The Ecological Approach to Visual Perception*. Boston: Houghton Mifflin.

Gilhuly and Worman 2014: Gilhuly, K. and N. Worman, eds. (2014), *Space, Place, and Landscape in Ancient Greek Literature and Culture*. Cambridge: Cambridge University Press.

Gill 2019: Gill, C. (2019), Enactivism and embodied cognition in Stoicism and Plato's *Timaeus*, Anderson, M., D. Cairns, and M. Sprevak, (eds.), *Distributed Cognition in Antiquity*, Edinburgh Univ. Press, 150–168

Gils, van, de Jong, and Kroon 2019: Gils, L. van, I. de Jong, & C. Kroon (2019, eds.), *Textual Strategies in Ancient War Narrative: Thermopylae, Cannae and beyond*, Amsterdam studies in classical philology; Vol. 29. Leiden: Brill.

Giordano 2022: Giordano, M. 2022. From Oral Theory to Neuroscience: a Dialogue on Communication". *Rethinking Orality I: Codification, Transcodification and Transmission of 'Cultural Messages'*, ed. by A. Ercolani and L. Lulli, Berlin, Boston: De Gruyter, 167–198.

Golab 2023: Golab, H. (2023), Spectating ancient dramas: the Athenian audience and its emotional response, in: F. Budelmann, I. Sluiter (eds.), *Minds on Stage. Greek Tragedy and Cognition*, Oxford: OUP, 135–152

Goldberg 2003: Goldberg, A. (2003), Constructions: A new theoretical approach to language. *Trends in Cognitive Sciences*, 7 (5), 219–224.

Goldberg 2006: Goldberg, A. (2006). *Constructions at Work. The nature of generalization in language.* Oxford: Oxford University Press.

Goody 1988: Goody, J. (1988), *The interface between the written and the oral*, Cambridge University Press.

Gosden 2014: Gosden, C. (2014), Cognitive landscapes: The origins of the English village, L. Malafouris, C. Gosden and K. A. Overmann (eds.), *Creativity, Cognition and Material Culture* [*Pragmatics & Cognition* 22:1] Amsterdam/Philadelphia: John Benjamins Publishing Company, 93–108.

Gottschall 2012: Gottschall, J. (2012). *The storytelling animal: How stories make us human.* Houghton Mifflin Harcourt.

Gowlett 1979: Gowlett, J. (1979), Complexities of cultural evidence in the Lower and Middle Pleistocene. *Nature* 278:14–17.

Grady 2007: Grady, J. E. (2007), Metaphor, D. Geeraerts and H. Cuyckens (eds.), *The Oxford handbook of Cognitive Linguistics.* Oxford: Oxford University Press, 188–213

Grand-Clément 2023: Grand-Clément, A. (2023), *Au plaisir des dieux : expériences du sensible dans les rituels en Grèce ancienne*, Anacharsis, Toulouse.

Grand-Clément and Ribeyrol 2022: Grand-Clément, A. and C. Ribeyrol, eds. (2023), *The smells and senses of antiquity in the modern imagination.* Bloomsbury Academic, London e.a.

Graubard 1988: Graubard, S. R., ed. (1988), *The Artificial Intelligence Debate: False Starts, Real Foundations*, The MIT Press.

Graziosi, Haubold, Cowen-Breen, & Brooks 2023: Graziosi, B., Haubold, J., Cowen-Breen, C., & Brooks, C. (2023). Machine Learning and the Future of Philology: A Case Study. *TAPA 153*(1), 253–284

Greaves et al. 2022: Greaves D. A., Pinti P., Din S., Hickson R., Diao M., Lange C., Khurana P., Hunter K., Tachtsidis I., Hamilton A. F. C. (2022), Exploring Theater Neuroscience: Using Wearable Functional Near-infrared Spectroscopy to Measure the Sense of Self and Interpersonal Coordination in Professional Actors. *J Cogn Neurosci.* 34(12):2215–2236.

Grethlein 2013: Grethlein, J. (2013). *Experience and teleology in ancient historiography*, Cambridge Univ. Press.

Grethlein 2015: Grethlein, J. (2015). Social Minds and Narrative Time: Collective Experience in Thucydides and Heliodorus. *Narrative.* 23. 123–139.

Grethlein 2017: Grethlein, J. (2017). *Aesthetic experiences and classical antiquity: the content of form in narratives and pictures*, Cambridge Univ. Press.

Grethlein 2018: Grethlein, J. (2018), More than minds: experience, narrative, and plot, *Partial answers* 16/2:279–290.

Grethlein 2019: Grethlein, J. (2019). Odysseus and his bed. From significant objects to thing theory in Homer, *The Classical Quarterly* 69, 2: 467–82.
Grethlein 2023a: Grethlein, J. (2023), Gorgias' *apatê*, Sophocles' *Electra*, and cognitive criticism, in: F. Budelmann, I. Sluiter (eds.), *Minds on Stage. Greek Tragedy and Cognition*, Oxford, 153–172
Grethlein 2023b: Grethlein, J. (2023), *Ancient Greek texts and modern narrative theory: towards a critical dialogue*. Cambridge Univ. Press.
Grethlein, Huitink, and Tagliabue 2020: Grethlein, J., L. Huitink, A. Tagliabue, eds. (2020), *Experience, Narrative, and Criticism in Ancient Greece. Under the Spell of Stories*. Oxford: Oxford University Press.
Grieser and Johnston 2017: Grieser, A. K. and Johnston, J. (2017), *Aesthetics of Religion: A Connective Concept*, Berlin, Boston: De Gruyter.
Grosz 1994: Grosz, E. (1994), *Volatile Bodies: Toward a Corporeal Feminism*, Indiana University Press.
Grosz 2017: Grosz, E. (1994), *The Incorporeal: Ontology, Ethics, and the Limits of Materialism*, Columbia University Press.
Gruber 1986: Gruber, W. E. (1986), *Comic Theaters: Studies in Performance and Audience Response*, University of Georgia Press.
Grusin 2015: Grusin, R., ed. (2015). *The Nonhuman Turn*. University of Minnesota Press.
Guidorizzi and Beta 2000: Guidorizzi, G. & Beta, S. (2000). *La metafora: Testi greci e latini*, trad. and comm. Pisa: Edizioni ETS.
Gumpel 1984: Gumpel, L. (1984). *Metaphor reexamined: A non-Aristotelian perspective*. Bloomington: Indiana University Press.
Guthrie 1993: Guthrie, S. E. (1993), *Faces in the Clouds: A New Theory of Religion*, Oxford University Press.
Habinek and Reyes 2019: Habinek, T., H. Reyes (2019). Distributed Cognition and its discontents: a dialogue across history and artistic genre, M. Anderson, D. Cairns, and M. Sprevak, eds., *Distributed Cognition in Antiquity*, Edinburgh Univ. Press, 225–239
Hagen and Tushingham 2019: Hagen, E. H., S. Tushingham (2019), The Prehistory of Psychoactive Drug Use, T. B. Henley, M.J. Rossano, E. P. Kardas (eds.), *Handbook of Cognitive Archaeology: Psychology in Prehistory*, Routledge New York, 471–498
Hakemulder, Kuijpers, Tan, Bálint, and Doicaru 2017: Hakemulder, F., M. M. Kuijpers, E. S. Tan, K. Bálint & M. M. Doicaru, eds. (2017). *Narrative Absorption*. Amsterdam: John Benjamins.
Hallet and Neumann 2009: Hallet, W. and Neumann, B. (2009), *Raum und Bewegung in der Literatur: Die Literaturwissenschaften und der Spatial Turn*, Bielefeld: transcript Verlag.
Halliwell 2022: Halliwell, S. (2022), *On the Sublime / Pseudo-Longinus*, ed. with an introduction, translation, and commentary. Oxford – New York: OUP.
Halpern 2000: Halpern, D. (2000), *Sex differences in cognitive abilities*. Mahwah, NJ: Lawrence Erlbaum.
Hamilakis 2013: Hamilakis, Y. (2013), *Archaeology and the Senses: Human Experience, Memory, and Affect*, Cambridge: Cambridge University Press.
Hampe 2005: Hampe B. (2005), "Image Schemas in Cognitive Linguistics: Introduction", in B. Hampe, J. E. Grady (eds,), *From Perception to Meaning: Image Schemas in Cognitive Linguistics*, Berlin/New York: De Gruyter, 1–12.
Harré 2002: Harré, R. (2002), *Cognitive Science: A Philosophical Introduction*. SAGE Publications Ltd.
Harris 2021: Harris, R. A. (2021), *The Linguistics Wars: Chomsky, Lakoff, and the Battle over Deep Structure*, 2nd ed., revised. Oxford Univ. Press, Oxford (1st ed. 1993).
Harvey 1996: Harvey, D. (1996), *Justice, Nature and the Geography of Difference*, Wiley-Blackwell.

Havelock 1963: Havelock, E. A. (1963), *Preface to Plato. A History of the Greek Mind*. Cambridge and London: The Belknap Press of Harvard University Press.

Havelock 1986: Havelock, E. A. (1986), *The Muse Learns to Write: Reflections on Orality and Literacy from Antiquity to the Present*. New Haven and London: Yale University Press.

Hawes 2017: Hawes, G. ed. (2017), *Myths on the map: the storied landscapes of Ancient Greece*, Oxford, OUP.

Hawkes 2011: Hawkes, D. (2011), Against Materialism in Literary Theory. In: Cefalu, P., Reynolds, B. (eds) *The Return of Theory in Early Modern English Studies*. Palgrave Macmillan, London, 237–257.

Heidegger 1951: Heidegger, M. (1951), "Das Ding", in: *Gestalt und Gedanke: ein Jahrbuch. 1951*, ed. by C. Podewils and Bayerische Akademie der Schönen Künste, Berlin, Boston: Oldenbourg Wissenschaftsverlag, 128–149.

Heintz 2004: Heintz, C. (2004). Introduction: Why There Should Be a Cognitive Anthropology of Science, *Journal of Cognition and Culture*, 4(3–4), 391–408.

Heintz 2011: Heintz, C. (2011), Cognitive history and cultural epidemiology, L. H. Martin, J. Sørensen (eds.), *Past Minds: Studies in Cognitive Historiography*, Routledge, 11–28.

Henle 1958: Henle, P. (1958). Metaphor. P. Henle (Ed.), *Language, thought, and culture*. Ann Arbor: University of Michigan Press, 173–195.

Henley, Rossano, and Kardas 2019: T. B. Henley, M.J. Rossano, E. P. Kardas, eds. (2019), *Handbook of Cognitive Archaeology: Psychology in Prehistory*, Routledge New York.

Herman 2011: Herman, D. (ed., 2011), *The Emergence of Mind: Representations of Consciousness in Narrative Discourse in English*, Lincoln.

Hernández Garcés 2021: Hernández Garcés, C. (2021), "Forgetfulness as a Narrative Device in Herodotus' Histories", K. Mawford and E. Ntanou (eds.), *Ancient Memory: Remembrance and Commemoration in Graeco-Roman Literature*, Berlin, Boston: De Gruyter, 267–290.

Hernando 2002: Hernando, A. (2002), *Arqueología de la identidad*, Madrid: Ediciones Akal.

Herz 2016: Herz, R. S. (2016), The Role of Odor-Evoked Memory in Psychological and Physiological Health, *Brain Sci.*;6(3):22.

Heyes 2012: Heyes C. (2012), New thinking: the evolution of human cognition. *Philos Trans R Soc Lond B Biol Sci.* 367(1599):2091–6

Hick 2006: Hick, J. (2006), *The New Frontier of Religion and Science: Religious Experience, Neuroscience and the Transcendent*, Palgrave MacMillan.

Hodder 2012: Hodder, I. (2012), *Entangled: An Archaeology of the Relationships Between Humans and Things*, Chichester: Wiley-Blackwell.

Hölscher 2018: Hölscher, T. (2018), *Visual Power in Ancient Greece and Rome. Between Art and Social Reality*. University of California Press, Oakland.

Holloway and Hubbard 2001: Holloway, L., Hubbard, P. (2001), *People and place. The extraordinary geographies of everyday life*. Harlow: Prentice Hall.

Holter, Muth and Schwesinger 2018: Holter, E., S. Muth and S. Schwesinger (2018), Sounding out public space in late republican Rome, in: Butler, S., S. Nooter, eds. (2018), *Sound and the Ancient Senses*, Routledge, 44–60.

Hopper and Thompson 1980: P. J. Hopper; S. A. Thompson (1980), Transitivity in Grammar and Discourse. *Language* 56/2: 251–299

Horn 2015a: Horn, F. (2015), "Visualising Hom. *Il*. 3.57: "Putting on the Shirt of Stone" ", *Rheinisches Museum für Philologie* 158,1: 1–7

Horn 2015b: Horn, F. (2015), " "Sleeping the brazen slumber" – a cognitive approach to Hom. *Il.* 11.241", *Philologus* 159,2: 197–206.
Horn 2016a: Horn, F. (2016), "Metaphor and Spatial Conceptualization: Observations on Orientational Metaphors in Lycophron's Alexandra", F. Horn/C. Breytenbach (eds.): *Spatial Metaphors: Ancient Texts and Transformations*, Edition Topoi: Berlin, 85–102.
Horn 2016b: Horn, F. (2016), " "Building in the Deep": Notes on a Metaphor for Mental Activity and the Metaphorical Concept of Mind in Early Greek Epic ", *Greece & Rome* 63,2: 163–174.
Horn 2018: Horn, F. (2018), "Dying is Hard to Describe: Metonymies and Metaphors of Death in the *Iliad* ", *Classical Quarterly* 68,2: 359–383.
Horn 2020: Horn, F. (2020), " "Entering the House of Hades": The Formulaic Language for Metaphors of Death and the Question of Deliberateness in Early Greek Poetry ", in: C. Di Biase-Dyson/M. Egg (eds.): *Drawing Attention to Metaphor. Case Studies Across Time Periods, Cultures and Modes*, Amsterdam/Philadelphia: John Benjamins Publishing Company, 159–187.
Horn 2021: Horn, F. (2021), "On a Razor's Edge" (*Il.* 10.173): Iliadic Images of Imbalance and Uncertainty, *Greek, Roman, and Byzantine Studies* 61,4: 446–455
Horn 2025: Horn, F. ed., (2025), *Metaphors of the Ancient World: Conceptual Metaphor Theory and Ancient Sources.* De Gruyter: Berlin/New York.
Horn and Breytenbach 2016: F. Horn/C. Breytenbach. eds., (2016): *Spatial Metaphors: Ancient Texts and Transformations*, Edition Topoi: Berlin.
Hornstein 2011: Hornstein, S. (2011), *Losing Site: Architecture, Memory and Place*, Routledge.
Hubbard 2021: Hubbard, T. K. (2021). Comic somatisation and the body of evidence in Aeschines' *Against Timarchus*, in: Papaioannou, S. and Serafim, A. (eds.). *Comic Invective in Ancient Greek and Roman Oratory*, Berlin, Boston: De Gruyter, 171–190.
Huettel, Song, and McCarthy 2014: S. A. Huettel, A. W. Song, and G. McCarthy (2014), *Functional Magnetic Resonance Imaging*, 3rd Edition, Oxford Univ. Press.
Huffman 1986: Huffman, T. N. (1986), Cognitive Studies of the Iron Age in Southern Africa. *World Archaeology*, 18(1), 84–95.
Huitink 2019: Huitink, L. (2019), *Enargeia*, Enactivism and the Ancient Readerly Imagination, Anderson, M., D. Cairns, and M. Sprevak, (eds.), *Distributed Cognition in Antiquity*, Edinburgh Univ. Press, 169–189
Huitink 2020: Huitink, L. (2020). *Enargeia* and Bodily Mimesis. In J. Grethlein, L. Huitink, & A. Tagliabue (Eds.), *Experience, Narrative, and Criticism in Ancient Greece: Under the Spell of Stories*, Oxford: Oxford University Press, 188–209.
Hunter and Laemmle 2020: Hunter, R., R. Laemmle, 2020. *Euripides: Cyclops*, Cambridge, CUP.
Huth 2013: Huth, C. (2013), Kognitive Archäologie, A. Stephan, S. Walter (hrsg.), *Handbuch Kognitionswissenschaft*, Metzler, Stuttgart – Weimar, 514–517.
Hutmacher 2019: Hutmacher, F. (2019), Why Is There So Much More Research on Vision Than on Any Other Sensory Modality? *Front. Psychol., Sec. Theoretical and Philosophical Psychology*, 10:02246
Hutto 2000: Hutto, D. D. (2000), *Beyond Physicalism*, Amsterdam/Philadelphia: John Benjamins Publishing Company.
Hutto 2008: Hutto D. D. (2008). *Folk psychological narratives: The socio-cultural basis of understanding reasons.* Cambridge, MA: MIT Press.
Hutto and Myin 2012: Hutto, D. D., Myin, E. (2013). *Radicalizing enactivism: Basic minds without content.* MIT Press.

Iovino and Oppermann 2012: Iovino, S., Oppermann, S. (2012), Material ecocriticism: Materiality, agency, and models of narrativity, *Ecozon@: European Journal of Literature, Culture and Environment* 3/1: 75–91

Iovino and Oppermann 2014: Iovino, S., Oppermann, S., eds. (2014). *Material Ecocriticism*. Indiana University Press.

Iser 1971: Iser, W. (1971), *Die Appellstruktur der Texte; Der Lesevorgang; Die Wirklichkeit der Fiktion. Elemente eines funktionsgeschichtlichen Textmodells*, Konstanz.

Iser 1972: Iser, W. (1972), *Der implizite Leser. Kommunikationsformen des Romans von Bunyan bis Beckett*, Fink, München.

Iser 1976: Iser, W. (1976), *Der Akt des Lesens: Theorie ästhetischer Wirkung*, Fink, München.

Jakobson 1956: Jakobson, R. (1956), "Two Aspects of Language and Two Types of Aphasic Disturbances." *Selected Writings II: Word and Language.* Mouton Paris 1971, 239–259.

James 1884: James, W. (1884), What is an Emotion? *Mind* 9/34: 188–205

Janik 2020: Janik, L. (2020), *The Archaeology of Seeing, Science and Interpretation, the Past and Contemporary Visual Art*, Routledge.

Janowski and Ingold 2012: Janowski, M., & Ingold, T. (Eds.) (2012). *Imagining Landscapes: Past, Present and Future*, Routledge.

Jauß 1967: Jauß, H. R. (1967), *Literaturgeschichte als Provokation der Literaturwissenschaft*, Universitätsverlag Konstanz.

Jauß 1982: Jauß, H. R. (1982), *Ästhetische Erfahrung und literarische Hermeneutik.* Frankfurt a.M.: Suhrkamp.

Jauß 1994: Jauß, H. R. (1994), *Wege des Verstehens*, München, Fink.

Jauß 1998: Jauß, H. R. (1998), *Die Theorie der Rezeption. Rückschau auf ihre unerkannte Vorgeschichte.* Abschiedsvorlesung von Hans Robert Jauß am 11. Februar 1987 anläßlich seiner Emeritierung, Universitätsverlag Konstanz.

Johnson 1987: Johnson, M. (1987). *The body in the mind: The bodily basis of meaning, imagination, and reason.* University of Chicago Press.

Johnson 2015: Johnson, M. (2015). Embodied Understanding, *Frontiers in psychology* 6:875.

Johnson 2018: Johnson, M. (2018), 'The Embodiment of Language', A. Newen, L. De Bruin, and S. Gallagher (eds), *The Oxford Handbook of 4E Cognition*, OUP Oxford, 623–639

Jola and Hansen 2021: Jola C., Hansen P. (2021), Editorial: Performance in Theatre and Everyday Life: Cognitive, Neuronal, and Applied Aspects of Acting. *Front Psychol.* 732233 https://www.frontiersin.org/articles/10.3389/fpsyg.2021.732233/full, last access June 3rd 2024.

Kampakoglou and Novokhatko 2018: Kampakoglou, A. and Novokhatko, A. (eds., 2018) *Gaze, Vision, and Visuality in Ancient Greek Literature*, Berlin, Boston: De Gruyter.

Kaster 2005: R. A. Kaster (2005), *Emotion, Restraint, and Community in Ancient Rome.* Oxford: Oxford University Press.

Kazantzidis 2019: Kazantzidis, G. (2019), Cognition, Emotions and the Feeling Body in the Hippocratic Corpus, Anderson, M., D. Cairns, and M. Sprevak, (eds.), *Distributed Cognition in Antiquity*, Edinburgh Univ. Press, 132–149

Keller and Young 2023: Keller, A. and B. D. Youngs, eds. (2023), *Theoretical perspectives on smell.* Routledge.

Kemp and McConachie 2018: Kemp, R., B. McConachie (eds., 2018), *The Routledge Companion to Theatre, Performance and Cognitive Science*, London, Routledge.

Keogh, Pearson, and Zeman 2021: Keogh, R., Pearson, J., and Zeman, A. (2021), 'Aphantasia: The Science of Visual Imagery Extremes', *Handbook of Clinical Neurology* 178: 277–96.

Kirby 1997: Kirby, V. (1997), *Telling Flesh: The Substance of the Corporeal.* Routledge, New York.
Kirchhoff 2018: Kirchhoff, M. (2018). Predictive processing, perceiving and imagining: Is to perceive to imagine, or something close to it? *Philosophical studies* 175: 751–767
Kiverstein 2018: Kiverstein, J. (2018), Extended Cognition, A. Newen, L. De Bruin, and S. Gallagher (eds), *The Oxford Handbook of 4E Cognition,* OUP Oxford, 19–40
Klein, Damm, and Giebeler 1983: Klein, J., Damm, V., Giebeler, A. (1983). An outline of a theory of imagination. *Journal for General Philosophy of Science* 14 (1):15–23.
Heirman and Klooster 2013: Heirman, J., J. Klooster, eds. (2013), *The Ideologies of Lived Space in literary texts: Ancient and Modern,* Ginkgo Academia Press, Gent.
Knapp 2014: Knapp, J. A. (2014), Beyond Materiality in Shakespeare Studies, *Literature Compass* 11/10 (2014): 677–690
Knappett and Malafouris 2008: Knappett, C., L. Malafouris, eds. (2008), *Material Agency: Towards a Non-Anthropocentric Approach,* Berlin: Springer.
Kolonas 2020: Κολώνας, Λ. (2020), *Βούντενη Ι : ένα σημαντικό μυκηναϊκό κέντρο της Αχαΐας,* τόμος 2, Αθήνα, Ταμείο Αρχαιολογικών Πόρων και Απαλλοτριώσεων.
Konstan 1997: Konstan, D. (1997), *Friendship in the Classical World.* Cambridge: CUP.
Konstan 2003a: Konstan, D. (2003). Aristotle on anger and the emotions: The strategies of status, S. Braund & G. Most (Eds.), *Ancient Anger: Perspectives from Homer to Galen* (Yale Classical Studies, 99–120). Cambridge: Cambridge University Press.
Konstan 2003b: Konstan, D. (2003). Shame in ancient Greece. *Social Research: An International Quarterly* 70 (4):1031–1060.
Konstan 2006a: Konstan, D. (2006), *The Emotions of the Ancient Greeks: Studies in Aristotle and Classical Literature,* University of Toronto Press.
Konstan 2006b: Konstan, D. (2006). The concept of "emotion" from Plato to Cicero, *Méthexis* 19: 139–151.
Konstan 2017: Konstan , D. (2017), "Ancient Views on Emotion ," in A. Chaniotis, N. Kaltsas, and I. Mylonopoulos (eds), *A World of Emotions: Greece, 700 BC-200 AD,* New York: Onassis Foundation USA, 39–49.
Konstan and Rutter 2003: D. Konstan, N. K. Rutter, eds. (2003), *Envy, spite and jealousy: the rivalrous emotions in ancient Greece.* Edinburgh: Edinburgh University Press.
Körtner 1994: Körtner, U. H. J. (1994), *Der inspirierte Leser: zentrale Aspekte biblischer Hermeneutik,* Vandenhoeck & Ruprecht.
Kosslyn 1980: Kosslyn, S. M. (1980) *Image and Mind.* Cambridge, MA.
Kosslyn, Thompson, and Ganis 2005: Kosslyn, S. M., Thompson, W. L., and Ganis, G. (2005), *The Case for Mental Imagery.* Oxford.
Kövecses 2010: Kövecses, Z. (2010), *Metaphor: A Practical Introduction,* 2nd Edition, Oxford University Press.
Kövecses 2015: Kövecses, Z. (2015), "How does context produce metaphors?: A contextualist view of conceptual metaphor theory". J. Daems, E. Zenner, K. Heylen, D. Speelman and H. Cuyckens (eds.), *Change of Paradigms – New Paradoxes: Recontextualizing Language and Linguistics,* Berlin, München, Boston: De Gruyter Mouton, 109–116
Kreider 2014: Kreider, K. (2014). *Poetics and Place: The Architecture of Sign, Subjects and Site,* London: I.B.Tauris.
Kroon 1995: Kroon, C. (1995), *Discourse Particles in Latin: A Study of nam, enim, autem, vero and at,* Brill.

Küchler 2005: Küchler, S. (2005), "Materiality and Cognition: The Changing Face of Things". D. Miller (ed.), *Materiality*, New York, USA: Duke University Press, 206–230.

Kukkonen 2014: Kukkonen, K. (2014), Presence and prediction: the embodied reader's cascades of cognition, *Style* 48.3: 367–384

Kukkonen 2017: Kukkonen, K. (2017). Fantastic cognition. M. Burke & E. T. Troscianko (Eds.), *Cognitive literary science: Dialogues between literature and cognition* (151–167). Oxford University Press.

Kukkonen and Caracciolo 2014: Kukkonen, K., and Caracciolo, M. (2014). Introduction. What Is the 'Second Generation'? *Style* 48.3: 261–274.

Kundtová Klocová and Geertz 2019: Kundtová Klocová, E., and Geertz, A. W. (2019). Ritual and embodied cognition, R. Uro, J. J. Day, R. E. Demaris, & R. Roitto (Eds.). *The Oxford handbook of early Christian ritual*, 74–94, Oxford: Oxford University Press.

Kyselo 2013: Kyselo, M. (2013), Enaktivismus, A. Stephan, S. Walter (hrsg.), *Handbuch Kognitionswissenschaft*, Metzler, Stuttgart – Weimar, 197–201.

Ladda, Wallwork, and Lotze 2020: Ladda A. M., Wallwork S. B., Lotze M. (2020), Multimodal Sensory-Spatial Integration and Retrieval of Trained Motor Patterns for Body Coordination in Musicians and Dancers. *Front Psychol.* 576120

Lakoff 1987a: Lakoff, G. (1987), A Cognitive Theory of Metaphor. *Philosophical Review* 96 (4):589–594.

Lakoff 1987b: Lakoff, G. (1987), *Women, Fire, and Dangerous Things: What Categories Reveal About the Mind*, Univ. of Chicago Press.

Lakoff 1993: Lakoff, G. (1993), The Contemporary Theory of Metaphor. A. Ortony (ed.), *Metaphor and Thought*. 2nd ed., Cambridge, 202–251.

Lakoff 2008: Lakoff, G. (2008). The neural theory of metaphor, W. Gibbs (Ed.), *The Cambridge handbook of metaphor and thought* (17–38). Cambridge: Cambridge University Press.

Lakoff 2012: Lakoff, G. (2012). Explaining Embodied Cognition Results. *Topics in Cognitive Science* 4, 773–785

Lakoff and Johnson 1980: Lakoff, G. and M. Johnson (1980), *Metaphors we live by*. The Univ. of Chicago.

Lakoff and Turner 1989: Lakoff, G., Turner, M. (1989), *More Than Cool Reason: A Field Guide to Poetic Metaphor*. Chicago: University of Chicago Press.

Langacker 1987: Langacker R. W. (1987), *Foundation of Cognitive Grammar* (Vol. 1). *Theoretical Prerequisites*. Stanford: Stanford University Press.

Langacker 1991: Langacker R. W. (1991), *Concept, Image and Symbol. The Cognitive Basis of Grammar.* Berlin; New York: Mouton de Gruyter.

Langacker 1993: Langacker R. W. (1993), Reference-Point Constructions. *Cognitive Linguistics*, 4, 1–38.

Langacker 2005: Langacker R. W. (2005), "Construction Grammars: cognitive, radical, and less so". *Cognitive Linguistics: Internal Dynamics and Interdisciplinary Interaction*, F. J. Ruiz de Mendoza Ibáñez and M. S. Peña Cervel, Berlin, New York: De Gruyter Mouton, 101–162.

Larson 2016: Larson, J. (2016), *Understanding Greek Religion. A Cognitive Approach*. London/New York, Routledge.

Larsson, Svensson, and Nordin 2020: Larsson, J. Svensson, G., A. Nordin, eds. (2020), *Building Blocks of Religion. Critical Applications and Future Prospects*, Equinox Publishing.

Lather 2019: Lather, A. (2019), Staging artificial intelligence, P. Meineck, W. M. Short, J. Devereaux, eds., *The Routledge Handbook of Classics and Cognitive Theory*, Routledge, 345–355

Lather 2021: Lather, A. (2021). *Materiality and Aesthetics in Archaic and Classical Greek Poetry*. Edinburgh University Press.

Lauwers, Schwall, and Opsomer 2018: Lauwers, J., Schwall, H. and Opsomer, J. (eds., 2018), *Psychology and the Classics: A Dialogue of Disciplines*, Berlin, Boston: De Gruyter.
Lavelle 2022: Lavelle J. S. (2022), *Mindreading and Social Cognition*. Cambridge University Press.
Lavocat 2016: Lavocat, F. (2016), *Fait et fiction. Pour une frontière*, SEUIL.
Lawson 2004: Lawson, E. T. (2004), "The Wedding of Psychology, Ethnography and History: Methodological Bigamy or Tripartite Free Love?", H. Whitehouse and L. H. Martin (eds.), *Theorizing Religions Past: archaeology, history, and cognition*, Altamira Press, 1–6
Lazarus 1991: Lazarus, R. S. (1991), *Emotion and adaptation*. New York, OUP.
Le Goff 1992: Le Goff, J. (1992). *History and memory*. Tr. by S. Rendall and E. Claman. New York: Columbia University Press.
Lech 2009: Lech, M. (2009), Marching Choruses? Choral Performance in Athens, *Greek, Roman and Byzantine studies* 49(3): 343–361
Lee 2001: Lee, D. (2001), *Cognitive Linguistics: An Introduction*. Oxford: Oxford University.
Lee 2010: Lee, J. H. (2010). *Paul's gospel in Romans: a discourse analysis of Rom 1:16–8:39*. Leiden – Boston.
Leech and Short 1981: Leech, G.and M. Short, (1981), *Style in Fiction: A Linguistic introduction to English Fictional Prose*. London and New York: Longman,.
Lefebvre 1974: Lefebvre, H. (1974), *La production de l'espace*. Paris (Anthropos).
Leidhold 2022: Leidhold, W. (2022), *The History of Experience: A Study in Experiential Turns and Cultural Dynamics from the Paleolithic to the Present Day* (Routledge Studies in Cultural History), Routledge, London.
Lemke 2021: Lemke, T. (2021), *The Government of Things: Foucault and the New Materialisms*, NYU Press.
Leverage e. a. 2011: Leverage, P., H. Mancing, R. Schweickert, and J. M. William (eds.), *Theory of Mind and Literature*, West Lafayette.
Levin 2022: Levin, M. (2022), Technological Approach to Mind Everywhere: An Experimentally-Grounded Framework for Understanding Diverse Bodies and Minds, *Front Syst Neurosci.* 16:768201.
Lewicka 2011: Lewicka, M. (2011), On the Varieties of People's Relationships With Places: Hummon's Typology Revisited, *Environment and Behavior* 43/5: 676–709
Lewis-Williams 2002: Lewis-Williams, D. (2002), *The mind in the cave: consciousness and the origins of art*. London: Thames and Hudson.
Lex 1979: Lex, B.W. (1979). "The Neurobiology of Ritual Trance", E. D'Aquili, C.D. Laughlin, and J. McManus (eds.), *The Spectrum of Ritual*, New York: Columbia University Press, 117–51.
Ley 2007: Ley, G. (2007), *The theatricality of Greek tragedy*, The university of Chicago Press, Chicago and London.
Littlemore and Taylor 2014: J. Littlemore, J. R. Taylor eds., (2014), *The Bloomsbury Companion to Cognitive Linguistics*, Bloomsbury Academic.
Livingstone 2011: Livingstone, N. (2011), Silent Voices? Cultural Memory and the Reading of Inscribed Epigram in Classical Athens, M. Bommas (ed.), *Cultural Memory and Identity in Ancient Societies*, Continuum Publishing Corporation, New York, 26–42
Louwerse and Van Peer 2009: M. Louwerse, W. van Peer (2009), How cognitive is cognitive poetics? Adding a symbolic approach to the embodied one. G. Brone & J. Vandaele, eds., *Cognitive Poetics. Goals, Gains and Gaps*, Berlin / New York: Mouton de Gruyter, 423–444.
Low and Altman 1992: Low, S. M., Altman, I. (1992). Place attachment: A conceptual inquiry, *Human Behavior & Environment: Advances in Theory & Research* 12, 1–12.

Luhrmann e.a. 2021: Luhrmann, T. M., Weisman K., Aulino F., Brahinsky J. D., Dulin J. C., Dzokoto V. A., Legare C. H., Lifshitz M., Ng E., Ross-Zehnder N., Smith R. E. (2021), Sensing the presence of gods and spirits across cultures and faiths, *Proc Natl Acad Sci U S A* 118(5):e2016649118

Lupack 2022: Lupack; S. (2022), The Mycenaeans and Ecstatic Ritual Experience, D. Stein, S. K. Costello, K. Polinger Foster (eds.), *The Routledge Companion to Ecstatic Experience in the Ancient World*, Routledge, 284–295

Luraghi 2003: Luraghi, S. (2003). *On the Meaning of Prepositions and Cases. The expression of semantic roles in Ancient Greek*. Amsterdam/Philadelphia: John Benjamins Publishing Company.

Luraghi 2010: Luraghi, S. (2010). Philip Baldi & Pierluigi Cuzzolin (eds), *Adverbial phrases. In A New Historical Syntax of Latin*, 19–107. Berlin: Mouton de Gruyter.

Luraghi 2014: Luraghi, S. (2014), Plotting diachronic semantic maps. The role of metaphors, S. Luraghi and H. Narrog (eds.), *Perspectives on Semantic Roles*, Amsterdam/Philadelphia: John Benjamins Publishing Company, 99–150

Luraghi 2021: Luraghi, S. (2021), *Experiential Verbs in Homeric Greek: A Constructional Approach*, Brill, Leiden.

Lutterbie 2011: Lutterbie, J. (2011). *Toward a General Theory of Acting. Cognitive Science and Performance.* Palgrave Macmillan.

Lyre 2013: Lyre, H. (2013), Verkörperlichung und situative Einbettung, A. Stephan, S. Walter (hrsg.), *Handbuch Kognitionswissenschaft*, Metzler, Stuttgart – Weimar, 186–192

MacCorquodale 1970: MacCorquodale, K. (1970), On Chomsky's review of Skinner's "Verbal behavior." *Journal of the Experimental Analysis of Behavior* 13(1): 83–99.

MacDowell 2000: MacDowell, D. M. (2000), *Demosthenes, On the False Embassy.* Oxford University Press.

Malafouris 2004: Malafouris, L. (2004), The cognitive basis of material engagement: where brain, body and culture conflate, DeMarrais, E., Gosden, C., Renfrew, C. (eds.), *Rethinking materiality: the engagement of mind with the material world*, McDonald Institute for Archaeological Research, Cambridge, 53–62

Malafouris 2007: Malafouris, L. (2007), The sacred engagement: outline of a hypothesis about the origin of human 'religious intelligence', Barrowclough, D. A., Malone, C. (eds.), *Cult in context: reconsidering ritual in archaeology*, Oxbow, 198–204

Malafouris 2008: Malafouris, L. (2008), At the Potter's Wheel: An Argument for Material Agency, C. Knappett, L. Malafouris (eds.), *Material Agency: Towards a Non-Anthropocentric Approach*, Springer, 19–36

Malafouris 2009: Malafouris, L. (2009), "Neuroarchaeology": exploring the links between neural and cultural plasticity, J. Chiao (ed.), *Cultural Neuroscience: Cultural Influences on Brain Function*, Elsevier, 253–261

Malafouris 2012: Malafouris, L. (2012), More than a brain: human mindscapes, *Brain* 135/12: 3839–3844

Malafouris 2013: Malafouris, L. (2013), *How things shape the mind: A theory of material engagement*, MIT Press.

Malafouris 2014: Malafouris, L. (2014), Creative thinging: the feeling of and for clay, *Pragmatics and Cognition* 22/1: 140–158

Malafouris 2016: Malafouris, L. (2016), Material Engagement and the Embodied Mind, T. Wynn, F. L. Coolidge (eds.), *Cognitive Models in Palaeolithic Archaeology*, Oxford University Press, 69–88

Malafouris 2019a: Malafouris, L. (2019), Thinking as "thinging": psychology with things, *Current Directions in Psychological Science* 29/1: 3–8

Malafouris 2019b: Malafouris, L. (2019), Mind and material engagement, *Phenomenology and the Cognitive Sciences* 18, 1–17
Malafouris 2020: Malafouris, L. (2020), How does thinking relate to tool making? *Adaptive Behavior* 29(2) 107–121
Malafouris 2021: Malafouris, L. (2021), Making hands and tools: steps to a process archaeology of mind, *World archaeology* 53:1, 38–55.
Malafouris 2022: Malafouris, L. (2022), 'What Is Cognitive Archaeology? The Material Engagement Approach', T. Wynn, K. A. Overmann, and F. L. Coolidge (eds), *The Oxford Handbook of Cognitive Archaeology*, Oxford Univ. Press, C54.S1–C54.S5
Malafouris and Koukouti 2022: Malafouris L., Koukouti M.-D. (2022), Where the touching is touched: the role of haptic attentive unity in the dialogue between maker and material, *Multimodality and Society* 2/3: 265–287
Malafouris and Renfrew 2010: Malafouris, L., C. Renfrew, eds. (2010), *The Cognitive Life of Things. Recasting the Boundaries of the Mind*, McDonald Institute for Archaeological Research, University of Cambridge.
Malpas, J. (1999). *Place and Experience: A Philosophical Topography*. Cambridge/New York: Cambridge University Press.
Manzo and Devine-Wright 2021: Manzo, L. C. and P. Devine-Wright, eds. (2021), *Place attachment: advances in theory, methods, and applications*, Routledge.
Mar, Oatley, Djikic, and Mullin 2011: Mar, R. A., Oatley, K., Djikic, M., & Mullin, J. (2011), Emotion and narrative fiction: Interactive influences before, during, and after reading. *Cognition and Emotion*, 25(5): 818–833.
Mar, Djikic, Oatley 2008: Mar, R.A., Djikic, M., & Oatley, K. (2008), Effects of reading on knowledge, social abilities, and selfhood: Theory and empirical studies, in S. Zyngier, M. Bortolussi, A. Chesnokova, J. Auracher (eds.), *Directions in Empirical Literary Studies*, Amsterdam/Philadelphia: John Benjamins Publishing Company, 127–137.
Marcinkowski and Wilgaux 2004: Marcinkowski, A. & Wilgaux, J. (2004), Automates et créatures artificielles d'Héphaïstos: entre science et fiction. *Techniques & Culture*, 43–44, 9.
Markowitsch, Enlegen, Tscherepanow, Welzer 2013: Markowitsch, H., E.-M. Enlegen, M. Tscherepanow, H. Welzer (2013), Gedächtnis und Erinnern, A. Stephan, S. Walter (hrsg.), *Handbuch Kognitionswissenschaft*, Metzler, Stuttgart – Weimar, 289–303.
Marseglia 2023: Marseglia, R. (2023), Le chœur entre spectacle et spectateurs: médiations chorales, émotions et pragmatique poétique, in: E. Valette and S. Wyler (eds.), *Spectateurs grecs et romains: Corps, régimes de présence, modalités d'attention*, Paris: Hermann, 65–77.
Martin 2018: Martin, L. H. (2018), *Studies in Hellenistic Religions*, Cascade Books, Eugene Oregon.
Martin and Sauter 1995: Martin, J. and Sauter, W. eds. (1995). *Understanding Theatre: Performance Analysis in Theory and Practice*. Stockholm: Almqvist and Wiksell.
Martin and Sørensen 2011: Martin, L. H., J. Sørensen, eds. (2011), *Past Minds: Studies in Cognitive Historiography*, Routledge.
Mascia-Lees 2011: Mascia-Lees, F. E. 2011. Aesthetics: aesthetic embodiment and commodity capitalism, in: F. E. Mascia-Lees (ed.), *A Companion to the Anthropology of the body and embodiment*, Wiley-Blackwell, 3–23.
Matzner 2016: Matzner, S. (2016), *Rethinking Metonymy: Literary Theory and Poetic Practice from Pindar to Jakobson*, Oxford: OUP.
Mayor 2018: Mayor, A. (2018), *Gods and Robots: Myths, Machines, and Ancient Dreams of Technology*, Princeton Univ. Press.

McAuley 1999: McAuley, G. (1999), *Space in performance: making meaning in the theatre*. Ann Arbor: University of Michigan Press.
McCauley and Lawson 1990: Lawson, E. T., and McCauley, R. N. (1990). *Rethinking religion: Connecting cognition and culture*. Cambridge University Press.
McCauley and Lawson 2002: McCauley, R. N., and Lawson, E. T. (2002). *Bringing ritual to mind: Psychological foundations of cultural forms*. Cambridge University Press.
McCauley and Lawson 2007: McCauley, R. N., and Lawson, E. T. (2007). Cognition, Religious Ritual, and Archaeology, E. Kyriakidis (ed.), *The archaeology of ritual, of cult, and of religion*, Cotsen Institute of Archaeology Press, Los Angeles 209–254.
McConachie 2008: McConachie, B. (2008). *Engaging Audiences. A Cognitive Approach to Spectating in the Theatre*, Palgrave Macmillan London.
McConachie 2013: McConachie, B. (2013). *Theatre & mind*. Hampshire: Palgrave Macmillan.
McConachie 2015: McConachie, B. (2015). *Evolution, Cognition, and Performance*. Cambridge: Cambridge University Press.
McCorduck 2004: McCorduck, P. (2004), *Machines Who Think: A Personal Inquiry into the History and Prospects of Artificial Intelligence*, Routledge.
Meijs et al. 2018: Meijs, E. L., Slagter, H. A., de Lange, F. P., van Gaal, S. (2018), Dynamic Interactions between Top-Down Expectations and Conscious Awareness. *J Neurosci*. 38(9):2318–2327.
Meineck 2011: Meineck, P. (2011), The neuroscience of the tragic mask, *Arion* 19: 113–158
Meineck 2012: Meineck, P. (2012). The Embodied Space: Performance and Visual Cognition at the Fifth Century Athenian Theatre. *New England Classical Journal*. 39. 1–47.
Meineck 2016: Meineck, P. (2016), Cognitive Theory and Aeschylus: Translating beyond the Lexicon, S. E. Constantinidis (ed.) *The Reception of Aeschylus' Plays through Shifting Models and Frontiers*, Leiden and Boston: Brill, 147–175
Meineck 2017: Meineck, P. (2017). *Theatrocracy: Greek drama, cognition, and the imperative for theatre*. Routledge.
Meineck 2019: Meineck, P. (2019), Mask as Mind Tool: A Methodology of Material Engagement, Anderson, M., D. Cairns, and M. Sprevak, eds. *Distributed Cognition in Classical Antiquity*. Edinburgh University Press: 71–91
Meineck and Konstan 2014: Meineck, P., D. Konstan (eds.), *Combat Trauma and the Ancient Greeks*. The New Antiquity. New York: Palgrave Macmillan.
Meineck, Short and Devereaux 2019a: P. Meineck, W. M. Short, J. Devereaux, eds. (2019), *The Routledge Handbook of Classics and Cognitive Theory*, Routledge.
Meineck, Short, and Devereaux 2019b: P. Meineck, W. M. Short, J. Devereaux (2019), Introduction, P. Meineck, W. M. Short, J. Devereaux, eds., *The Routledge Handbook of Classics and Cognitive Theory*, Routledge, 1–18
Michaelian and Sutton 2013: Michaelian, K. Sutton, J., eds. (2013). *Distributed Cognition and Memory Research* (special issue). *Review of Philosophy and Psychology*.
Millidge, Seth, and Buckley 2022: Millidge, B., Seth, A.K., Buckley, C.L. (2021). Predictive Coding: a Theoretical and Experimental Review. *ArXiv, abs*/2107.12979.
Mills 2014: Mills, S. (2014), *Auditory Archaeology: Understanding Sound and Hearing in the Past*, Walnut Creek, CA: Left Coast Press.
Minchin 2001: Minchin, E. (2001), *Homer and the resources of memory: some applications of cognitive theory to the Iliad and the Odyssey*. Oxford: Oxford University Press.
Minchin 2005: Minchin, E. (2005), Homer on Autobiographical Memory: The Case of Nestor, R. Rabel (ed.), *Approaches to Homer, Ancient and Modern*, Swansea, Classical Press of Wales, 55–72.

Minchin 2007: Minchin, E. (2007), *Homeric voices: discourse, memory, gender.* Oxford: Oxford University Press.
Minchin 2008: Minchin, E. (2007), "Chapter One. Spatial Memory And The Composition Of The Iliad", E. A. Mackay (ed.), *Orality, Literacy, Memory in the Ancient Greek and Roman World.* Leiden, Niederlande: Brill, 9–34.
Minchin 2016: Minchin, E. (2016), Voice and Voices: Homer and the Stewardship of Memory, Slater, N. W. (ed.), *Voice and Voices in Antiquity: Orality and Literacy in the Ancient World*, Leiden, Niederlande: Brill, 11–30
Minchin 2019: Minchin, E. (2019), The cognition of deception: falsehoods in Homer's Odyssey and their audiences, Anderson, M., D. Cairns, and M. Sprevak, eds. *Distributed Cognition in Classical Antiquity.* Edinburgh University Press: 109–121
Misic and Graham 2024: Misic, B. and A. Graham, eds. (2024), *Senses, cognition, and ritual experience in the Roman world*, Cambridge: CUP.
Mitchell 2002: Mitchell, W. J. T., ed. (2002), *Landscape and Power*, Second Edition (1st ed. 1994), The University of Chicago Press.
Mithen 1996: Mithen, S. (1996), *The Prehistory of Mind.* London: Thames and Hudson.
Mocciaro and Short 2019a: Mocciaro, E. and Short, W. M. eds., (2019). *Toward a Cognitive Classical Linguistics: The Embodied Basis of Constructions in Greek and Latin*, Warsaw, Poland: De Gruyter Open Poland.
Mocciaro and Short 2019b: Mocciaro, E. and Short, W. M. (2019). "Introduction. Toward a cognitive classical linguistics", Mocciaro, E. and Short, W. M. eds., *Toward a Cognitive Classical Linguistics: The Embodied Basis of Constructions in Greek and Latin*, Warsaw, Poland: De Gruyter Open Poland, 1–15
Montello 2018: Montello, D. R. (2018), Behavioural and cognitive geography: introduction and overview, D. R. Montello (ed.), *Handbook of behavioural and cognitive geography*, Edward Elgar Cheltenham, UK, Northampton, MA, USA, 3–15
Morgan e.a. 2017: Morgan, B., Park., and Spolsky, E. eds., (2017), *Situated cognition and the study of culture.* Special issue of *Poetics Today* 38.2.
Morley 2014: Morley, N. (2014), Urban smells and roman noses, in: Bradley, M., ed., *Smell and the Ancient Senses*, Routledge, 110–119.
Moutoussis 2016: Moutoussis K. (2016), The machine behind the stage: A neurobiological approach toward theoretical issues of sensory perception. *Front Psychol.* 7:1357.
Nagy 2015: Nagy, G. (2015). *Masterpieces of Metonymy: From Ancient Greek Times to Now.* Hellenic Studies Series 72. Washington, DC: Center for Hellenic Studies.
Neumann and Thomason 2022: Neumann, K., A. Thomason, eds. (2022), *The Routledge handbook of the senses in the ancient Near East.* Abingdon; New York: Routledge.
Newen, De Bruin and Gallagher 2018: Newen, A., De Bruin, L. and Gallagher, S. (2018), *The Oxford Handbook 4E Cognition.* Oxford University Press, New York.
Ng 2019: Ng, D. (2019), Roman-period theatres as distributed cognitive micro-ecologies, Anderson, M., D. Cairns, and M. Sprevak, (eds.), *Distributed Cognition in Antiquity*, Edinburgh Univ. Press, 117–131
Nikiforidou 1991: Nikiforidou, K. (1991), "The meanings of the genitive: A case study in semantic structure and semantic change", *Cognitive Linguistics* 2/2: 149–206.
Nilsson 2009: Nilsson, N. L. (2009), *The Quest for Artificial Intelligence*, CUP Cambridge.
Nisbett 2003: Nisbett, R. (2003), *The Geography of Thought: How Asians and Westerners Think Differently...and Why*, Free Press.

Noë 2004: Noë, A. (2004). *Action in Perception*, Cambridge, MA: MIT Press.
Noë 2009: Noë, A. (2009), *Out of our heads: Why you are not your brain, and other lessons from the biology of consciousness*. Hill & Wang.
Noel 2013: Noel, A.-S. (2013), Le vêtement-piège et les Atrides : métamorphoses d'un objet protéen, B. Le Guen, S. Milanezi, éd., *L'appareil scénique dans les spectacles de l'Antiquité*. Saint-Denis, Presses universitaires de Vincennes, 159–182.
Noel 2019: Noel, A.-S. (2019), What do we actually see on stage? A cognitive approach to the interactions between visual and aural effects in the performance of Greek tragedy, P. Meineck, W. M. Short, J. Devereaux, eds., *The Routledge Handbook of Classics and Cognitive Theory*, Routledge, 297–309.
Noel 2023a: Noel, A.-S. (2023), "Thinking through things: extended cognition as a consolatory fiction in Greek tragedy," F. Budelmann, I. Sluiter, eds., *Minds on stage: Greek tragedy and Cognition*, Oxford: Oxford University Press, 117–132.
Noel 2023b: Noel, A.-S. (2023), La vie des objets dans le théâtre antique : dramaturgie et ontologie. Introduction, *Cahiers du Théâtre Antique*, 2023, Dossier : *La vie des objets dans le théâtre antique : dramaturgie et ontologie*, 6, 11–38.
Noel forthcoming: Noel, A.-S. (forthcoming) *Playing with objects in Greek tragedy: Poets, actors, spectators*, Oxford: Oxford University Press.
Nooter 2019a: Nooter, S. (2019), Review: The Materialities of Greek Tragedy: Objects and Affect in Aeschylus, Sophocles, and Euripides, Mario Telò, Melissa Mueller, The Materialities of Greek Tragedy: Objects and Affect in Aeschylus, Sophocles, and Euripides. London: Bloomsbury, 2018, *BMCR* 2019.11.03, https://bmcr.brynmawr.edu/2019/2019.11.03/, last access June 3rd 2024.
Nooter 2019b: Nooter, S. (2019). Sounds of the stage, S. Butler and S. Nooter (eds.), *Sound and the Ancient Senses*, Routledge, 198–211.
Nooter 2023: Nooter, S. (2023). *Greek Poetry in the Age of Ephemerality*. Cambridge: Cambridge University Press.
Nooter 2024: Nooter, S. (2024), Aristophanes and the flying sound, S. Nooter and M. Telò (eds.), *Radical formalisms: reading, theory, and boundaries of the Classical*, Bloomsbury, 85–104.
Norberg-Schulz 2000: Norberg-Schulz, C. (2000). *Architecture: Presence, Language and Place*. Skira Editore.
Nordgren 2015: Nordgren, L. (2015), *Greek Interjections: Syntax, Semantics and Pragmatics*, Berlin, München, Boston: De Gruyter Mouton.
Nöth 1985: Nöth, W. (1985), Semiotic aspects of metaphor, W. Paprotté & R. Dirven (Eds.), *The ubiquity of metaphor: Metaphor in language and thought*. Amsterdam/Philadelphia: John Benjamins Publishing Company, 1–16.
Nöth 1990: Nöth, W. (1990). *Handbook of Semiotics*. Bloomington: Indiana University Press.
Novokhatko 2014: Novokhatko, A. (2014), Ancient theories of metaphor, G. K. Giannakis (ed.), *Encyclopedia of ancient Greek language and linguistics*, vol. 2 (414–418). Leiden/Boston: Brill.
Novokhatko 2016: Novokhatko, A. (2016), The use of the term 'metaphor' in Latin linguistic discourse before Quintilian, P. Poccetti (ed.), *Latinitatis rationes. Descriptive and historical accounts for the Latin language*, Berlin/Boston: De Gruyter, 395–409.
Novokhatko 2017: Novokhatko, A. (2017), The linguistic treatment of metaphor in Quintilian, *Pallas* 103, 311–318.
Novokhatko 2019: Novokhatko, A. (2019), The typology of linguistic metaphor in 1st c. CE Roman thought, *Lemmata Linguistica Latina*. Vol. 1: *Words and Sounds*, N. Holmes, M. Ottink, J. Schrickx, M. Selig (eds.), De Gruyter, Berlin / New York, 384–398.

Novokhatko 2021a: Novokhatko, A. (2021), Contemporary Metaphor Studies and Classical Texts, *Mnemosyne* 74,4: 682–703
Novokhatko 2021b: Novokhatko, A. (2021), Images and cognitive metaphor in 1st c. CE Roman discourse, A. M. Martín Rodríguez (ed.), *Linguisticae Dissertationes. Current Perspectives on Latin Grammar, Lexicon and Pragmatics*, Madrid, Ediciones clásicas, 149–160
Novokhatko 2023: Novokhatko, A. (2023), *Greek Comedy and Embodied Scholarly Discourse*. De Gruyter, Berlin / New York.
Novokhatko 2024: Novokhatko, A. (2024), "Fronto's Theory of Metaphor? An Enactivist and Psycholinguistic Perspective". In: *Recent Trends and Findings in Latin Linguistics: Volume I: Syntax, Semantics and Pragmatics. Volume II: Semantics and Lexicography. Discourse and Dialogue*, ed. by C. Cabrillana, Berlin, Boston: De Gruyter: 569–585.
Novokhatko 2025a: Novokhatko, A. (2025), Joy and Tears in Situ: The Perception of Theatre in Early Greek Sources, M. Ornaghi (ed.), *Chronology and history of the Attic theatre: towards a reappraisal*, De Gruyter, Berlin / New York (forthcoming)
Novokhatko 2025b: Novokhatko, A. (2025), Multimodality of Metaphor in Old Greek Comedy, in: F. Horn (ed.), *Metaphors of the Ancient World: Conceptual Metaphor Theory and Ancient Sources*, De Gruyter, Berlin/ New York (forthcoming).
O' Regan and Noë 2001: O' Regan, J. K. and Noë, A., (2001), 'A Sensorimotor Account of Vision and Visual Consciousness', *Behavioral and Brain Sciences* 24: 883–917
Oatley 2004: Oatley, K. (2004). *Emotions: A brief history.* Blackwell Publishing.
Oatley 2009: Oatley, K. (2009). Changing our minds, *Greater Good* 5/3. https://greatergood.berkeley.edu/article/item/chaning_our_minds, last access June 3rd 2024.
Oatley and Jenkins 1996: Oatley, K., Jenkins, J. M. (1996). *Understanding emotions.* Blackwell Publishing.
Oesterreich 2020: Oesterreich, N. (2021). *Kognitionswissenschaftliche Perspektiven auf biblische Visionserzählungen.* Leiden: Brill.
Olofsson e.a. 2020: Olofsson, J. K., I. Ekström, J. Lindström, E. Syrjänen, A. Stigsdotter-Neely, L. Nyberg, S. Jonsson, M. Larsson (2020), Smell-Based Memory Training: Evidence of Olfactory Learning and Transfer to the Visual Domain, *Chemical Senses* 45/7: 593–600.
Olsen 2017: Olsen, S. (2017), "Kinesthetic Choreia: Empathy, Memory, and Dance in Ancient Greece." *Classical Philology* 112: 153–174.
Olsen 2019: Olsen, S. (2019), Sappho's kinesthetic turn: agency and embodiment in archaic Greek poetry, P. Meineck, W. M. Short, J. Devereaux, eds., *The Routledge Handbook of Classics and Cognitive Theory*, Routledge, 281–296
Olsen 2021: Olsen, S. (2021), *Solo Dance in Archaic and Classical Greek Literature: Representing the Unruly Body.* Cambridge University Press.
Ong 1982: Ong, W. J. (1982), *Orality and Literacy: The Technologizing of the Word*, Routledge, London – New York.
Ostenfeld 2018: Ostenfeld, E. N. (2018), *Ancient Greek Psychology and the Modern Mind-Body Debate*, 2nd ed., Baden-Baden, Academia.
Overmann and Coolidge 2019: Overmann, K. A. and F. L. Coolidge (2019), Introduction: Cognitive Archaeology at the Crossroads, Overmann, K. A. and F. L. Coolidge (eds.), *Squeezing Minds From Stones: Cognitive Archaeology and the Evolution of the Human Mind*, Oxford University Press, 1–12.
Overmann and Wynn 2019: Overmann, K.A. and Wynn, T. (2019), Materiality and Human Cognition, *Journal of Archaeological Method and Theory* 26, 457–478.

Pachis 2014: Pachis, P. (2014), Data from Dead Minds? Dream and Healing in the Isis / Sarapis Cult During the Graeco-Roman Age, *Journal of Cognitive Historiography* 1(1): 52-71

Pachis 2019: Pachis, P. (2019), 'Waves of emotion' in Apuleius' "Metamorphoses", book XI: an approach according to cognitive historiography, in: A. K. Petersen, I. S. Gilhus, L. H. Martin (eds.), *Evolution, cognition, and the history of religion: a new synthesis*, Leiden: Brill, 490–505.

Pachis 2020: Pachis, P. (2020), The Rites of the Day of Blood (*dies sanguinis*) in the Graeco-Roman Cult of Cybele and Attis: A Cognitive Historiographical Approach. *Journal of Cognitive Historiography*, 5(1–2): 37–55.

Pagan 2014: Pagan, N. O. (2014), *Theory of Mind and Science Fiction*, Palgrave Macmillan.

Palmer 2004: Palmer, A. (2004), *Fictional minds*, Lincoln, NE.

Palmer 2010: Palmer, A. (2010), *Social minds in the novel*, Columbus.

Panagiotidou 2014: Panagiotidou, O. (2014), The Asklepios Cult: Where Brains, Minds, and Bodies Interact With the World, Creating New Realities, *Journal of Cognitive Historiography* 1(1):14–23

Panagiotidou 2022: Panagiotidou, O. (2022), Emotional Arousal, Sensory Deprivation and "Miraculous Healing" in the Cult of Asclepius, D. Stein, S. K. Costello, K. Polinger Foster (eds.), *The Routledge Companion to Ecstatic Experience in the Ancient World*, Routledge, 296–313

Panagiotidou and Beck 2017: Panagiotidou, O. and R. Beck (2017), *The Roman Mithras Cult: A Cognitive Approach*, New York, Bloomsbury.

Parker and Gibson 1979: Parker, S., and K. Gibson (1979), A developmental model for the evolution of language and intelligence in early hominids. *Behavioral and Brain Sciences* 2:367–408.

Pelliccia 1995: Pelliccia, H. (1995), *Mind, body, and speech in Homer and Pindar*. Göttingen: Vandenhoeck & Ruprecht.

Peponi 2013: Peponi, A.-E. (2013), 'Theorizing the Chorus in Greece', J. Billings, F. Budelmann, and F. Macintosh (eds), *Choruses, Ancient and Modern*, Oxford Univ. Press, 15–34

Perdicoyianni-Paléologou 2014: Perdicoyianni-Paleologou, H. (2014) 'Discourse Analysis and Greek', G. K. Giannakis (ed.), *Encyclopedia of Ancient Greek Language and Linguistics*. Vol. 1: A-F. Leiden-Boston, Brill, 509–512.

Perry 2001: Perry, C. ed. (2001). *Material Culture and Cultural Materialisms in the Middle Ages and Renaissance*, Turnhout: Brepols.

Petsalis-Diomidis 2010: Petsalis-Diomidis, A. (2010), *Truly Beyond Wonders: Aelius Aristides and the Cult of Asklepios*. Oxford, OUP.

Pillière 2013: Pillière, L. (2013), "Mind Style: Deviance from the Norm?", *Études de stylistique anglaise* 4, 67–80.

Pirenne-Delforge 2018: Pirenne-Delforge, V. (2018). Greek Gods and Cognitive Sciences: About Jennifer Larson's Understanding Greek Religion. *Journal of Cognitive Historiography*, 4(1), 47–52.

Plamper 2010: Plamper, J. (2010). The History of Emotions: An Interview with William Reddy, Barbara Rosenwein, and Peter Stearns. *History and Theory* 49: 237–265.

Poignault 2002: Poignault, R. 2002. " Deux îles, des poulets et quelques divinités : images des rapports de parenté dans la famille impériale selon la correspondance de Fronton ", *Hommages à C. Deroux, II : Prose et linguisitique, médecine*, Latomus, 357–371.

Porter 2003: Porter, J. I. (2003), The materiality of classical studies, *Parallax* 9/4: 64–74.

Porter 2010: Porter, J. I. (2010), *The Origins of Aesthetic Thought in Ancient Greece: Matter, Sensation, and Experience*. Cambridge, UK: Cambridge University Press.

Porter 2016: Porter, J. I. (2016), *The Sublime in Antiquity*. Cambridge: CUP.

Porter and Carson 1995: Porter, S. E., Carson, D. A., eds. (1995), *Discourse Analysis and Other Topics in Biblical Greek*, Bloomsbury Academic.

Porter and Reed 1999: Porter, S. E., and J. T. Reed eds., (1999), *Discourse Analysis and the New Testament: Approaches and Results*, Shefield: Shefield Academic Press.

Portugali 2018: Portugali, J. (2018), History and theoretical perspectives of behavioural and cognitive geography, D. R. Montello (ed.), *Handbook of behavioural and cognitive geography*, Edward Elgar Cheltenham, UK, Northampton, MA, USA, 16–38

Pragglejaz Group 2007: Pragglejaz Group (2007) MIP: A Method for Identifying Metaphorically Used Words in Discourse, *Metaphor and Symbol*, 22:1, 1–39

Premack and Woodruff 1978: Premack, D. and Woodruff, G. (1978). Does the chimpanzee have a theory of mind? *Behavioral and Brain Sciences*, 1(4), 515–526

Prinz 2004: Prinz, J. J. (2004). Embodied emotions. In R. C. Solomon (Ed.), *Thinking about feeling: Contemporary philosophers on emotions* (44–58). Oxford University Press.

Prinz 2007: Prinz, J. J. (2007). *The emotional construction of morals*. Oxford: Oxford University Press.

Proietti 2019: Proietti, G. (2019), "Can an Ancient Truth Become an Old Lie? A Few Methodological Remarks Concerning Current Comparative Research on War and its Aftermath", in M. Giangiulio – E. Franchi G. Proietti (eds.), *Commemorating War and War Dead. Ancient and Modern*, Stuttgart, 71–92.

Proietti 2021: Proietti, G. (2021), *Prima di Erodoto. Aspetti della memoria delle Guerre persiane* (Hermes Einzelschriften 120), Stuttgart: Franz Steiner.

Proietti 2022: Proietti, G. (2022), A Collective War Trauma in Classical Athens? Coping with War Deaths in Aeschylus' *Persians*, in O. Rees, K. Hurlock, J. Crawley (eds.), *Combat Stress in Premodern Europe*, London: Palgrave Macmillan, 37–61.

Proust and Fortier 2018: Proust, J. and M. Fortier (2018), Metacognitive Diversity across cultures: an introduction, Proust, J. and M. Fortier (eds.), *Metacognitive Diversity: An Interdisciplinary Approach*, OUP Oxford, 1–22.

Pühringer 2004: Pühringer, R. (2004), Als es weder Kilos noch das Einmaleins gab: Gedanken über ein urzeitliches Maßsystem als Ordnungsprinzip. *Experimentelle Archäologie in Europa* 3: 15–23.

Purves 2014: Purves, A. 2014, "In the Bedroom: Interior Space in Herodotus' Histories," in K. Gilhuly & N. Worman, eds., *Space, Place, and Landscape in Ancient Greek Literature and Culture*. Cambridge University Press, 94–129.

Purves 2017: Purves, A., ed. (2017), *Touch and the Ancient Senses*, Routledge.

Pylyshyn: 2003a: Pylyshyn, Z. (2003), *Seeing and Visualising: It's Not What You Think*. Cambridge, MA.

Pylyshyn: 2003b: Pylyshyn, Z. (2003), 'Return of the Mental Image: Are There Really Pictures in the Brain?', *Trends in Cognitive Sciences* 7: 113–18.

Raccanelli 1998: Raccanelli, R. (1998), *L' 'amicitia' nelle commedie di Plauto: un'indagine antropologica*, Edipuglia.

Raccanelli 2010: Raccanelli, R. (2010), *Esercizi di dono: pragmatica e paradossi delle relazioni nel "De beneficiis" di Seneca*, Palumbo.

Raccanelli 2012: Raccanelli, R. (2012), *Cicerone, "Post reditum in senatu" e "Ad Quirites". Come disegnare una mappa di relazioni*, Bologna, Pàtron Editore.

Raible 2016: Raible. W. (2016), "Metaphors as models of thinking ", F. Horn/C. Breytenbach (Hgg.): *Spatial Metaphors: Ancient Texts and Transformations*, Edition Topoi: Berlin, 21–42

Reddy 1979: Reddy, M. J. (1979). The conduit metaphor: A case of frame conflict in our language about language. A. Ortony, ed., *Metaphor and Thought*, 284–310. Cambridge: Cambridge University Press.

Rehm 2002: Rehm, R. 2002. *The Play of Space. Spatial Transformation in Greek Tragedy*. Princeton and Oxford: Princeton University Press.

Reinarz 2014: Reinarz, J. (2014), *Past Scents: Historical Perspectives on Smell*, University of Illinois Press.
Reinhardt 2020: Reinhardt, K. (2020), Digitaler Humanismus. Jenseits von Utopie und Dystopie. *Berliner Debatte Initial* 31:111–123.
Reitz and Finkmann 2020. Reitz, C. and Finkmann, S. eds., (2020), *Structures of Epic Poetry:* Vol. I: *Foundations.* Vol. II.1/II.2: *Configuration.* Vol. III: *Continuity*, Berlin, Boston: De Gruyter.
Renfrew 1982: Renfrew, C. (1982), *Towards an archaeology of mind: an inaugural lecture delivered before the University of Cambridge on 30 November 1982*, Cambridge: Cambridge University Press.
Renfrew 1989: Renfrew C. (1989), Comments on archaeology into the 1990s. *Nor. Archaeol. Rev.* 22: 33–41.
Renfrew 1993: Renfrew, C. (1993), Cognitive archaeology: Some thoughts on the archaeology of thought. *Cambridge Archaeological Journal* 3.2: 248–250.
Renfrew 1994: Renfrew C. (1994), Towards a cognitive archaeology, C. Renfrew, E. B. W. Zubrow (eds): *The Ancient Mind: elements of cognitive archaeology*, 3–12. Cambridge University Press, Cambridge.
Renfrew 2004: Renfrew C. (2004), Towards a theory of material engagement. In: DeMarrais E., Gosden C., and Renfrew C. (eds.), *Rethinking materiality: the engagement of mind with the material world.* McDonald Institute; Cambridge, 23–32.
Renfrew 2006: Renfrew, C. (2006), Becoming human: The archaeological challenge, *Proceedings of the British Academy* 139: 217–238
Renfrew 2007: Renfrew, C. (2007), *Prehistory: The Making of the Human Mind*, Weidenfeld & Nicolson.
Renfrew and Bahn 1991: Renfrew, A.C. and Paul Bahn (1991), *Archaeology: Theories, Methods and Practice*, London: Thames & Hudson.
Renfrew and Zubrow 1994: Renfrew, A.C. and E. B. W. Zubrow, eds. (1994), *The ancient mind: elements of cognitive archaeology.* Cambridge: Cambridge University Press.
Renfrew, Frith, and Malafouris 2008: Renfrew C., Frith C., Malafouris L. (2008), Introduction. The sapient mind: archaeology meets neuroscience. *Philos Trans R Soc Lond B Biol Sci.* 363(1499):1935–8.
Rengakos 2022: Rengakos, A. (2022), Μετα-ανθρωπισμός, ανθρωπισμός και αρχαιότητα, in: *Praktika tis Akadimias Athinon* 97: 19–32.
Rengakos 2024: Rengakos, A. (2024), Classical Studies (*Altertumswissenschaft*) in the Anthropocene, Giannakis, G. K., Papanghelis, T. and Rengakos, A. eds. *The Future of the Past: Why Classical Studies still matter. Athenian Dialogues IV*, De Gruyter: Berlin-Boston, 201–211.
Revermann 2006: Revermann, M. (2006), The Competence of Theatre Audiences in Fifth- and Fourth-Century Athens, *The Journal of Hellenic Studies*, 126: 99–124
Revuelta Puigdollers 2017: Revuelta Puigdollers, A. R. (2017), Illocutionary force and modality. How to tackle the issue in Ancient Greek, O. Spevak & C. Denizot (eds.), *Pragmatic Approaches to Latin and Ancient Greek*, 17–43. Amsterdam/Philadelphia: John Benjamins Publishing Company.
Reynolds and Reason 2012: Reynolds, D. and M. Reason, eds. (2012): *Kinesthetic Empathy in Creative and Cultural Practices.* Bristol, UK: Intellect Ltd.
Richardson 2004: Richardson, A. (2004). "Studies in Literature and Cognition: A Field Map." A. Richardson and E. Spolsky, eds., *The Work of Fiction: Cognition, Culture, and Complexity*, 1–29. Aldershot, UK: Ashgate.
Rickheit, Weiss, and Eikmeyer 2010: Rickheit, G., S. Weiss. H.-J. Eikmeyer (2010), *Kognitive Linguistik. Theorien, Modelle, Methoden.* Narr Francke, Tübingen.

Riggsby 2019: Riggsby, A. M. (2019), Distributed cognition and the diffusion of information technologies in the Roman World, Anderson, M., D. Cairns, and M. Sprevak, (eds.), *Distributed Cognition in Antiquity*, Edinburgh Univ. Press, 57–70

Ritchie 2008: Ritchie, L. D. (2008), X is a journey: Embodied simulation in metaphor interpretation. *Metaphor and Symbol*, 23(3), 174–199.

Rivera Arrizabalaga 1998: Rivera Arrizabalaga, Á. (1998), Arqueología del lenguaje en el proceso evolutivo del Género Homo, *Espacio Tiempo y Forma, Serie I, Prehistoria y Arqueología* 11: 13–43.

Rivera Arrizabalaga 2005: Rivera Arrizabalaga, Á. (2005), *Arqueología cognitiva: Origen del simbolismo humano*, Madrid: Arco Libros.

Robson 2017: Robson, J. (2017). Humouring the masses: the theatre audience and the highs and lows of Aristophanic comedy. In Grig, L. (ed.), *Popular culture in the ancient world*, Cambridge: Cambridge University Press, 66–87.

Roby 2019: Roby, C. (2019), Physical sciences: Prolemy's extended mind, Anderson, M., D. Cairns, and M. Sprevak, (eds.), *Distributed Cognition in Antiquity*, Edinburgh Univ. Press, 37–56

Rohde 2013: Rohde, M. (2013), Evolutionäre Robotik, organic computing und Künstliches Leben, A. Stephan, S. Walter (hrsg.), *Handbuch Kognitionswissenschaft*, Metzler, Stuttgart – Weimar, 180–183.

Rohrer 2007: Rohrer, T. (2007): Embodiment and experientialism, Geeraerts, D., H. Cuyckens (eds), *The Oxford Handbook of Cognitive Linguistics*. Oxford, Oxford University Press, 25–47.

Rokotnitz 2011: Rokotnitz, N. (2011). *Trusting Performance. A Cognitive Approach to Embodiment in Drama*. Palgrave Macmillan.

Rolls 2021: Rolls, E. T. (2021). Mind causality: a computational neuroscience approach. *Front. Comp. Neurosci*. 15:5.706505

Ronnick 1997: Ronnick, M. V. 1997. " Substructural Elements of Architectonic Rhetoric and Philosophical Thought in Fronto's Epistles ", in W. J. Dominik (ed.), *Roman Eloquence. Rhetoric in Society and Literature*, London and New York: Routledge, 229–245

Roselli 2011: Roselli, D. K., (2011). *Theater of the People: Spectators and Society in Ancient Athens*. University of Texas Press.

Rosenwein 2006: Rosenwein, B. H. (2006), *Emotional Communities in the Early Middle Ages*, Cornell University Press.

Rosenwein 2020: Rosenwein, B. H. (2020), *Anger. The Conflicted History of an Emotion*, New Haven: Yale University Press

Ross, Spurrett, Stephens, Kincaid 2007: Ross, D., Spurrett, D., Kincaid, H., Stephens, G. L., eds. (2007). *Distributed Cognition and the Will: Individual Volition and Social Context*. MIT Press.

Rouby et al. 2002: Rouby, C., B. Schaal, D. Dubois, R. Gervais, A. Holley, eds. (2002), *Olfaction, taste, and cognition*, Cambridge: CUP.

Rowlands 1999: Rowlands, M. (1999). *The Body in Mind: Understanding Cognitive Processes*. Cambridge University Press.

Rowlands 2010: Rowlands, M. (2010). *The New Science of the Mind: From Extended Mind to Embodied Phenomenology*. The MIT Press.

Rubin, Atwood and Olson 2019: Rubin, J. D., Atwood, S., Olson, K. R. (2019), Studying Gender Diversity, *Trends Cogn Sci*. 24(3):163–165.

Rudolph 2017: Rudolph, K. C., ed. (2017), *Taste and the Ancient Senses*, Routledge.

Rueckert 1978: Rueckert, W. (1978), "Literature and Ecology: An Experiment in Ecocriticism." *Iowa Review* 9.1: 71–86.

Ruffell 2008: Ruffell, I. (2008), Audience and Emotion in the Reception of Greek Drama, in M. Revermann, and P. Wilson (eds), *Performance, Iconography, Reception: Studies in Honour of Oliver Taplin*, Oxford, OUP, 37–58.

Russell 1964: Russell, D. (1964), *'Longinus' On the Sublime*, ed. with introduction and comm. Oxford, Clarendon Press.

Ryan 2015: Ryan, M.-L. (2015). *Narrative as Virtual Reality Narrative as Virtual Reality 2: Revisiting Immersion and Interactivity in Literature and Electronic Media*. Baltimore, MD.: Johns Hopkins University Press.

Sanford and Emmot 2012: Sanford, A. J., Emmott, C. (2012). *Mind, brain, and narrative*. Cambridge University Press.

Scarinzi 2015: Scarinzi, A. (2015), ed., *Aesthetics and the embodied mind: beyond art theory and the Cartesian mind-body-dichotomy*, Springer Dordrecht Heidelberg, New York, London.

Scherer 2009: Scherer, K. R. (2009) The dynamic architecture of emotion: Evidence for the component process model, *Cognition and Emotion*, 23:7, 1307–1351

Schiewer 2014: Schiewer, G. L. (2014), *Emotionsforschung. Theorien, Anwendungsfelder, Perspektiven*, WBG Darmstadt.

Schjoedt and Andersen 2017: Schjoedt, U., M. Andersen (2017), How does religious experience work in predictive minds? *Religion Brain & Behavior* 7(3):1–4

Schlicht, Vetter, Thaler, Moss 2013: Schlicht, T., P. Vetter, L. Thaler, C. F. Moss. (2013), Wahrnehmung, A. Stephan, S. Walter (hrsg.), *Handbuch Kognitionswissenschaft*, Metzler, Stuttgart – Weimar, 472–487

Schliephake 2016: Schliephake, C. ed., (2016), *Ecocriticism, Ecology, and the Cultures of Antiquity*, Lanham, MD: Lexington Books.

Schmid 2010: Schmid, C. (2010), *Stadt, Raum und Gesellschaft: Henri Lefebvre und die Theorie der Produktion des Raumes*, Steiner Wiesbaden.

Schmid 2013: Schmid, U. (2013), Künstliche-Intelligenz-Forschung, A. Stephan, S. Walter (hrsg.), *Handbuch Kognitionswissenschaft*, Metzler, Stuttgart – Weimar, 44–47

Schmitt 1934: Schmitt, A. (1934), *Das Bild als Stilmittel Frontos*. Diss. München.

Schneider 2000: Schneider, R. (2000), *Grundriß zur kognitiven Theorie der Figurenrezeption am Beispiel des viktorianischen Romans*, Tübingen: Stauffenburg.

Schneider 2012: Schneider, R. (2012), "The Cognitive Theory of Character Reception: An Updated Proposal," *Anglistik* 24: 117–134

Scholz 2013: Scholz, O. R. (2013), Soziale und verteilte Kognition (*social/distributed cognition*), A. Stephan, S. Walter (hrsg.), *Handbuch Kognitionswissenschaft*, Metzler, Stuttgart – Weimar, 202–206.

Schouwenburg 2015: Schouwenburg, H. (2015), Back to the Future? History, Material Culture and New Materialism, *International Journal for History, Culture and Modernity*, 3/1: 59–72

Schwarz-Friesel 2012: Schwarz-Friesel, M. (2012). "On the status of external evidence in the theories of cognitive linguistics". *Language Sciences* 34 (6): 656–664

Scodel 2008: Scodel, R. (2008), *Epic Facework: Self-presentation and Social Interaction in Homer*. Swansea: Classical Press of Wales.

Scodel 2012: Scodel, R. (2012), "ἦ and Theory of Mind in the *Iliad*". *Homer, gedeutet durch ein großes Lexikon: Akten des Hamburger Kolloquiums vom 6.–8. Oktober 2010 zum Abschluss des Lexikons des frühgriechischen Epos*, ed. by M. Meier-Brügger, Berlin, Boston: De Gruyter, 319–334.

Scodel 2014: Scodel, R. (2014), "Narrative focus and elusive thought in Homer", D. L. Cairns and R. Scodel (eds.), *Defining Greek Narrative*, Edinburgh: Edinburgh University Press, 55–74.

Scodel 2023: Attribution and Antigone, in F. Budelmann and I. Sluiter (eds.), *Minds on stage: Greek tragedy and cognition*, Oxford OUP, 81–97.

Scott 1986: Scott, J. W. (1986), Gender: A Useful Category of Historical Analysis, *The American Historical Review*, 91/5: 1053–1075

Scott 1991: Scott, J. W. (1991), The Evidence of Experience, *Critical Inquiry*, 17/4: 773–797

Scott 2022: Scott, M. (2022), Walls and the Ancient Greek ritual experience: the sanctuary of Demeter and Kore at Eleusis, Eidinow, E., A. W. Geertz and J. North (eds.), *Cognitive Approaches to Ancient Religious Experience*, Cambridge: Cambridge University Press, 193–217.

Semino 2002: Semino, E. (2002), "A Cognitive Stylistic Approach to Mind Style in Narrative Fiction." In: *Cognitive Stylistics: Language and Cognition in Text Analysis*. E. Semino and J. Culpeper (eds.), Amsterdam, John Benjamins, 95–122

Semino 2005: Semino, E. (2005), "Mind style." *Elsevier Encyclopaedia of Language and Linguistics*, 142–48.

Semino 2007: Semino, E. (2007), 'Mind style 25 years on', *Style* 41, 2, 153–203.

Semino 2008: Semino, E. (2008), *Metaphor in Discourse*, Cambridge: Cambridge University Press.

Semino and Culpeper 2002: Semino, E. and Culpeper, J., eds. (2002), *Cognitive Stylistics: Language and Cognition in Text Analysis*. Amsterdam/Philadelphia: John Benjamins Publishing Company.

Semsch 2005: Semsch, K. (2005), Rezeptionsästhetik, G. Ueding (Hrsg.), *Historisches Wörterbuch der Rhetorik*. Band 7, Niemeyer, Tübingen, 1363–1374.

Sharag-Eldin et al. 2019: Sharag-Eldin, A., Xinyue Ye, B. Spitzberg, Ming-Hsiang Tsou (2019), "The role of space and place in social media communication: two case studies of policy perspectives," *Journal of Computational Social Science*, Springer, vol. 2(2): 221–244.

Shargel and Prinz 2017: Shargel, D., & Prinz, J. (2017). An Enactivist Theory of Emotional Content. In: H. Naar & F. Teroni (Eds.), *The Ontology of Emotions* (pp. 110–129). Cambridge: Cambridge University Press.

Shay 1995: Shay, J. (1995), *Achilles in Vietnam: Combat Trauma and the Undoing of Character*, New York.

Shay 2002: Shay, J. (2002), *Odysseus in America: Combat Trauma and the Trials of Homecoming*, New York.

Shepherd-Barr 2020: Shepherd-Barr, K., ed. (2020). *The Cambridge Companion to Theatre and Science*, Cambridge: Cambridge University Press.

Short 2008: Short, W. M. (2008), Thinking Places, Placing Thoughts: Spatial Metaphors of Mental Activity in Roman Culture, *Quaderni del Ramo d'Oro* 1, 106–129.

Short 2009: Short, W. M. (2009). Eating Your Words: 'Oral' Metaphors of Perception in Roman Culture, *Quaderni del Ramo d'Oro* 2, 111–123.

Short 2012: Short, W. M. (2012). A Roman Folk Model of the Mind, *Arethusa* 45(1), 109–147.

Short 2013a: Short, W. M. (2013). 'Transmission' Accomplished? Latin's Alimentary Metaphors of Communication. *American Journal of Philology* 134(2), 247–275.

Short 2013b: Short, W. M. (2013). Getting to the Truth: Metaphors of Mistakenness in Greek and Latin. *Arion* 21(2), 111–140.

Short 2014: Short, W. M. (2014). Metafora, Bettini, M., Short W. M. (Eds.), *Con i Romani: Un'antropologia della cultura antica*, Bologna: Il Mulino, 329–352

Short 2016: Short, W. M. (2016), Spatial Metaphors of Time in Roman Culture. *Classical World* 109(3), 381–412

Short 2017: Short, W. M. (2017), *Paene quicquid loquimur figura est:* Metaphorical Themes in Roman Culture. Beta, S. (ed.) *A Maurizio Bettini: Pagine stravaganti per un filologo stravagante*, Milan: Mimesis, 371–375

Short 2018a: Short, W. M. (2018), Metaphors. Bettini, M., Short W. M. (Eds.), *The World through Roman Eyes: Anthropological Studies of the Ancient World*, Cambridge: Cambridge University Press, 47–70

Short 2018b: Short, W. M. (2018), The Spatial Metaphorics of Ambiguity in Roman Culture, Fontaine, M., McNamara, C., Short, W. M. (eds.) *Quasi Labor Intus: Ambiguity in Latin Literature, Papers in honor of Reginald Thomas Foster, OCD*, Gowanus, the Paideia Institute, New York. https://ore.exeter.ac.uk/repository/bitstream/handle/10871/31855/short-ambiguity-metaphors.pdf?sequence=2&isAllowed=y, last access June 3rd 2024.

Short 2019a: Short, W.M. (2019). Roman Cultural Semantics. P. Meineck, W. M. Short, J. Devereaux, eds., *The Routledge Handbook of Classics and Cognitive Theory*, Routledge, 79–92.

Short 2019b: Short, W.M. (2019). Embodied, Extended and Distributed Cognition in Roman Technical Practice, M. Anderson, D. Cairns, and M. Sprevak, eds., *Distributed Cognition in Antiquity*, Edinburgh Univ. Press, 92–116.

Short and Duffy 2016: Short, W. M., Duffy, W. (2016). Metaphor as Ideology: the Greek Folk Model of the Epic Tradition, Cánovas C. P., Antovic M. (Eds.) *Oral Poetics and Cognitive Science*, Berlin: De Gruyter, 52–78

Silverman 2022: Silverman, K. (2022). The Androids of Hephaestus: Between Human and Machine in the *Iliad. Selected Proceedings of the Classics Graduate Student Symposia at the University of Florida*, 1. https://doi.org/10.32473/pcgss.v1i.130426, last access October 2nd 2024

Simon 1988: Simon, G. (1988), *Le regard, l'être, et l'apparence dans l'optique de l'antiquité*, Paris.

Skempis and Ziogas 2014: Skempis, M. and I. Ziogas, eds. (2014), *Geography, topography, landscape: configurations of space in Greek and Roman epic*, Berlin – Boston: De Gruyter.

Slaney 2017: Slaney, H. (2017), In the Body of the Beholder: Herder's Aesthetics and Classical Sculpture, in: Purves, A., ed. (2017), *Touch and the Ancient Senses*, Routledge, 105–120.

Slotnick 2017: Slotnick, S. D. (2017). *Cognitive neuroscience of memory*. Cambridge University Press.

Small 1997: Small, J. P. (1997), *Wax Tablets of the Mind: Cognitive Studies of Memory and Literacy in Classical Antiquity*, Routledge.

Smith 2018a: Smith, J. S. (2018), Introduction: Putting place back in place attachment research, J. S. Smith (ed.), *Explorations in Place Attachment*, Routledge, 1–16.

Smith 2018b: Smith, J. S., ed., (2018), *Explorations in Place Attachment*, Routledge.

Sneis 2018: Sneis, J. (2018), *Phänomenologie und Textinterpretation: Studien zur Theoriegeschichte und Methodik der Literaturwissenschaft*, Berlin, Boston: De Gruyter.

Snell 1946: Snell, B. (1946), *Die Entdeckung des Geistes. Studien zur Entstehung des europäischen Denkens bei den Griechen*. Hamburg, Claassen & Goverts.

Soja 1996: Soja, E. W. (1996). *Thirdspace: Journeys to Los Angeles and Other Real-and-imagined Places*. Blackwell.

Solomon 1993a: Solomon, R. C. (1993 [1976]), *The passions: emotions and the meaning of life*, Indianapolis: Hackett.

Solomon 1993b: Solomon, J., ed. (1993), *Accessing antiquity: the computerization of classical studies*, University of Arizona Press.

Sourvinou-Inwood 1989: Sourvinou-Inwood, C, (1989), "Assumptions and the Creation of Meaning: Reading Sophocles' *Antigone*" *The Journal of Hellenic Studies* 109: 134–48.

Sørensen 2007a: Sørensen, J. (2007), *A Cognitive Theory of Magic*, Rowman Altamira.

Sørensen 2007b: Sørensen, J. (2007), Acts That Work: A Cognitive Approach to Ritual Agency, *Method & Theory in the Study of Religion* 19(3):281–300

Spence 2021: Spence, C. (2021), Scent in the Context of Live Performance, *i-Perception* 11(6):1–28

Squillace 2020: Squillace, G. (2020), *Il profumo nel mondo antico, con la traduzione italiana del "Sugli odori" di Teofrasto*. Firenze: Leo S. Olschki editore.

Squire 2015: Squire, M., ed. (2015), *Sight and the Ancient Senses*, Routledge.

Stanford (1936): Stanford, W. B. (1936), *Greek Metaphor.* Blackwell.

Steen 2007: Steen, G. J. (2007), *Finding Metaphor in Grammar and Usage. A methodological analysis of theory and research*, Amsterdam/Philadelphia: John Benjamins Publishing Company.

Steen 2011: Steen, G. J. (2011). The Contemporary Theory of Metaphor: Now New and Improved. *Review of Cognitive Linguistics* 9(1): 26–64

Stein, Costello, and Polinger Foster 2022: D. Stein, S. K. Costello, K. Polinger Foster, eds. (2022), *The Routledge Companion to Ecstatic Experience in the Ancient World*, Routledge.

Steiner 2021: Steiner, D. T. (2021), *Choral constructions in Greek culture: the idea of the chorus in the poetry, art and social practices of the Archaic and early Classical period*. Cambridge; New York: Cambridge University Press.

Stewart, Gapenne, Di Paolo 2010: Stewart, J., O. Gapenne, and E. A. Di Paolo (eds) (2010). *Enaction: Towards a New Paradigm for Cognitive Science*, Cambridge, MA: MIT Press.

Stocker 2015: Stocker, K. (2015). Toward an Embodied Cognitive Semantics. *Cognitive Semantics* 1(2): 178–212.

Stockwell 2002: Stockwell, P. (2002), *Cognitive Poetics: An Introduction.* Routledge, London.

Stockwell 2007: Stockwell, P. (2007), "Cognitive Poetics and Literary Theory ", *Journal of Literary Theory* 1/1: 135–152.

Stockwell 2009: Stockwell, P. (2009), *Texture – A Cognitive Aesthetics of Reading*, Edinburgh Univ. press.

Storey 2011: Storey I. C. 2011. *Fragments of Old Comedy.* Ed. and transl. vol. 2. Loeb, Cambridge, Mass.

Struck 2016: Struck, P. T. (2016), *Divination and Human Nature: A Cognitive History of Intuition in Classical Antiquity*, Princeton Univ. Press.

Sutton and Keene 2017: Sutton, J. and N. Keene (2017), Cognitive History and Material Culture, D. Gaimster, T. Hamling, C. Richardson (Eds.), *The Routledge Handbook of Material Culture in Early Modern Europe* (44–56). London: Routledge.

Talmy 2000: Talmy, L. (2000), *Toward a Cognitive Semantics.* Vol. 1: *Concept Structuring Systems.* Vol. II: *Typology and process in concept structuring.* Cambridge: MIT Press.

Taves 1999: Taves, A. (1999), *Fits, Trances, and Visions: Experiencing Religion and Explaining Experience from Wesley to James*, Princeton Univ. Press.

Taves 2009: Taves, A. (2009), *Religious Experience Reconsidered: A Building-Block Approach to the Study of Religion and Other Special Things*, Princeton Univ. Press.

Taylor 1989: Taylor, J. R. (1989), *Linguistic Categorization: Prototypes in Linguistic Theory*, Oxford Clarendon Press.

Taylor et al. 2015: Taylor, P., Hobbs, J., Burroni, J. et al. (2015), The global landscape of cognition: hierarchical aggregation as an organizational principle of human cortical networks and functions. *Sci Rep* 5, 18112.

Telò 2013: Telò, M. (2013), "Aristophanes, Cratinus and the Smell of Comedy," S. Butler and A. Purves, (eds.), *Synaesthesia and the Ancient Senses.* London: Acumen, 2013: 53–69.

Telò 2018: Telò, M. (2018), The boon and the woe: friendship and the ethics of affect in Sophocles' *Philoctetes*, Telò, M., M. Mueller, (eds.), *The Materialities of Greek Tragedy: Objects and Affect in Aeschylus, Sophocles, and Euripides*. London: Bloomsbury, 133–152.

Telò and Mueller 2018a: Telò, M., M. Mueller, eds. (2018), *The Materialities of Greek Tragedy: Objects and Affect in Aeschylus, Sophocles, and Euripides*. London: Bloomsbury.

Telò and Mueller 2018b: Telò, M., M. Mueller (2018), Introduction: Greek tragedy and the New Materialisms, Telò, M., M. Mueller, (eds.), *The Materialities of Greek Tragedy: Objects and Affect in Aeschylus, Sophocles, and Euripides*. London: Bloomsbury, 1–15.

Thagard 2021: Thagard, P. (2021), *Bots and Beasts: What Makes Machines, Animals, and People Smart?* The MIT Press.

Thein 2022: Thein, K. (2022), *Ecphrastic shields in Graeco-Roman literature: the world's forge. Image, text, and culture in classical antiquity*. Abingdon, Oxon; New York, NY: Routledge.

Theodorou 2013: Theodorou, S. (2013). Metaphor and Phenomenology. *Internet Encyclopedia of Philosophy*. https://iep.utm.edu/met-phen/#H6, last access September 22nd, 2024

Thiering 2018: Thiering, M. (2018). *Kognitive Semantik und Kognitive Anthropologie: Eine Einführung*, Berlin, Boston: De Gruyter.

Thomas 1999: Thomas, N. J. T. (1999), 'Are Theories of Imagery Theories of Imagination? An Active Perception Approach to Conscious Mental Content', *Cognitive Science* 23: 207–245.

Thomas 2016: Thomas, N. J. T. (2016) 'Mental Imagery', in E. N. Zalta (ed.), *Stanford Encyclopedia of Philosophy.* http://plato.stanford.edu/archives/sum2016/entries/mental-imagery/, last access June 3rd 2024.

Tomasello 2014: Tomasello, M. (2014). The ultra-social animal. *European Journal of Social Psychology*, 44(3), 187–194.

Toner 2014a: Toner, J., ed. (2014). *A Cultural History of the Senses in Antiquity*. London and New York: Bloomsbury Academic.

Toner 2014b: Toner, J. (2014). Sensory studies – Butler, Purves, *Synaesthesia and the ancient senses*, Durham: Acumen publishing, 2013, *The Classical Review* 64 (2):343–345.

Tribble 2011: Tribble, E. (2011), *Cognition in the Globe: Attention and Memory in Shakespeare's Theatre*, New York: Palgrave Macmillan.

Trigg 2012: Trigg, D. (2012), *The Memory of Place: A Phenomenology of the Uncanny*, Ohio University Press.

Tsur 1983: Tsur, R. (1983), *What is Cognitive Poetics?* Katz Research Institute for Hebrew Literature, Tel Aviv University.

Tsur 2008: Tsur, R. (2008), *Toward a Theory of Cognitive Poetics:* Second, Expanded & Updated Edition, Sussex Academic Press.

Tsur 2017: Tsur, R. (2017), *Poetic Conventions as Cognitive Fossils*. New York: Oxford University Press.

Trostle 2005: Trostle, J. (2005). *Epidemiology and Culture*, Cambridge Studies in Medical Anthropology, Cambridge: Cambridge University Press.

Tuan 1975: Tuan, Y.-F. (1975), Place: An Experiential Perspective, *Geographical Review*, 65/2:151–165

Tuan 1977: Tuan, Y.-F. (1977), *Space and Place: The Perspective of Experience*. Minneapolis, MN: University of Minnesota Press.

Tuan 1990: Tuan, Y.-F. (1990), *Topophilia: A Study of Environmental Perception, Attitudes, and Values*, Columbia University Press.

Ünal and Papafragou 2018: Ünal, E. and Papafragou, A. (2018). Relations Between Language and Cognition: Evidentiality and Sources of Knowledge. *Topics in Cognitive Science*. 12/4: 1–21

Unceta Gómez and Berger 2022: Unceta Gómez, L. and L. Berger, eds. (2022), *Politeness in Ancient Greek and Latin*. Cambridge: CUP.
Underwood 2018: Underwood, C. (2018), *Mythos and Voice: Displacement, Learning and Agency in Odysseus' World*, Lexington Books.
Ungerer and Schmid 1996: Ungerer, F. H., Schmid, H. J. (1996). *An Introduction to Cognitive Linguistics*. London & New York Longman.
Ustinova 2009: Ustinova, Y. (2009), *Caves and the Ancient Greek Mind. Descending Underground in the Search for Ultimate Truth*. Oxford/New York: Oxford University Press.
Ustinova 2018: Ustinova, Y. (2018), *Divine mania: alteration of consciousness in ancient Greece*, London, Routledge.
Ustinova 2022a: Ustinova, Y. (2022), To the Netherworld and Back. Cognitive Aspects of the Descent to Trophonius, E. Eidinow, A. Geertz and J. North (eds), *Cognitive Approaches to Ancient Religious Experience*. Cambridge University Press, Cambridge, 44–66.
Ustinova 2022b: Ustinova, Y. (2022), Apolline and Dionysian Ecstasy at Delphi, D. Stein, S. K. Costello, K. Polinger Foster (eds.), *The Routledge Companion to Ecstatic Experience in the Ancient World*, Routledge, 332–350.
Vaesen 2012: Vaesen, K. (2012), The cognitive bases of human tool use, *Behavioral and Brain Sciences* 35(4): 203–18
Van Dam, Parise, and Ernst 2014: van Dam L, Parise C., Ernst, M. O. (2014), Modeling Multisensory Integration, Bennett D., Hill C. (Eds.), *Sensory Integration and the Unity of Consciousness*. MIT Press: 209–229.
Van den Hout 1999: Van den Hout, M. P. J. (1999). *A commentary on the Letters of M. Cornelius Fronto*. Brill Leiden-Boston-Köln.
Van Duijn 2012: Van Duijn M. (2012). *The biocognitive spectrum: Biological cognition as variations on sensorimotor coordination*. Diss. University of Groningen, Groningen, The Netherlands.
Van Emde Boas 2017: Van Emde Boas, E. (2017), *Language and Character in Euripides' Electra*, Oxford OUP.
Van Emde Boas 2021: Van Emde Boas, E. (2021), 'The Linguistic Characterisation of Oedipus in *OT*: A Pragmatics-Based Approach to "Mind Style"', in G. Martin, F. Iurescia, S. Hof and G. Sorrentino (eds.), *Pragmatic Approaches to Drama: Studies in Communication on the Ancient Stage*, 96–120, Leiden: Brill.
Van Emde Boas 2022: Van Emde Boas, E. (2022), 'Mind Style, Cognitive Stylistics, and *Ethopoeia* in Lysias', in A. Serafim and A. Vatri (eds.), *Trends in Classics* 14.2: 233–254 (special issue *Style and the Ancient City: Form and Functions of Language and Style in Attic Oratory*).
Van Essen-Fishman 2023: Van Essen-Fishman, L. (2023), 'Remember to what of man you give this favour': Looking back on Sophocles' Ajax, in: F. Budelmann and I. Sluiter (eds.), *Minds on stage: Greek tragedy and cognition*, Oxford OUP, 98–116.
Van Laer, de Ruyter, Visconti and Wetzels 2014: van Laer, T., K. de Ruyter, L. M. Visconti, M. Wetzels (2014). 'The Extended Transportation-Imagery Model: A Meta-Analysis of the Antecedents and Consequences of Consumers' Narrative Transportation', *Journal of Consumer Research* 40: 797–817
Van Leeuwen and van Elk 2018: Van Leeuwen, N. M. van Elk (2018), Seeking the supernatural: the Interactive Religious Experience Model, *Religion, Brain & Behavior*, 9:3, 221–251
Van Rooy 2016: Van Rooy, R. (2016). The Relevance of Evidentiality for Ancient Greek: Some Explorative Steps through Plato. *Journal of Greek Linguistics*. 16/1: 3–46
Varela, Thompson, and Rosch 1991: Varela, F. J., Thompson, E., Rosch, E. (1991), *The Embodied Mind*, The MIT Press, Cambridge MA, London, England.

Vermeule 2010: Vermeule, B. (2010), *Why Do We Care about Literary Characters?* Baltimore: Johns Hopkins university Press.
Villacèque 2013: Villacèque, N. (2013), *Spectateurs de paroles! Délibération démocratique et théâtre à Athènes à l'époque classique*. Rennes, Presses Universitaires de Rennes.
Villard 2002: Villard, L. (2002) (ed.) *Couleurs et vision dans l'Antiquité classique*, Rouen.
Villard 2005: Villard, L. (2005) (ed.) *Études sur la vision dans l'Antiquité classique*, Rouen.
Vint 2020: Vint S., ed. (2020), *After the Human: Culture, Theory and Criticism in the 21st Century*. Cambridge University Press.
Visvardi 2015: Visvardi, E. (2015), *Emotion in Action: Thucydides and the Tragic Chorus*. Leiden, Niederlande: Brill.
Wachsmuth, Lenzen, and Knoblich 2008: Wachsmuth, I., Lenzen, M., Knoblich, G. eds. (2008). *Embodied Communication in Humans and Machines*. Oxford University Press.
Walter 2013: Walter, S. (2013), Erweiterte Kognition (*extended cognition*), A. Stephan, S. Walter (hrsg.), *Handbuch Kognitionswissenschaft*, Metzler, Stuttgart – Weimar, 193–197
Watson 1994: Watson, G. (1994), "The concept of 'Phantasia' from the Late Hellenistic period to early Neoplatonism", in *ANRW* II 37, 7, 4765–4810.
Webb 2009: Webb, R. (2009), *Ekphrasis, imagination and persuasion in Ancient rhetorical theory and practice*, London/New York, Routledge.
Webster 1970: Webster, T. B. L. (1970), *The Greek chorus*. London: Methuen.
Weinrich 1976: Weinrich, H. (1976), *Sprache in Texten*. Stuttgart, Klett.
Weiss 2018: Weiss, N. (2018), "Speaking Sights and Seen Sounds in Aeschylean Tragedy", in M. Telò – M. Mueller (eds.), *The Materialities of Greek Tragedy. Objects and Affect in Aeschylus, Sophocles and Euripides*, London, 169–84.
Weiss 2023: Weiss, N. (2023), *Seeing theatre: the phenomenology of Classical Greek Drama*, Univesity of California Press, Oakland.
Wescoat and Ousterhoust 2012: Wescoat, B., Ousterhout, R. (Eds.). (2012), *Architecture of the Sacred: Space, Ritual, and Experience from Classical Greece to Byzantium*. Cambridge: Cambridge University Press.
Wheeler 2005: Wheeler, M. (2005), *Reconstructing the Cognitive World: The Next Step*, Cambridge, MA: MIT Press.
Whitehouse 2004: Whitehouse, H. (2004), *Modes of Religiosity: A Cognitive Theory of Religious Transmission*, AltaMira Press.
Whitley and Hays-Gilpin 2008: Whitley, D. S., K. Hays-Gilpin (2008), Religion Beyond Icon, Burial and Monument: An Introduction, D. S. Whitley, K. Hays-Gilpin (eds.), *Belief in the Past: Theoretical Approaches to the Archaeology of Religion*, Routledge, 11–22.
Whitmarsh 2013: Whitmarsh, T. (2013), Radical cognition: metalepsis in Classical Greek drama, *Greece & Rome*, Second Series, 60/1: 4–16
Wierzbicka, 1988: Wierzbicka, A. (1988), *The Semantics of Grammar*, Amsterdam/Philadelphia: John Benjamins Publishing Company.
Willey and Phillips 1958: Willey, G.R., Phillips, P.W. (1958). Method and theory in American archaeology, *American Anthropologist*, New Series, 55/5/1: 615–633
Wilson 2000: Wilson, P. (2000), *The Athenian institution of the choregia: the chorus, the city, and the stage*. Cambridge: CUP.
Winko and Köppe 2008: Winko, S., T. Köppe (2008), Rezeptionsästhetik. In: T. Köppe, Winko, S. (Hrsg.): *Neuere Literaturtheorien. Eine Einführung*. Metzler, 85–96.

Wolfe, Butcher, Lee, and Hyle 2003: Wolfe, J. M., Butcher, S. J., Lee, C., Hyle, M. (2003). Changing your mind: On the contributions of top-down and bottom-up guidance in visual search for feature singletons. *Journal of Experimental Psychology: Human Perception and Performance*, 29(2), 483–502.

Wood 2017: Wood, M.S. (2017), Aristotle's Theory of Metaphor Revisited. *Mouseion: Journal of the Classical Association of Canada* 14(1), 63–90.

Worman 2021: Worman, N. (2021), *Tragic bodies: edges of the human in Greek drama.* London – New York: Bloomsbury.

Wynn 1979: Wynn, T. (1979), The intelligence of later Acheulean hominids. *Man* 14:371–391.

Wynn, Overmann and Coolidge 2022: Wynn, T., K. A. Overmann, and F. L. Coolidge, eds. (2022), *The Oxford Handbook of Cognitive Archaeology,* Oxford University Press.

Xygalatas 2014: Xygalatas, D. (2014). Cognitive Science of Religion. Leeming, D. A., K. Madden, S. Marlan (eds.), *Encyclopedia of Psychology and Religion.* Springer, Boston, MA, 343–347.

Yakhlef 2008: Yakhlef, A. (2008), Towards a post-human distributed cognition environment, *Knowledge Management Research & Practice* 6(4):287–297

Zahavi 2014: Zahavi, D. (2014), *Self and other: Exploring subjectivity, empathy, and shame.* Oxford: Oxford University Press.

Zakowski 2018: Zakowski, S. (2018), The evolution of the Ancient Greek deverbal pragmatic markers áge, íthiand phére, *Journal of Historical Pragmatics* 19/1:55–91

Zanker 2016: Zanker, A. T. (2016), *Greek and Latin Expressions of Meaning. The Classical Origins of a Modern Metaphor.* München Beck.

Zanker 2018: Zanker, A. T. (2018) "Metaphor in Latin Expressions of Reading and Meaning", *PhaoS: Revista de Estudos Clássicos* 18, 97–118.

Zanker 2019: Zanker, A. T. (2019), *Metaphor in Homer: Time, Speech, and Thought.* Cambridge: Cambridge University Press.

Zanker 2020: Zanker, A. T. (2020), "Metaphor in the Speech of Achilles (*Iliad* 9.308–429)" *The Yearbook of Ancient Greek Epic* 4, 95–121.

Zbikowski 2009: Zbikowski, L. M. (2009), " Music, language, and multimodal metaphor", C. J. Forceville and E. Urios-Aparisi, *Multimodal Metaphor,* Berlin, New York: De Gruyter Mouton, 359–382.

Zhang and Patel 2006: Zhang, J., Patel, V. L. (2006), Distributed cognition, representation, and affordance, *Pragmatics and Cognition* 14(2):333–341

Zube, Sell, and Taylor 1982: Zube, E.H., Sell, J.L. and Taylor, L.G. (1982) Landscape Perception: Research, Application and Theory. *Landscape and Urban Planning* 9: 1–33.

Zunshine 2006: Zunshine, L. (2006). *Why We Read Fiction: Theory of Mind and the Novel.* Ohio State University Press.

Zunshine 2015a: Zunshine, L. ed. (2015). *The Oxford Handbook of Cognitive Literary Studies.* New York: Oxford University Press.

Zunshine 2015b: Zunshine, L. (2015). Introduction, L. Zunshine, ed., *The Oxford Handbook of Cognitive Literary Studies*, 1–9. New York: Oxford University Press.

Zunshine 2022: Zunshine, L. (2022). *The secret life of literature.* The MIT Press. Cambridge, Mass., London, England.

General Index

Adema, Suzanne 108–109
Aeschylus 81, 99
agency 10, 21, 40–41, 49, 51, 58, 68, 115–116, 120, 125, 155, 160
Alexis 72–73
Amphis 65, 68, 75
Antović, Mihailo 53
Aristophanes 75, 81–84
Aristotle 81, 86–89, 93, 132–134, 136, 151, 154
Armstrong, Paul 29
Arnold, Magda 126–127
artificial intelligence 8, 11, 23–27, 28, 30, 35, 48, 160
Assmann, Aleida 17
Assmann, Jan 16, 17

Barad, Karen 40
Barrett, Lisa 127
Barrett, Felix 161
Barsalou, Lawrence W. 104, 118
Bennett, Jane 40
Bentein, Klaas 15
Berti, Monica 25
Binford, Lewis 32
Blair, Rhonda 79
blending theory (conceptual blending) 99
Bodard, Gabriel 25
Bol, Cornelis 36
Bradley, Mark 111
Braidotti, Rosi 40
Brennan, Susan E. 35
Breytenbach, Cilliers 101–102
Brook, Peter 65
Budelmann, Felix 1–2, 19, 21
Butler, Shane 111, 113

Cairns, Douglas 1, 10, 17, 52, 91, 98, 125, 128, 130, 145–156, 158, 159
Canevaro, Lilah Grace 49–51, 60
Cánovas, Cristóbal Pagán 52–53, 99
Caracciolo, Marco 90, 108, 109
Chalmers, David 6

Chaniotis, Angelos 10, 125, 128, 129–130, 138–144, 158, 159
Charles, David 132–133
Chomsky, Noam 12
chorus 68, 69, 71, 73, 75, 81–84, 121–124
Cicero 55, 87, 91, 92, 94, 95, 113
Clark, Andy 6, 43, 80, 146–147
Clark, Herbert H. 35
cognitive *passim*
– archaeology 10, 24, 28, 32–39, 44, 48, 57, 60, 70, 76, 111, 114, 139, 141, 157, 159–162
– geography 28, 58, 60–76, 159
– history 39, 63–65, 121, 158
– linguistics 11–16, 22, 35, 52–55, 94, 97, 104, 106–110
– poetics 21–23, 125, 160
– stylistics 19–21, 23, 97, 99, 101, 108

D'Angour, Armand 82–83
DeLanda, Manuel 40
Democritus 102
Demosthenes 68
Derrida, Jacques 120
Descartes, René (Renatus Cartesius) 2, 4–5, 8–9, 41, 52, 91
Devereaux, Jennifer 55
Dewey, John 28, 123–124
Di Biase-Dyson, Camilla 102–103
Dolan, Raymond 140, 143–144

Eagleton, Terry 152
ecocriticism 23, 49, 51, 62, 77
4E-cognition 8–10, 41, 43, 57, 145, 147
ekphrasis 77–78
embodiment 6, 8–10, 12–14, 26, 28, 30–31, 37, 40, 41, 42, 44, 46, 48, 52–57, 58, 59, 64, 78–79, 84, 90, 92, 97–98, 101, 104, 107, 109–110, 116, 118, 121, 122, 127, 132–133, 145, 159, 160
emotions 2, 4, 6, 10, 18–19, 21, 28, 30, 37, 38, 40, 48, 49, 52, 54, 55, 57, 58, 60, 64–69, 72, 76, 78–79, 81, 91–94, 98, 99, 101, 109, 113–115, 118, 121, 125–156, 157–160

enactivism 6, 8–10, 16, 28–29, 43, 46, 48, 68, 73, 74, 90–92, 94, 112, 116, 123, 127, 145–147, 159
enargeia 91–92, 94, 122, 150–151
environment 2, 6–10, 12, 16, 28–30, 33, 35, 37, 41–42, 49, 52–53, 56, 58, 60–62, 64, 66, 68–71, 73–76, 104, 109–112, 114–115, 119, 126, 146–147, 149–150, 155, 157–159
Eupolis 68, 75
Euripides 22, 46, 72–73
evidentiality 106–108
experience 4, 9–10, 12–13, 16–17, 19, 22, 28–32, 35–40, 46, 48–49, 52, 55–61, 63–64, 66, 69–71, 73–74, 76, 78–82, 84, 86, 89–92, 94–98, 101–104, 106–124, 126–128, 132, 139, 142–143, 152–155, 159–162
experientiality 10, 28, 90, 106–109, 115, 125

Fedriani, Chiara 54, 98–99
Flavius Josephus 150
Fludernik, Monika 90, 98–99, 107–108
Foucault, Michel 61, 120
Fowler, Roger 23
Fronto, Marcus Cornelius 3–4, 86, 87–91, 96
functional Magnetic Resonance Imaging 79–80

Gadamer, Hans-Georg 161
Gallagher, Shaun 159
García Jurado, Francisco 53
Gibson, James 29
Goffman, Erving 153
Grand-Clément, Adeline 115
Grethlein, Jonas 20, 106, 109–110
Grosz, Elizabeth 40

Heidegger, Martin 51, 159
Herder, Johann Gottfried 112–113
hermeneutics 109, 160–161
Hermippus 73–75
Herodotus 65
Hesiod 25, 46, 60, 100
Holter, Erika 113
Homer 14, 20–21, 46, 48, 72, 87, 99–101, 109, 136–137, 152–153
Horn, Fabian 98–99, 101–104

Huffman, Thomas 35
Huitink, Luuk 8, 92, 94
Husserl, Edmund 57, 159
Hutto, Daniel 159

imagination 3–4, 10, 29, 36, 40, 42, 46, 52, 53, 56, 60, 71–74, 75, 76, 77–105, 109, 125, 158, 160–161

James, William 133
Jeannerod, Marc 113
Johnson, Mark 4, 88, 94, 95, 97–99

Kahneman, Daniel 148
Kirby, Vicki 40
Konstan, David 10, 20, 125, 128–131, 131–138, 158, 160
Kukkonen, Karin 12, 109–110

Lakoff, George 4, 12, 88, 92, 98, 99
landscape 38–39, 49, 51, 58–61, 65, 67–72, 74, 75, 77, 151
Langacker, Ronald 12
Lange, Carl 127
Lather-Mars, Amy 25, 46–48
Lazarus, Richard 126
LeDoux, Joseph 140
Lefebvre, Henri 61
Leucippus 102
Luraghi, Silvia 15

Malafouris, Lambros 34–35, 39, 41–44, 55
Marcus Aurelius 3–4, 90
mask 48–50, 75, 78, 80, 123, 172
Material Engagement Theory 23, 39–44, 46
materialities, material turn 2, 10, 28–30, 32–57, 58–60, 64, 69, 74, 75, 115, 125, 129, 138–144, 149, 154, 158, 160–162
McAuley, Gay 65
McConachie, Bruce 79
McCulloch, Warren 5
Meineck, Peter 8, 20, 25, 48–50, 55, 80–81
memory 4, 11, 16–19, 34, 56, 60, 77, 117–118, 123, 143–145, 157–158, 160
Merleau-Ponty, Maurice 159

Metaphor   3–5, 11, 13, 29, 52–56, 77, 82–83, 86–89, 92–94, 97–105, 107, 111, 140, 151–153, 155, 159
– conceptual theory of   4, 53, 77, 97–105
Minchin, Elizabeth   18, 20
mindreading   19–20, 23
mind theory (theory of mind)   5, 11, 19–21, 23, 28, 35, 41, 146–147, 154
mirror neuron system   79
Morley, Neville   112
Mueller, Melissa   44
music   48, 65, 68–69, 78, 81–84, 110, 113–114, 122, 130
Muth, Susanne   113
Mycenaean Linear script B   42

new materialisms   1, 39–41, 46
Nikiforidou, Kiki   54
Noë, Alva   1, 31, 43, 91, 159
Noel, Anne-Sophie   40, 78, 81
Nooter, Sarah   40, 44, 82, 83, 113
Nussbaum, Martha   138, 146

Oatley, Keith   126
Oberender, Thomas   161
Olsen, Sarah   123

Palmer, Alan   19–20
Philodemus   86
Pitts, Walter   5
place   6, 36, 41, 58–76, 78, 89, 91, 95, 104, 157
place attachment   65–68, 69, 77
Plato   10, 65, 66, 68, 69, 87, 93, 108, 151
Plato comicus   75
Plutarch   86–87
predictive coding   58, 80, 119
Prinz, Jesse   127
Pseudo-Longinus   80, 87, 92–93, 134
Pühringer, Elisabeth   36
Purves, Alex   111, 112

Quintilian   87, 91, 93–96

Raible, Wolfgang   102
Reddy, Michael   100
Reddy, William   125–126

religious studies   2, 17, 37–39, 59, 63–65, 106, 112, 114–121, 121–124, 139
Renfrew, Colin   34–35
Rosenwein, Barbara   126–128, 140
Roudet, Léonce   102
Rowlands, Mark   8
Rudolph, Kelli   113
Rueckert, William   62
Russell, James   127

Scherer, Klaus   126–127
Schwesinger, Sebastian   113
Scodel, Ruth   20
Scott, Joan   120
semantics   12–13, 42, 52–55, 87, 102, 107
semiotics   35, 41, 46, 92
Seneca   87–88, 91–92, 136
senses, 'sensory turn'   39, 57, 59, 61–62, 69–70, 73, 76, 78–79, 106–124,142
Short, Michael William   8, 18, 53–55, 98–99
sight   77–105, 111
Slaney, Helen   112–113
smell   43, 72, 73, 80, 110–112, 115–118, 150
Snell, Bruno   20, 136
social cognition   60–63, 154
Soja, Edward   71
Solomon, Robert   126, 146
sound   28, 79–84, 110–111, 113–114, 142
Sourvinou-Inwood, Christiane   73
space, 'spatial turn'   6, 10, 18, 34–35, 38, 48, 53, 58–76, 79, 89, 99, 102–104, 107, 109, 160
Squire, Michael   111
Steiner, Deborah   91, 122
synaesthesia   81–82, 101, 112–113

taste   40, 66, 110–115, 142
Taves, Ann   63
Telò, Mario   44–46
theatre   8, 18, 28, 48–50, 55–58, 60–61, 65–71, 73, 75, 77–80, 82–85, 104, 114, 118, 130, 160–161
Theophrastus   86, 88
touch   35, 43–44, 80, 112–113, 115
Tuan, Yi-Fu   59–61, 66
Turing, Alan Mathison   5
Tversky, Amos   148

van Emde Boas, Evert 22
Van Rooy, Raf 108
vision 10, 26, 30, 64, 77–105, 111, 118–119

Weiss, Naomi 65, 73, 79, 81
Wilson, Peter 122

Wittgenstein, Ludwig Josef Johann 152
Worman, Nancy 46, 70

Zahavi, Dan 8, 159
Zanker, Andreas 88, 98–102
zooming devices 73
Zunshine, Lisa 19–21

Index of Greek and Latin passages

Alcaeus fr. 140, 3–10 Voigt 48
Alcman *Parth.* 1, 66 PMG 48
Alexis *Tarantinoi* fr. 224, 1–4 PCG 72–73
Amphis *Erithoi* fr. 17, 4 PCG 65, 68
Anacreon fr. 358 PMG 48
Aristophanes *Birds* 209–222 83–84
Aristophanes *Birds* 223–224 83–84
Aristophanes *Birds* 255–262 83–84
Aristophanes *Birds* 305–307 83–84
Aristophanes *Frogs* 205–268 82–83
Aristotle *Metaphysica* A4 985b4 102

Cicero *Philippica* 2, 25 and 2, 67 55
Cicero *Verrines* 5, 86 95

Demosthenes 19, 60; 209 68

Eupolis *Cities* frs. 245–247 PCG 75
Euripides *Cyclops* 113–129 72–73
Euripides *Helen* 71–74 26

Flavius Josephus *Bellum Iudaicum* 6 150
Fronto *Epist. ad M. Caes. et Inv.* 3.7; 3.8 3–4, 88–91

Hermippus *Basket-bearers* fr. 63 PCG 73–75
Herodotus 6, 21, 2 65
Hesiod *Opera et dies* 60

Ilias 13, 130–135 48
Ilias 18, 372–380 25
Ilias 18, 469–473 25
Ilias 18, 599–601 48
Ilias 22, 440–441 46–47
Ilias 3, 125–128 46–47

'Longinus' *De Sublimitate* 15, 1–2 92–93
'Longinus' *De Sublimitate* 20, 2 92

Odyssey 9, 181–193, 213–223 72

Pindar fr. 194 Snell-Maehler 48
Pindar *Nemean* 4, 14 48
Pindar *Nemean* 5, 28 48
Pindar *Olympian* 1, 29 48
Pindar *Olympian* 6, 87 48
Pindar *Pythian* 8, 46 48
Pindar *Pythian* 10, 46 48
Plato *Ion* 530b 87
Plato *Leges* 2, 659a-c 65, 69
Plato *Leges* 3, 701a 65, 69
Plato *Symposion* 194a-b 65, 69

Quintilian *Institutio* 10, 7, 15 95
Quintilian *Institutio* 12, 10, 6 95
Quintilian *Institutio* 8, 2, 6 87
Quintilian *Institutio* 6, 2, 27 94
Quintilian *Institutio* 6, 2, 31–32 94
Quintilian *Institutio* 8, 3, 63–64 91, 95
Quintilian *Institutio* 8, 3, 71 95–96
Quintilian *Institutio* 8, 3, 88 95
Quintilian *Institutio* 8, 6, 11 93–94

Sappho fr. 98a-b Voigt 48
Seneca *Benef.* 2, 18, 5 88
Seneca *Benef.* 4, 12, 1 88
Seneca *Epist.* 114, 10 87–88
Seneca *Epist.* 9, 20 87
Sophocles *Philoctetes* 44–46

Theocritus *Eidyllia* 1, 32–38 49–51
Theocritus *Eidyllia* 7, 25–26 51
Theocritus *Eidyllia* 7, 39–48 51

www.ingramcontent.com/pod-product-compliance
Lightning Source LLC
Chambersburg PA
CBHW061939220426
43662CB00012B/1961